# Insurance Law in Spain

# Insurance Law in Spain

## Second Edition

**Juan Bataller Grau**
**Nuria Latorre Chiner**
**Jesús Olavarría Iglesia**
**Javier Vercher Moll**
**Irene Córdoba Mochales**

This book was originally published as a monograph in the International Encyclopaedia of Laws/Insurance Law.

Founding Editor: Roger Blanpain
General Editor: Frank Hendrickx
Volume Editor: Herman Cousy

Wolters Kluwer

*Published by:*
Kluwer Law International B.V.
PO Box 316
2400 AH Alphen aan den Rijn
The Netherlands
E-mail: international-sales@wolterskluwer.com
Website: lrus.wolterskluwer.com

*Sold and distributed by:*
Wolters Kluwer Legal & Regulatory U.S.
7201 McKinney Circle
Frederick, MD 21704
United States of America
Email: customer.service@wolterskluwer.com



ISBN 978-94-035-3940-9

e-Book: ISBN 978-94-035-3970-6
web-PDF: ISBN 978-94-035-3971-3

# The Authors

Prof. Dr Juan Bataller Grau is doctor at the University of Valencia, Spain, where he obtained the extraordinary prize for degree in Law and the extraordinary prize for doctorate in Law. He is currently a full-time professor of Commercial Law in the Faculty of Business Administration at the Polytechnic University of Valencia. His research works include diverse areas of commercial law, especially insurance and corporation law. His dedication to the insurance sector has led him to produce a variety of national and international scientific publications, including such essays as *The Duty to Declare the Risk, Claims Liquidation in Property Insurance and Multiple.* He has also coordinated and authored the following collective works: *The Insurance Contract in the Jurisprudence of the Supreme Court, Comments to the Insurance Contract Law, Comments to the Mediation Law of Private Insurance and Reinsurance and Insurance Supervisión Law (Solvency II).*

Prof. Dra. Nuria Latorre Chiner is doctor of law at the University of Valencia where she is currently a full-time professor in Commercial Law. Her scientific work lies mainly within the insurance field and in corporate law. She has contributed to the study of insurance law in her essay *The Aggravation Risk in Insurance Law* and with her outstanding participation in various works such as *The Insurance Contract in the Jurisprudence of the Supreme Court, Comments to the Insurance Contract Law* and *Comments to the Mediation Law of Private Insurance and Reinsurance.*

## The Authors

Prof. Dr Jesús Olavarría Iglesia is Professor of Commercial Law at the University of Valencia and doctor at the same university. He has published in different areas of commercial law and his contributions about collective practice of liberal professions or the increase of capital in public limited companies are outstanding. With regard to insurance law, he has published on premium payment, liability insurance and zoning norms. In addition, he has coordinated and authored collective works, such as *The Insurance Contract in the Jurisprudence of the Supreme Court* and *Comments to the Insurance Contract Law*.

Prof. Dr Javier Vercher Moll is doctor of law at the University of Valencia. He was awarded the extraordinary prize for doctorate in Law. His publications have focused on the planning, supervision and solvency of insurance companies. He also has several publications on the system of governance of insurance companies, the management of their risks, and the requirements of honesty and competence of the directors of insurance companies. He was also CEO of a mutual insurance company. He is also the author of several international publications such as: *Towards a European Supervisory Authority*, *Insurance Law Journal*, University of Connecticut.

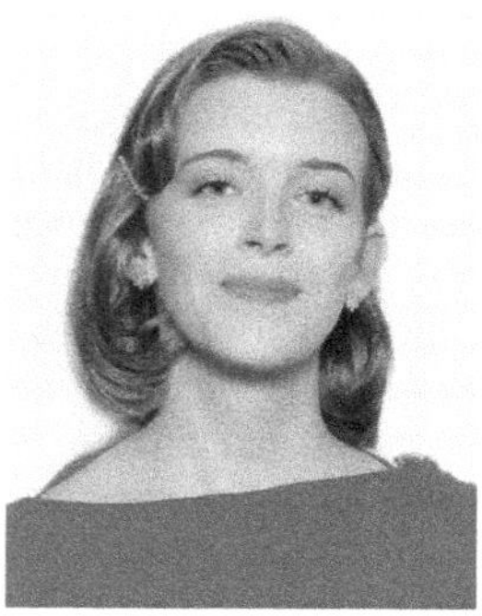

Irene Córdoba Mochales graduated with Double Degree of Law and Criminology from the University of Valencia, and also Master's in Practice of Law. She is currently doing her PhD in Commercial Law at the University of Valencia. Among her recent publications can be mentioned *Capital Riesgo y la Responsabilidad Social de la* Empresa, *Principios de Derecho del Contrato de Reaseguro*, and she has also taken part in Spanish translation of the *Principles of Reinsurance Contract Law*.

# Table of Contents

# List of Abbreviations

| | Spanish | English |
|---|---|---|
| AA.VV. | *Autores Varios* | Various Authors |
| AC | *Aranzadi Civil* | Aranzadi Civil |
| Act. Civ. | *Actualidad Civil* | Actualidad Civil |
| ADC | *Anuario de Derecho Civil* | Civil Law Year Book |
| AJ | *Actualidad Jurídica* | Actualidad Jurídica |
| Art. (Arts.) | *Artículo (artículos)* | Article/Articles |
| BOE | *Boletín Oficial del Estado* | Spanish government's official state journal |
| CC | *Código civil* | Civil Code |
| CCJC | *Cuadernos Civitas de Jurisprudencia Civil* | Cuadernos Civitas on Civil Case law |
| Ccom | *Código de comercio* | Commercial Code |
| CCS | *Consorcio de Compensación de Seguros* | Insurance Compensation Consortium |
| CDC | *Cuadernos de Derecho y Comercio* | Cuadernos on Law and Commerce |
| CDJ | *Cuadernos de Derecho Judicial* | Cuadernos on Judicial Law |
| CEE | *Comunidad Económica Europea* | European Economic Community |
| CGPJ | *Consejo General del Poder Judicial* | General Council of the Judicial Power |
| CNMV | *Comisión Nacional del Mercado de Valores* | National Commission for Securities Market |
| CP | *Código Penal* | Criminal Code |
| D. | *Decreto* | Decree |
| DdS | *Derecho de Sociedades* | Corporations law Review |
| Dir.Ec.Ass. | *Diritto ed economia dell'assicurazione* | Law and economy of insurance |

## List of Abbreviations

| | Spanish | English |
|---|---|---|
| Disp. Ad. | *disposición adicional* | Additional dispositive |
| Disp. Transit. | *disposición transitoria* | Transitional dispositive |
| DGSFP | *Dirección General de Seguros y Fondos de Pensiones* | General Direction for Insurance and Pension Funds |
| DN | *Derecho de los Negocios* | Business Law Review |
| EEE | *Espacio económico europeo* | European Economic Area |
| ELCCS | *Real Decreto Legislativo 7/2004, de 29 de octubre, por el que se aprueba el Texto refundido del Estatuto Legal del Consorcio de Compensación de Seguros* | Royal Legislative Decree 7/2004, 29 October, which approved the consolidated text of the Legal Estatute for the Insurance Compensation Consortium |
| ENESA | *Entidad Estatal de Seguros Agrarios* | Spanish Agency of Agricultural Insurance |
| FIVA | *Fichero informativo de vehículos asegurados* | Informative card index of insured vehicles |
| HPE | *Hacienda Pública Española* | Ministry of Public Finances |
| IPC | *Índice de precios al consumo* | Consumer price index |
| LCGC | *Ley de Condiciones Generales de la Contratación* | Law for General Provisions for Contracts |
| LCS | *Ley de Contrato de Seguro* | Insurance Contract Law |
| LEC | *Ley de Enjuiciamiento Civil* | Civil Procedure Law |
| LECrim | *Ley de Enjuiciamiento Criminal* | Criminal Procedure Law |
| LEN | *Ley 25/1964, de 29 de abril, sobre Energía Nuclear* | Law 25/1964, 29 April on nuclear energy |
| LGDCU | *Ley General para la Defensa de los Consumidores y Usuarios* | General law for the defence of consumers and users |
| LGSS | *Ley General de la Seguridad Social* | General law for social security |

| | Spanish | English |
|---|---|---|
| LMSRP | *Ley 26/2006, de 30 de abril, de Mediación en Seguros y Reaseguros Privados* | Law 26/2006, 30 April on mediation for private insurance and reinsurance |
| LOE | *Ley de Ordenación de la Edificación* | Law for zoning and development |
| LOPJ | *Ley Orgánica del Poder Judicial* | Law for organization of the judiciary |
| LOSSP de 1995 | *Ley 30/1995, de 8 de noviembre, de Ordenación y Supervisión de los Seguros Privados* | Law 30/1995, 8 November for organization and supervision of private insurance |
| LOTT | *Ley de Ordenación del Transporte Terrestre* | Law for Organization of Ground Transport |
| LSAC | *Ley 87/1978, de 28 de diciembre, de Seguros Agrarios Combinados* | Law 87/1978, 28 September on combined agricultural insurance |
| NotUE | *Noticias de la Unión Europea* | European Union news Review |
| núm. | *Número* | Number |
| OFESAUTO | *Oficina española de aseguradores de Automóviles* | Spanish office for vehicle insurers |
| párr. | *Párrafo* | Paragraph |
| p. ej. | *por ejemplo* | For example |
| Previse | *Previsión y seguro* | Prevision and insurance |
| RAEA | *Registro Administrativo de Entidades Aseguradoras* | Administrative Registry for Insurers |
| RAJ | *Repertorio Aranzadi de Jurisprudencia* | *Repertorio Aranzadi* of case law |
| RCRN | *Decreto 2177/1967, de 22 de julio, por el que se aprueba el Reglamento sobre cobertura de riesgos nucleares* | Decree 2177/1967, 22 July, which approves the regulation on coverage for nuclear risks |
| RD | *Real Decreto* | Royal Decree |
| RDBB | *Revista de Derecho Bancario y Bursátil* | Review of Banking and Securities Law |

**List of Abbreviations**

| | Spanish | English |
|---|---|---|
| RDCir. | *Revista de Derecho de la Circulación* | Review of Circulation Law |
| RDLeg | *Real Decreto Legislativo* | Royal Legislative Decree |
| RDley | *Real Decreto-ley* | Royal Law Decree |
| RDM | *Revista de Derecho Mercantil* | Review of Commercial Law |
| RDP | *Revista de Derecho Privado* | Review of Private Law |
| RDSP | *Revista de Derecho de los Seguros Privados* | Review of Private Insurance Law |
| RES | *Revista Española de Seguros* | Review of Spanish Insurance |
| Rev. RC | *Revista de Responsabilidad Civil, Circulación y Seguro* | Review of Liability, Circulation and Insurance |
| RGD | *Revista General de Derecho* | General Review of Law |
| RJC | *Revista Jurídica de Cataluña* | Juridical Review of Cataluña |
| RMPS | *Reglamento de Mutualidades de Previsión Social, aprobado por RD 1430/ 2002, de 27 de diciembre* | Regulation of social mutual societies approved by RD 1430/2002, 27 December |
| RPFP | *Real Decreto Legislativo 1/2002, de 29 de noviembre, por el que se aprueba el texto refundido de la Ley reguladora de los Planes y Fondos de Pensiones* | Royal Decree 1/2002, 29 November, which approves the consolidated text of the law for organization of plans and pension funds |
| RRC SCVM | *Real Decreto 1507/2008, de 12 de September, por el que se aprueba el Reglamento sobre responsabilidad civil y seguro en la circulación de vehículos a motor* | Royal Decree 1507/2008, 12 September, which approved the regulation on liability and insurance for motor vehicle circulation |

| | Spanish | English |
|---|---|---|
| RRE | *Real Decreto 300/2004, de 20 de febrero, por el que se aprueba el Reglamento de Riesgos Extraordinarios* | Royal Decree 300/2004, 20 February, which approves the regulation of extraordinary risks |
| ROSSP | *Reglamento de Ordenación y Supervisión de los Seguros Privados* | Regulation for organization and supervision of private insurance |
| RSAC | *Real Decreto 2329/1979, de 14 de septiembre, por el que se aprueba el Reglamento para la aplicación de la Ley de Seguros Agrarios Combinados* | Royal Decree 2329/1979, 14 September, which approves the Regulation for the Application of Combined Crop Insurance Law |
| RyS | *Riesgo y Seguro* | Risk and insurance Review |
| SOA | *Seguro obligatorio de automóviles* | Compulsory vehicle insurance |
| SRC | *Seguro de responsabilidad civil* | Liability Insurance |
| ss. | *Siguientes* | following (ff.) |
| STC (SSTC) | *Sentencias (s) del Tribunal Constitucional* | Constitutional Court decisions |
| STS (SSTS) | *Sentencia (s) del Tribunal Supremo* | Supreme Court decisions |
| TRLOSSP | *Real Decreto Legislativo 6/2004, de 29 de octubre, por el que se aprueba el Texto refundido de la Ley de Ordenación y Supervisión de los Seguros Privados* | Royal Legislative Decree 6/2004, 29 October, which approves the consolidated law for Organization and Supervision of Private Insurance |

**List of Abbreviations**

| | Spanish | English |
|---|---|---|
| TRRC SCVM | *Real Decreto Legislativo 8/2004, de 29 de octubre, por el que se aprueba el Texto Refundido de la Ley sobre responsabilidad civil y circulación en la circulación de vehículos a motor* | Royal Legislative Decree 8/2004, 29 October, which approves the consolidated law on liability and circulation of motor vehicles |
| UE | *Unión Europea* | European Union |
| últ. | *Último* | last |

# General Introduction

## §1. General Background Information

*1.* Spain is located in southern Europe, bordering Portugal to its western side, France to its north and the Mediterranean Sea and African continent to its south. It occupies a total area of 505,955 $km^2$.

It has a population of 46,704,314 inhabitants,[1] (January 2013), who are mainly concentrated along the coast (especially along the Mediterranean Sea), on the islands and in the big cities. During the past years, there has been a constant increase in population due to immigration, as has been the case in most countries of the European Union.

### I. Political and Legal System

*2.* Spain is a parliamentary monarchy as established by section 1.3 of its 1978 Constitution. The king is the chief of state who supervises the regular functioning of the institutions and also assumes the highest representation of the Spanish State in international relations.

The coronation of King Juan Carlos I of Bourbon occurred in 1975 when General Franco died, ending a forty-year dictatorship regimen. The first general elections were held on 15 June 1977 in which the Democratic Centre Unity (DCU) won a relative majority with 165 seats and its founder, Adolfo Suárez, was proclaimed the president of the State. The democratic transition period (1975–1978) brought important changes; basically, a multiparty parliamentary system was established, and the State was decentralized with the formation of autonomous communities. In 1982, the first socialist government (PSOE) was formed and it ran the country until 1996. That year the Popular Party (PP) won the elections with Jose María Aznar. From 2004 till 2011, the socialist party ran the government with its José Luis Rodriguez Zapatero. In the last elections (November 2011), PP, chaired by Mariano Rajoy, won the majority in the Congress of Deputies.

*3.* The fundamental law in the Spanish legal system is the Constitution of 1978, which was approved by referendum on 6 December. Its section 1 declares that Spain is a social and democratic State and proclaims as superior values freedom, justice,

1. Data from Instituto Nacional de Estadística (www.ine.es).

equality and the pluralist political system. It also establishes that the national sovereignty lies in the Spanish people from whom the State powers come (legislative, executive and judicial) and that Spain is a parliamentary State. The Constitution recognizes an extensive list of citizens' rights and confirms the existence of its autonomous regions.

Spain is a politically and administratively decentralized country that has seventeen autonomous communities and two autonomous cities (Ceuta and Melilla). Each of them has a fundamental law called 'Statute of Autonomy', which regulates the functioning of the Parliament and of the autonomous government, their administrative organization and their responsibilities.

*4.* The legislative power lies with the Cortes Generales (General Courts) formed by two chambers: the Congress and the Senate. The first has 350 representatives and the second 266 senators (who are territorial representatives). Congressional representatives and senators are elected for four years. Law projects and proposals are presented and analysed first by the Congress and later by the Senate, which has the right to amend them if necessary. Law proposals then return to Congress for definitive approval. Congress also has the power to proclaim the president and to provoke the presidential dismissal by approving a motion of no confidence or by refusing support to the government.

The executive branch is represented by the government, which has the power to submit law proposals; govern by way of urgent legislation; prepare the national budget; and lead internal and external politics, the civil and military administration and the State defence. Currently, the government includes the president and seventeen ministers.

Justice is administrated by judges and magistrates and its government agency is the General Council of the Judicial Power (CGPJ). The Supreme Court is the highest court for all cases not related to constitutional rights. The constitutionality of the laws is the prerogative of the Constitutional Court.

## II. Commerce and Industry

*5.* Agriculture is one of the most important sectors of the Spanish economy; it is based on the cultivation of fruits, vegetables, olive oil and wine. After a period characterized by a decrease in population engaged in agriculture, the number of people engaged in agriculture has stabilized at 1 million. With regard to agricultural insurance, there has been an increase in the risk coverage, and specific lines of business for local production have been created. The State invests around EUR 234 million in 2013 to subsidize agricultural insurance costs. Besides agriculture, Spain stands out as one of the most important fishery countries in the European Union and as a leader in the tourism industry due to the number of international visitors received and to the amount of foreign currency income generated by this sector.

In the decades before the global recession, the integration of Spain in the international markets brought the country's economy on levels comparable to the economies of Germany, France and Italy. The opening of its markets and the important increase of Spanish exports affected the flows of direct investment. Today, investment of Spanish companies abroad is still larger than the investment made within the country. Most exports are sent to countries in the European Union, the leading sectors being equipment, semi-finished goods and motor vehicles. The global recession of 2008 has had devastating consequences for Spain. The property boom, the banking crisis, financial sector restructuring and a dramatic rise in unemployment that reached 26.6% in September 2013 are the most significant impacts the recession has left in its wake in Spain.

## III. Financial Institutions

*6.* At the end of the twentieth century, the Spanish banking industry experienced deep changes, passing from an oligopolistic to a more competitive and expansionist market, and bringing the Spanish banks to the level of the leaders in Europe. However, the global recession had a serious impact on the Spanish financial sector. It revealed that Spanish banking organizations had major capital and funding issues, as well as structural problems in the specific case of its savings banks. Since the crisis began, banks and saving banks have been subject to a series of mergers and buyouts, and savings banks have been turned into banks, etc., which has led to a considerable reduction in the number of financial institutions.[2]

The Spanish insurance market has an intermediate size and its structure is similar to other markets in Europe. In the past years, there has been an increasing demand for life insurance, which apparently has allowed trade in the national market to stabilize. With regard to non-life insurance, motor vehicle (or automobile) insurance, health insurance and fully comprehensive insurance are most in demand. Mapfre is the most important insurance group in the country and it has 12.68% of the direct insurance market.[3]

## IV. Currency Legislation and Monetary Regulations

*7.* Spain, as a member of the European Union, adheres to the monetary policy fixed by the European Central Bank. The national government uses fiscal policy and structural reform of the markets of goods and factors to implement such monetary policy. In this sense, Spain has taken many measures to deregulate different sectors of its economy (electricity, gas, hydrocarbon and telecommunications). Old monopolies have disappeared, almost all public benefit corporations have been privatized, barriers have been eliminated and entry of new operators has been allowed. The regulation of the affected sectors has been modified. Currently, there

---

2. Royal Decree-Law 9/2009, of 26 July, created the Fund for Orderly Bank Restructuring (FROB), the aim of which is to manage the restructuring processes of credit institutions and help to strengthen these institutions' equity. Current regulation comes under Law 9/2012, of 14 November, on credit institution restructuring and resolution.
3. Ranking of direct insurance in 2006. Source: ICEA., October 2013 (www.icea.es).

is a simple general framework for economic agents, and the defensive policy of competition has been fortified to contribute to a greater functionality in the markets.

## V. Insurance Business, General Organization and Special Features

*8.* During 2012, the collection of premiums for direct insurance and reinsurance reached the amount of EUR 57,712 million.

Internationally, in 2012, there were thirty-nine branches in States in the European Economic Area, which corresponded to twenty-one Spanish insurance companies. They are mostly located in Portugal, and there are about 200 independent providers of services, mainly in France, Portugal, Germany and the United Kingdom.[4]

Insurance activity can only be performed by Spanish private entities formed as public limited companies, health insurance companies, cooperatives or mutual societies.[5] Their operations are supervised by the *Dirección General de Seguros y Fondos de Pensiones* (General Direction of Insurance and Pension Funds), which is an agency of the Ministry of Economy.[6] In 2012, foreign capital in Spanish entities represented 16.23% of the total capital in the sector.[7]

*9.* The insurance sector also has the 'Insurance Compensation Consortium', a public enterprise that has traditionally and exclusively been in charge of coverage of extraordinary risks.[8] Within the insurance sector, the consortium currently has other functions, such as those related to automobile liability insurance.[9] The consortium assumes the compulsory coverage of motor vehicles that are not accepted

4. 20052012 Report of the General Direction of Insurance and Pension Funds (DGSFP) (http://www.dgsfp.mineco.es/).
5. Section 7 of the Royal Legislative Decree 6/2004, passed on 24 October, approved the adapted text of the Law for Organization and Supervision of Private Insurance (TRLOSSP). It also establishes that all undertakings that are incorporated under any form of public law (such as public benefit corporations), and that have the purpose of pursuing insurance business and are attached to the same conditions applied by private insurance undertakings that will be allowed to operate in the insurance market (Art. 7 of the TRLOSSP).
6. In particular, the DGSFP is charged with controlling the precise requirements for access to the insurance business and for its expansion; with the regular supervision of its practice; with controlling the of requirements to be complied by managers and partners of insurance undertakings; with control of mergers, spin-offs and acquisitions between insurance companies; with the control over access for the insurance brokerage activity; with supervision of its practice and other surveillance functions; with control of compliance and access requirements by pension fund management firms; with regular supervision of its practice and so on.
7. Data extracted from the 20052012 DGSFP report about the insurance sector.
8. The consortium loses exclusivity of coverage for special risks upon the entry into force of its Legal Statute approved by s. 4 of Law 21/1990 of 10 December about the adaptation of the Spanish law to the first non-life Directive 88/357/EEC (BOE, n° 304, 20 Dec. 1990). The Legal Statute of the consortium is afterwards modified by the ninth additional disposition of Law 30/1995 of 8 November about organization and supervision of private insurance and by Law 44/2002, of 22 November about measures for the reform of the financial system until the current adapted text. Read Ch. 10, Part III for more information.
9. The Legal Statute of the Insurance Compensation Consortium also deals with other tasks in the insurance business with respect to nuclear risk insurance, the combined crop insurance and forestal risks, compulsory insurance for travellers and compulsory hunters liability insurance (see ss 6–13

by insurers and also covers the vehicles of the State, autonomous communities, local corporations and public agencies. In addition, the consortium will provide for coverage in cases where the vehicle cannot be identified, or does not have insurance, or is stolen or in cases where the insurer was declared insolvent or in liquidation by the consortium itself. According to Law 44/2002, on the reform of the financial system, the consortium is also responsible for the liquidation of insurance companies, a function that, until that moment, was a prerogative of the commission for liquidation of insurance companies (CLEA). Finally, the consortium has also public functions or non-insurance functions, strictly speaking, such as the administration of credit exports insurance by the State and the design of plans and programmes for the prevention and reduction of losses.

## §2. Historical Background of Insurance and Insurance Legislation

### I. The Insurance Contract

*10.* There has been much debate about the origin of insurance. According to the most respected doctrine, the first regulation for insurance contracts published in the world was the Ordinance about Maritime Insurances of Barcelona on 21 November 1435.[10] This law proclaims some of the principles that are valid even today in numerous regulations codes.[11] The evolution did not stop there; it continued with the Ordinances of Burgos for maritime insurance published on 29 September 1537, the Ordinances of Sevilla of 1555 for maritime insurance at the time of the sailing towards the West Indies and the Ordinances of Bilbao of 1737. With these codes, maritime insurance regulation has evolved to reach a high degree of perfection in legal techniques.

The 1829 code followed the Ordinances of Bilbao and took into account the French Commercial Code. In maritime insurance, it focuses on details and improves the systematization of regulations of which the inclusion of Title VIII of the second book about terrestrial transport insurance is the most important. This move allowed mercantilist authors of the time to elaborate on the doctrine on terrestrial insurance as would later on be reflected in the Commercial Code of 1885.

*11.* Title VII of the Commercial Code of 1885 focused on the insurance contract. It was divided into five sections: the first contained six sections on the insurance contract in general (Articles 380–385), the second (extensive) was on fire

Royal Legislative Decree 7/2004 of 29 October, which approved the consolidated text of the Legal Estatute for the Insurance Compensation Consortium (ELCCS)).

10. The Ordinances of the Maritime of Barcelona constitute the first general code for insurance law. In contrast to the Italian legislative work (Statutes of Geneva, Florence and Venice), which simply stopped abusive practices of the insurance activity, the Spanish legislator of the time analysed almost all the legal elements of the contract. The ordinances of Barcelona were five in number: the first was dated 21 Nov. 1435; the second was dated August 1436, the third in 1458, the fourth in 1461 and the fifth in 1484. For more information about them see J.J. Garrido y Comas, *El contrato de seguro* (Barcelona: Spes, 1954), 11 ss.

11. Prohibition for unjust enrichment, prohibition for double insurance, etc.

insurance (Articles 386–415), the third was on the applicable framework for life insurance (Articles 416–431), the fourth section was on terrestrial transport insurance (Articles 432–437) and the fifth contained one single article that recognized the possibility to contract other types of insurance different from the ones expressly dealt with by the Commercial Code. Article 737 and the following concerned maritime insurance and are still valid.

The described legal system is tributary to the liberal concept that inspired the codification, where the only restrictions to contractual freedom were justified by the traditional lack of trust towards the insured (prohibition of enrichment). Soon, it became obvious that the consolidation of big insurance companies, which imposed massive contracts, meant in fact to leave in the hands of one of the parties – the insurer – the regulation of the legal relationship derived from an insurance contract. These problems ended with the publication of the currently in force Law 50/1980 of October about insurance contract.

## II. Insurance Undertakings

*12.* Before the formation of insurance companies, insurance was contracted among merchants. The first insurance company properly incorporated was formed in Cádiz in 1763 and it was dedicated to marine insurance.[12] Together with the first marine insurance companies, the Real Company of Ground and Marine Insurance was born in 1789. Its goal was to provide insurance for homes, warehouses, goods, maritime risks of ships and merchandise. Other types of insurance began operating in the middle of the nineteenth century.

In contrast to the regulation of contracts, the legal framework for the insurance business took some time before being adopted. The first great effort was made by the law of 14 May 1908, followed then by the organized law of private insurance in 1954 and another in 1984.

*13.* The entry of Spain into the European Community (EC) caused an important process of reform. The implementation of successive Community Directives has been carried out basically through Royal Legislative Decree 1.255/1986 of 6 June by which certain Articles of Law 33/1984 are modified; the Organic Law for private insurance of 2 August with the purpose of adapting the legislation according to the Adhesion Treaty of Spain to the European Economic Community; Law 21/1990 of 19 December which implemented the Spanish law according to Directive 88/357/CEE about freedom of services for non-life insurance and private insurance latest update; and finally Law 30/1995 of 8 November about organization and supervision of private insurance.

During the past few years, there have been many reforms. As a result of the GESCARTERA scandal, Law 44/2002 of 22 November introduced measures to reform

12. There is information to sustain that in 1793 there were fifty-four small companies of maritime insurance operating in that city; between 1786 and 1787, there were seven in Barcelona, and another was incorporated in Bilbao by 1783 (J.J. Garrido y Comas, *El contrato de seguro* (Barcelona: Spes, 1954) 10, 19).

the financial system. Almost by surprise Law 34/2003 was promulgated on 4 November about modification and adaptation to the community law. Later on, seven royal decrees and the Order ECO/734/2004 of 11 March were enacted to regulate the departments and services for customer service and the consumer ombudsman for financial entities.

The speed in the reformist movement introduced by the legislator caused some confusion in determining the regulatory framework. Given the number of promulgated laws it was necessary to consolidate the existing regulatory framework. For this reason the following laws were approved: the consolidated text about organization and supervision of private insurance by Royal Legislative Decree 6/2004 of 29 October, the Royal Legislative Decree 7/2004 of 29 October by which the Consolidated Legal Statute of the Insurance Compensation Consortium (CCS) was approved and the Royal Legislative Decree 8/2004 of 29 October which approved the consolidated text for liability insurance and motor vehicle insurance.

Despite all these laws, there still existed a need for more changes. Indeed, Law 5/2005 of 22 April about supervision of financial conglomerates was complemented by the Royal Decree 1332/2005 of 11 November. Finally, Law 12/2006 of 16 May modified again the Legal Statute of the Insurance Compensation Consortium.

### III. Intermediation for Private Insurance

*14.* Intermediation for private insurance was Law 117/1969 of 30 December concerning the distribution of private insurance. It was the object of consolidation by Royal Decree 1347/1985, of 1 August, repealed by Law 9/1992 of 30 April concerning intermediation of private insurance. This law remained in force until Law 26/2006 of 17 July was enacted. This last law regulates intermediation of private insurance and reinsurance.

## §3. Sources of Insurance Law

### I. Legislation

*15.* Legal sources concerning private insurance can be classified into three groups. The first group includes norms that establish the statute of the manager and are mainly of public character – but also include private law, especially corporate law – and concentrate on regulating the constitution, operation and supervision of insurance undertakings. The second group is composed of dispositions for the statute of the collaborators of the insurance businessperson – commercial and labour laws related to intermediation of private insurance. The third group regulates exclusively the relationship between the parties of the insurance contract.

Within the first group the most important laws are the Royal Legislative Decree 6/2004 of 29 October, by which the consolidated text for the organization and supervision of private insurance is approved; the consolidated text for organization of private insurance and Royal Decree 7/2004, of 29 October, by which the consolidated text for the Legal Statute of the Insurance Compensation Consortium was approved;

Law 26/2006 of 17 July about mediation rules, mediation of private insurance and reinsurance; and the excellent Law 50/1980 of 8 October on the insurance contract. This last one establishes the rules on the insurance contract and its main types (theft, caution, fire, credit, legal defence, liability, life, accident, health, etc.). It is directly applicable to these types of insurance and subsidiarily applicable to other types that are governed by special regulations such as the Royal Decree 8/2004 of October 29 that approved the consolidated text for motor vehicle liability insurance given their broad use and frequent occurrence of losses.

## II. Governmental Regulations

*16.* All the regulations mentioned were issued by or have to be carried out by the government. Important ones are the regulation for organization and supervision of private insurance approved by Royal Decree 2486/1998 of 2 November, the regulation about motor vehicle liability approved by Royal Decree 7/2001 of 12 January, the regulation for extraordinary risks for persons and goods approved by Royal Decree 300/2004 of 20 February and regulation for compulsory insurance for travellers approved by Royal Decree 1575/1989 of 22 December.

## III. Regulation by Governmental Agencies

*17.* There is no Spanish entity or agency that has legislative power to regulate the insurance business besides the Parliament or the government through its power to legislate.

## IV. Private International Law

*18.* The legislator in the European Community has chosen the place where the risk is situated as the criterion to determine the framework to be applied in the case of international insurance contracts. When the risk occurs within the European Union, the conflict of law rules contained in Community Directives will be applied.[13] When the risk is located within the territory of a third State, the 1980 Rome Convention will be the appropriate law.

Articles 107–109 of the insurance contract law have regulations of an international private law nature and they implement the Second Directives in the Spanish legal system. They distinguish between property insurance damage (also non-life insurance for persons) and life insurance. For the first group the rules are as follows:

(a) When the risks are located within the Spanish territory and the policyholder has his habitual residence in Spain, Spanish Law will be applied.

13. Articles 7 and 8 of the Directive Second Non-life Directive 88/357/ECC (as modified by the Third Directive 92/49/CEE) and Art. 4 of the Second Life Insurance Directive 90/619/ECC.

(b) When the risks are located in Spanish territory and the policyholder does not have habitual residence in Spain, the parties will have to choose between the Spanish Law and the law of the policyholder's country of origin.
(c) For compulsory insurance imposed by Spanish Law, Spanish law will be applied.
(d) For large risks, the parties may choose the law to be applied.
(e) When the policyholder is a businessman or professional insured against risks related to the insurance business in different countries, the parties may choose between the law of the States where the risks are located and the law of the policyholder's residence.
(f) When the guarantee is limited to events that may occur in a Member State which is not Spain, the parties may choose the law of that State.

*19.* Regarding life insurance, it is possible to distinguish:

(a) When the policyholder is a physical person with habitual residence in Spain, Spanish law will be applied except when the policyholder is a national from another Member State and decides to apply the law of the own country.
(b) When the policyholder is a legal undertaking and its domicile or main establishment is in Spain, Spanish Law will be applied.
(c) When the policyholder is a Spanish national but resides in another State and there is a previous agreement with the insurer, Spanish Law will be applied.
(d) When there is group insurance contracted due to work relationship subject to Spanish legislation, Spanish Law will be applied.

## V. Jurisdiction

*20.* For most disputes arising out of an insurance contract, the ordinary civil courts have jurisdiction. Nevertheless, there are two main exceptions with respect to liability insurance originating from criminal offences and from accident insurance. When the liability covered by an insurance has its origin in crimes or offences that are identified by the Criminal Code, the legal action must be brought before the competent criminal court, even if the own Criminal Code gives the victim the choice as to the civil jurisdiction.[14] With regard to accident insurance, the appropriate forum is the 'social' court that has jurisdiction over disputes arising from accident

14. Article 109.2 of the CP. The Criminal Code deals with direct liability of insurers in Art. 117: 'Insurers underwriting the risks for pecuniary liability from the use or exploitation of any good, enterprise, industry or activity will be directly fully liable up to the level of indemnity as legally established or contracted for by the parties, without prejudice to the right of recourse against whoever bears liability when the insured risk occurs as consequence of an event cited by this Code.'

insurance policies contracted by employers to improve their workers' labour conditions or to complement the compulsory social security; if, on the contrary, the policies have been contracted by the workers' initiative, the disputes will be decided by the civil court.[15]

Article 24 of the insurance contract law determines territorial jurisdiction and expressly declares the judge from the insured domicile as the proper authority to decide on legal actions arising out of the insurance contract, any agreement on the contrary being null. The law is partially repealed by Article 52.1 of the law for civil procedure (Law 1/2000 of January 7), which gives jurisdiction to specific courts for certain cases. For example, in claims for indemnity arising out of motor vehicle insurance, Article 52.1.9 designates as an appropriate forum the court of the place where damages were caused. In disputes arising out of contract clauses with a motion to declare them null or motion to dismiss their inclusion into the contract, Article 52.1.14 gives jurisdiction to the court of the plaintiff's residence. When the type of claim is not included by Article 52.1 of the Civil Procedure Law (LEC), Articles 24 of the Insurance Contract Law (LCS) and 52.2 of the LEC[16] point to the criterion of the insured's residence.

## §4. Dispute Settlement and Arbitration

*21.* The conflictual nature of the insurance contract and the lack of satisfaction that sometimes lingers after the end of the litigation process have led to a constant search for alternative methods of dispute resolution.

The parties may choose to subject their differences to arbitration. Indeed, the Royal Legislative Decree 6/2004 (TRLOSSP) determines the possibility to use arbitration when the parties agree to do so in the insurance policy or after the conflict has arisen (Article 61 of the TRLOSSP). It is also stipulated that an arbitration clause in an insurance contract will be considered abusive and null when the insured is a consumer according to the general law for the defence (LGDCU), except in cases of arbitration for consumers (clause No. 26 of the First Additional Disposition of the LGDCU). The same law provides for the possibility of arbitration in consumer cases, including the possibility to choose for common arbitration even after the dispute has arisen – as described by the reform introduced by Article 31 LGDCU approved by Law 44/2006 of 29 December for the improvement of consumers and clients' protection.

If the insured is not a consumer, part of the Spanish doctrine interprets the arbitration clause that is limitative of the insured's rights, and which, in order to be valid, has to be expressly accepted by the insured. Only if the insurance risk is qualified as large risk, will the freedom of contract prevail and the clause to be subject disputes to arbitration will be admitted unconditionally.

---

15. Article 2 of Law 36/2011 of 10 October of the Labour Procedure Jurisdiction: 'The jurisdictional bodies of the orden social will decide legal disputes that are initiated:[ … ] cq) In the implementation of systems for the protection of the social security, like pension plans and insurance contracts, only when their cause derive from a labour contract or collective agreements[ … ].'
16. See sentence of TS 25-5-2004 (Civil). RAJ 2004/4619.

*22.* In addition, Law 44/2002 on the reform of the financial system has modified Article 63 of the TRLOSSP and now requires insurers to have a department for customer service aiming at resolving complaints and demands. Moreover, insurance undertakings are able to appoint individually or collectively as a client defender 'an independent person of known reputation' who will listen and solve complaints within the scope of the functioning manual. Decisions will be binding upon the insurer if they are favourable to the client. This being bound will not impede full exercise of the judicial protection or access to other dispute resolving mechanisms.

The customer service and/or defender for the insured do not have the necessary independency to keep away from the criteria 'suggested' by the insurer and there is a risk that they become a second instance within their own insurance company. Evidence of this assumption is necessary to preserve the independency of the persons designated by Order ECO/734/2004 of 11 March about departments, customer service and client defender for financial undertakings, and those included in the Recommendations of the Commission of 30 March 1998 and 4 April 2001, concerning the principles to be applied by relevant agencies responsible for alternative solution of disputes in consumers litigation.

Likewise Law 44/2002 has introduced the so-called Commissioner for the defence of the insured, who has the power to issue an equitable solution and solve disputes without, however, being able to implement or enforce them. Nevertheless, there appear to exist many difficulties putting this institution into practice.

*23.* Furthermore, mention must be made of the appointment of 'expert witnesses' proceeding for liquidation of the claim. Article 38 of the LCS provides in the case of property insurance for a compulsory and supplementary procedure.[17] The objective is the preparation of an expert report to be used as a proposal to determine the amount to be indemnified by the insurer, on the basis of an examination of the cause of the claim, of the existing relationship between the cause of the event and damages and also of the question whether the fact that caused those damages gives rise to insurance coverage.[18]

The dynamics described in Article 38 of the LCS runs, briefly, as follows: when there is lack of agreement in a forty-day period upon the date of declaration of the claims, each party is qualified to appoint an expert[19] and to require the other party to proceed in the same manner. A first problem arises when such appointment is not

17. They established the need to use expert witnesses and its respective proceedings if one of the parties requests so, SSTS 14-7-1992 (Civil). RAJ 1992/6288, 17-7-1992 (Civil). RAJ 6432, and 20-5-2002 (Civil). RAJ 2002/5345. It has been confirmed that it is not possible to claim the compulsory character of Art. 38 LCS when it has not been followed by any of the parties according to SSTS 10-5-1989 (Civil). RAJ 1989/3751, 1-12-1989 (Civil). RAJ 1989/8785, 17-5-1990 (Social). RAJ 1990/4351, y 31-1-1992 (Civil). RAJ 1992/538.

18. For more details about liquidation proceedings for property insurance, see L. De Angulo Rodríguez, *La liquidación del siniestro en los seguros contra daño en las cosas* (Barcelona: Escuela del Seguro de Barcelona, 1989); J. Bataller Grau, *La liquidación del siniestro en los seguros de daños* (Valencia: Tirant lo Blanch, 1997).

19. The requirements to be complied with by the expert are mentioned in the Additional Dispositive 5a. of the LOSSP in 1995. See J. Bataller Grau & J. Olavarría Iglesia, 'Los peritos de seguro en la Ley de Ordenación y Supervision de los Seguros Privados' in *Estudios y comentarios sobre Ley de Ordenación y Supervisión de los Seguros Privados*, AA.VV. (Madrid: Mapfre, 1997), 381ff.

made. In such case the legislator punishes this behaviour by leaving the preparation of the report exclusively in the hands of the expert who was appointed by the other party. If, on the contrary, an appointment is properly made, both experts appointed by the parties will try to reach an agreement. A second difficulty raised by the law occurs when the experts reach an agreement and the proceeding ends with the issue of the expert report. If the agreement is not reached, the parties are able to appoint a third expert to solve the existing disagreements between the parties' experts.[20]

The legislator makes the effects of the expert report depending on the parties' compliance with such report. When the report is challenged, the insurer will have to pay a sum in advance according to the claimant's circumstances at that moment. When the report cannot be challenged, the payment must be made with only a brief delay, that is, within five days from the day that the indemnity became unchallengeable. If, however, the insured is obliged to legally claim an unchallengeable indemnity, the total amount will be increased with the applicable interest pre-established by Article 20 of the LCS.[21] In any case, the amount will have to cover incurred costs made by the insured during the proceedings. The decision must mention the indemnity in any type of legal action.

## §5. Consumer Protection

*24.* Article 2 of the 1980 Insurance Contract Law shows an effort to protect the insured.[22] The law is compulsory and derogations from it are only allowed when they are to the benefit of the insured. Article 2 demonstrates that the legislator is also concerned with other aspects of protection of the insured: with the possibility that potentially abusive clauses or unlawful clauses will be forbidden and monitored (Article 3 of the LCS); with the fact that the contract should have been timely and well reflected (Articles 3, 5, 6 and 8 of the LCS); with the right to a fast indemnity (Article 18 of the LCS); with territorial jurisdiction in the insured's domicile (Article 24 of the LCS); with the right of repentance in life insurance (Article 83 of the LCS); and so on.

Other laws that are protective of the insured can be found within the supervisory legislation for insurance, in particular in the TRLOSSP. Despite the fact that this legislation does not have the goal to protect the insured, it contains some dispositions that actually serve that purpose (Articles 59–62).

20. The third expert is appointed by agreement of both parties or by the judge in a voluntary jurisdiction act. The SSTS 14-7-1987 (Civil). RAJ 1987/5492; 14-7-1992 (Civil). RAJ 1992/6288; 9-4-1999 (Civil). RAJ 1999/3139; and 16 Oct. 2000 (Civil). RAJ 2000/9195 confirms that the appointment of the third expert will have to be by party motion.
21. See Art. 20 LCS, epigraph 3, Part II, Ch. 5.
22. About insured protection, see J.M. Embid Irujo, 'Aspectos institucionales y contractuales de la tutela del asegurado en el Derecho español', RES, n°91, 7 ff; E. Caballero Sánchez, *El consumidor de seguros: protección y defensa* (Madrid: Mapfre, 1997); M.J. Peñas Moyano, *La protección del asegurado: Análisis de la problemática derivada de la pluralidad de normas aplicables*, (Madrid: McGraw-Hill, 1999).

These dispositions have been modified by Law 44/2002 concerning the reform of the financial system. It establishes a new set of regulations to protect insurers' clients.[23] One of them is the creation of the so-called Commissioner for the insured defence and for the participation in pension plans. This commissioner will be appointed by the general director for insurance and pensions funds considering persons of known reputation and experience in the sector. The commissioner will advise users about their rights to transparency and protection, will listen to their complaints and send the respective files containing evidence of breach of duty or violation of transparency regulations and/or client protection.

*25.* Moreover, regarding administrative protection, there is still the possibility to lodge a complaint with the General Direction for Insurance and Pension Funds against the insurers who are guilty of abusive practices or otherwise infringe on a contract. There is a prerequisite though, namely that the insured must have brought his or her complaint before the clients' defender or the respective customer service. The administrative sanction will be imposed by resolution issued by the General Direction for Insurance.[24]

Besides the means provided for by insurance regulations, consumer[25] law also offers protection to the so-called weakest party in the contract. It can affect the insured when he or she is also a consumer, that is to say, when the insured is also the final receptor of the insurance.[26] Indeed, a distinction can be made between the consumer insured and the non-consumer insured depending on the use of the insurance – for personal or company purposes. In the first situation, the law of insurance contract and the general law for the defence of consumers and users will be relevant, whereas in the second situation the insurance law will apply.

## §6. Compulsory Insurance

*26.* Currently, Spain is the country with the highest number of compulsory insurances. Next to the strictly compulsory insurance (of which obligatory compliance is based on a general legal text), there are many 'insurance obligations' related to

---

23. The law of reform measures for the financial system repeals many provisions of Arts 62 and 63 of the LOSSP, concerning the administrative protection and the institution of the insurance defender.
24. Article 62.2 LOSSP.
25. Consumer protection is laid down in the Spanish legal system in Art. 51 of the 1978 Constitution. To implement the constitutional mandate of defending and protecting consumers, Law 26/1984 concerning consumers' and users' defence was promulgated on 19 June, the main law of the whole system dedicated to consumers' protection. Together with the general regulation, there are many more protective laws. Among them, for example, are Law 21/1995, of 6 July on combined trips; Law 42/1998 of 15 December on the optimization by turns of real property for tourism use; Law 7/1995 of 23 March on consumer's credit; Law 3/1991 of 10 January on unfair competition; Law 26/1991 of 21 November on contracts performed by non-commercial establishments; Law 22/1994 of 6 July on civil liability for caused damages by defective products; Law 7/1998 of 13 April on general contracting conditions.
26. J.M. Embid Irujo, 'La protección del asegurado: su consideración como consumidor' (The insured protection: consumer's consideration), in *Derecho de seguros (Insurance Law)*, AA.VV. (Dir. Marco Cos) (Madrid: GCJP, 1995), 29.

activities or professions that have been imposed by the public administration or by professional associations as a prerequisite for admittance to the relevant professional practice or activity (e.g., obligatory insurances required for travel agencies, surveillance companies, clinical tests, transfer of funds abroad, radio ham antennas, communication installation).[27]

Article 75 of the LCS empowers the government to promulgate compulsory liability insurance through royal decrees and to develop compulsory insurance in a set of regulations. On the basis of this power, the government has issued Royal Decree 607/1999 concerning the compulsory insurance for recreational vessels. Other types of compulsory insurances are found in the regulations with legal standards within the State jurisdiction or the autonomous communities (compulsory liability insurance for the use and circulation of motor vehicles with liability insurance of hunters, compulsory traveller insurance, civil liability insurance for nuclear risk, etc.) This last type of insurance is governed by a special law that establishes the creation of a guarantee fund or any type of State or private guarantee to operate in case the insurer would not do so.

The Spanish legislator has also foreseen lack of compliance with compulsory insurance and has established civil and criminal sanctions. Article 75 of the insurance contract law proclaims that 'the lack of insurance when it is compulsory will be sanctioned administratively'. The Criminal Code punishes those who perform activities without liability insurance when it is compulsory with a fine from one to two months (Article 636 CrimC).

27. On the distinction between compulsory insurance and the duty to obtain insurance, see E. Pavelek, 'Seguros obligatorios y obligación de asegurarse' (Compulsory insurance and the duty to get insurance), *RES*, núm. 106, Apr.–Jun. 2001, 235ff.

# Part I. The Insurance Company

## Chapter 1. Organization[28] and Supervision of the Insurance Industry in Spain

*27.* The logic of economic mutuality implies that every insurance transaction requires that a premium is paid by a policyholder and/or insured (present obligation) that is sufficient to cover, at the very least, the degree of probability that the risk is realized (future obligation), as well in cases where the insurance business is organized through the intermediation of a limited company as in the case of mutualistic undertakings (cooperative company or social mutual societies).

It so appears that the insurance contract is a legal instrument that allows the participation of one or various persons in an insurance operation and at the same time an economic operation that provides reciprocal coverage of economic needs, which are fortuitous and pecuniary, on the basis of pecuniary contributions (premiums).

*28.* Insurance contract law is the basic law of private insurance law, including more than simply contractual regulation. To set up the regulatory framework, it is crucial that the legislation on the organization and supervision of private insurance contains different laws ranging from public to private law. It consists of three basic pieces of information:

(1) The law on the organization and supervision of private insurance, the consolidated text of which was approved by the Legislative RD 6/2004 of 29 October (TRLOSSP), which consists of two basic regulations: the regulation on the organization and supervision of private insurance approved by RD 2486/1998 of 20 November (regulation for organization and supervision of private insurance (ROSSP)) and the regulation on social mutual societies approved by RD 1.430/2002 of 27 December (regulation of social mutual societies approved by RD 1430 (RMPS)).
(2) Law 26/2006 of 17 July, on intermediaries in insurance and reinsurance (Law 26/2006 of 30 April on mediation for private insurance and reinsurance (LMSRP)).
(3) The Legal Statute of the Insurance Compensation Consortium, the consolidated text of which was approved by Legislative Royal Decree 7/2004 of 29 October (TRECCS).

28. In this text we use the term 'Organization' as the equivalent of the Spanish legal term 'Ordenación'.

*29.* From an economic viewpoint, the insurance contract implies the exchange of a present and certain obligation (premium) for another future and uncertain insurance payment, presupposing a mechanism of economic mutualization. Therefore, the whole insurance business is based on a process that is characterized by the inversion of the production cycle, in the sense that the insurer demands the premium from the policyholder in advance of the coverage period (income), whereas his or her obligation (the obligation to indemnify) is future and uncertain (at least with respect to the moment on which it will occur). Consequently, there is public interest to guarantee the effective insurance payment by the insurance undertakings when the event occurs. Such interest justifies the organization and supervision of the insurers by a public body in order to verify whether insurers have sufficient solvency to accomplish their corporate goals.

*30.* The legal framework for the organization and supervision of the State is based on the system of administrative authorization with permanent surveillance.[29] According to its text:

(a) Insurance undertakings are asked to comply with financial, technical and precise professional requirements which are a condition for the taking-up and pursuit of the business of insurance.
(b) There are capital requirements and compliance with both insurance contract law and accounting regulations is also controlled, throughout the period of insurance activities.
(c) Insurance undertakings that do not comply with the mentioned regulations are subject to supervisory measures. To this end certain special control measures can be issued and the granted administrative authorization can be repealed or the dissolution of the insurance undertaking can be ordered when the minimal requirements for continuing operation are not met.

*31.* All these actions are implemented by a system of information that includes:

(a) Imposing special obligations with respect to the information that must be complied by insurance undertakings for the taking-up and pursuit of insurance business.
(b) Providing the administration with sufficient powers to require information from the insurance undertakings.
(c) Extending the inspection capabilities of the supervisory personnel.

In comparison to other models, the Spanish system has opted for confiding the control and supervision functions of the insurance sector to the public State administration, specifically to the General Direction for Insurance and Pension Funds (hereinafter DGSFP), which both functionally and hierarchically depends on the Ministry of Economy.

29. See Exp. de Motives of the 1995 LOSSP.

# Chapter 2. The Insurance Company: Its Form

## §1. Insurance Undertakings in the Spanish Insurance Market

*32.* European Community legislation on private insurance obliges Member States to follow certain rules to organize the insurance business in accordance with rules laid down in the Insurance Directives. These rules aim at establishing an internal market of insurance. The system is based on the single authorization or 'license unique' allowing insurance undertakings to operate in the entire European Economic Area.

In Spain, undertakings may take up the business of insurance after having obtained the required authorization from the Ministry of Economy. Also those undertakings that are domiciled and authorized in any Member State can operate in Spain on the basis of their right to establishment and the freedom to provide services. Finally, undertakings domiciled in third countries, non-members of the European Community, that have the authorization of the Ministry of Economy to establish branch offices and pursue insurance business in Spain, may engage in insurance business in Spain.

## §2. Public and Private Nature and Legal Forms of Undertakings Authorized to Pursue Insurance Business in Spain

*33.* In accordance with the traditional view of insurance law that is also shared by the Member States of the European Community, Spanish law allows the insurance business to be carried out by undertakings of a private and public nature (Article 7 of the TRLOSSP).

With regard to private undertakings, the Spanish system sticks to traditional *numerous clausus* for legal forms. The insurance activity can only be performed by private undertakings with the legal form of a public limited society, of mutual societies, and of cooperative or social mutual societies (Articles 5.2 and 7.1 of the TRLOSSP).

The mutual forms (mutual societies, cooperative societies and social mutual societies) set aside the only authorized private corporate form in the public limited society.

*34.* Mutual societies, insurance cooperatives and social mutual societies can operate with fixed or variable premiums and are called fixed or variable premium mutual societies, fixed or variable insurance cooperatives and fixed or variable social mutual societies, respectively.

Our legal system expressly indicates that together with private insurance undertakings, those 'with any form of public law will also be allowed to engage in insurance business' (Article 7.2 of the TRLOSSP). In accordance with Articles 38 (freedom of enterprise) and 128 (public economic initiative) of the 1978 Spanish Constitution (EC) and Article 106 (ex Article 86) of the EEC Treaty, insurers that have any structural form of public law must have the purpose 'to engage in the insurance business and meet the same conditions as those under which private insurers operate'. Consequently, they must fully comply with the legislation for organization and supervision of private insurance and insurance contract law and they must submit to the civil courts' jurisdiction. To conclude, they shall compete with private insurers in the market and under equal conditions.

## I. The Public Limited Society

*35.* The regulatory framework for public limited insurance societies is found in the legislation on the organization and supervision of private insurance (TRLOSSP and ROSSP) and complementarily in the law on public limited societies (consolidated text of the law for public limited society approved by Royal Legislative. Decree 1/2010, of 2 of July) along with other regulations that are applicable to such societies.

The special framework for public limited insurance societies that are laid down in the legislation for organization deals with the requirements of access to and of the pursuit of the insurance business and will be examined in the following chapters.[30]

## II. The Mutualistic Insurance Entities: Insurance Mutual Societies

*36.* Insurance mutual societies can operate with a fixed or variable premium, as should be indicated in its denomination. Therefore, there exist fixed premium mutual societies and variable premium mutual societies.

Both have to make use of the legal framework described in the 2004 TRLOSSP and in the ROSSP. Additional regulations are the statutes of mutual societies and the law for public limited societies insofar as they do not contradict the specific framework for this type of undertaking (Article 21 of the ROSSP).

### A. *Fixed Premium Mutual Societies*

*37.* Fixed premium mutual societies are defined in Spanish legislation as non-profit private insurance undertakings that have the purpose of covering its partners, physical persons or legal entities, against insured risks through a fixed premium paid in the beginning of the risk period (Article 9 of the TRLOSSP).

Fixed premium mutual societies can operate in any insurance line of business and also assign or accept reinsurance in any line of their direct insurance business.

Mutual societies must have at least fifty associates or 'mutual partners'. The 'mutual partner' quality is inseparable from that of policyholder or insured (Article 9.2 (a) and (b) of the TRLOSSP). When the policyholder and the insured are not the same person, the qualification of mutual partner will be acquired by the policyholder except when the insurance policy expressly states the insured will take that

30. See Part I, Ch. 3.

condition. The by-laws (articles of association) of the undertaking must be delivered to the mutual partner at the moment of the insurance contract subscription.

*38.* The general rule is that mutual partners are not liable for corporate debts in fixed premium mutual societies. Nevertheless, the by-laws of the mutual societies can provide for the contrary. In that case the law (Article 9.2.d of the TRLOSSP) limits the liability of the mutual partners for the corporate debts to the equivalent sum of the payment for the annual premium, which must be underlined in the insurance policy.

The rights and obligations of mutual partners (Article 9.3 of the TRLOSSP) are such that no privilege can be bestowed upon any person; management bodies, management and control as well as every other aspect of the corporation should be organized to function in a democratic way.

In the fixed premium mutual societies, all the mutual partners have the same political, economic and information rights.

The governing bodies of the fixed premium mutual societies are the general assembly and the management board.

### *B. Variable Premium Mutual Societies*

*39.* Variable premium mutual societies are defined in Article 10.1 of the TRLOSSP as non-profit private undertakings based on the principle of reciprocal help with the objective to provide common account coverage for its partners (physical persons or legal entities) against insured risks through the collection of apportionments after the event occurs. The partners bear proportional and joint liability up to the sum of the insured capital of the undertaking.

The law that governs this type of undertaking is found in specific regulations, laws and rules that apply to fixed premium mutual societies except, as was previously mentioned, as far as the mutual partner liability system for corporate debts (see Article 10.2 of the TRLOSSP) is concerned.

## III. The Mutualistic Insurance Entities: Insurance Cooperatives

*40.* The TRLOSSP only authorizes the formation of consumer cooperatives that can be 'monovalente' (partners are also insured) or 'bivalente' (existence of insured partners next to work partners).

The insurance cooperatives may be on a fixed or variable premium basis. The laws applicable to fixed premium cooperatives are the laws applicable to the fixed premium mutual societies, except for the rules related to the dissolution of cooperatives, its members, social capital and cooperative return, and the references that contain the mutual societies, mutual partners, mutual fund and apportionments.

The laws applicable to variable premium cooperatives are the laws applicable to variable premium mutual societies, including cooperatives, cooperative partners and corporate capital. The reference includes mutual societies, mutual partners and mutual fund but 'the payment of the entry fee will be in the form of a contribution to the social capital'.[31]

## IV. The Mutualistic Insurance Entities: The Social Mutual Society ('*Mutualidades de Previsión Social*')

*41.* The current legal system[32] for social mutual societies is laid down in the TRLOSSP (basically in Chapter VII, Title II – Articles 64–68 – and in Article 69) and in Royal Decree 1430/2002 of 27 December, by which the regulation for social mutual societies is approved (hereinafter RMPS).

The non-profit private insurance undertakings are defined (Articles 64.1 of the LOSSP and 2.1 of the RMPS) as undertakings that voluntarily provide insurance services to complement the compulsory social security system through contributions in the form of fixed or variable premiums paid by mutual partners, physical persons and legal entities or by other undertakings or sponsors.

In order to qualify as a social mutual society, an undertaking has to 'cumulatively' comply with the requirements as described in Article 64 of the TRLOSSP.

The corporate purpose of the social mutual society is governed by Article 11 of the TRLOSSP. The *Mutualidades de previsión social* (SMS) can only assume specific obligations within the limits fixed by Article 65 of the TRLOSSP.[33]

---

31. For other matters fixed and variable premium cooperatives will be regulated:
    (a) By TRLOSSP regulations.
    (b) By appropriate regulations from the public limited societies' law as referred by TRLOSSP and also by other regulations that implement them.
    (c) As supplement legislation for cooperatives (Law 27/1999, of 16 July about cooperatives and laws for cooperatives in autonomous communities).
32. With these undertakings, historic precedent is found in the coverage for personal risks through associations and brotherhoods based solely on religious and/or professional inspiration. They have been excluded from the scope of the legislation for insurance organization and are subject to particular regulation according to the law of 6 Dec. 1941, which is closely related to the social security system. They are included in the Law of Organization of Private Insurance (LOSP) of 1984 establishing that they are subject to insurance legislation.
33. Specifically:
    (1) In relation to risk protection for persons, the contingencies that may be covered are death, widowhood, orphanage and retirement. They guarantee economic obligations in the form of capital or income. Moreover, they can also provide obligations for marriage, maternity, children and death. Additionally, they can provide insurance for accident, labour disability, sickness, legal defence and assistance, family aid to subsidize needs due to temporal interruption of professional practice caused by facts or legal acts. Guaranteed economic obligations cannot exceed EUR 30.000 as annual income neither the accounting equivalent as unique receiving of capital. That limit can be updated by the Ministry of Economy taking into consideration there is enough financial surety to satisfy updated obligations.
    (2) In relation to risk protection for goods, it is only possible to provide guarantees for the following and within the amount of these goods: (a) dwellings officially protected and others of social interest if they are inhabited by the mutual partner and family; (b) machinery, goods and work means of mutual partners who are small entrepreneurs (small entrepreneurs are defined as independent workers, professionals and entrepreneurs including those dedicated to

## Chapter 3. Access to Business

### §1. Administrative Authorization to Access and Pursue Insurance Business

*42.* In order to take up and pursue the business of insurance, it is required to obtain and keep an updated administrative authorization, which is granted if the required conditions are complied with.

It is about a 'confirming' authorization. The purpose is not only that the administration supervises undertakings whose plan is to take up the insurance business but also to install a permanent control so the insurance is developed according to the rules. The administration also has the power to adopt intervention measures that may include the withdrawal of the administrative authorization.

Obtaining the administrative authorization leads to an automatic registration in the administrative registry office for insurance undertakings (the Administrative Registry for Insurers (RAEA)) that is run by the DGSFP (Articles 5.7 and 74 of the TRLOSSP). The administrative authorization and automatic registration in the RAEA enable the undertaking to engage in insurance business within a determined branch and territorial scope. In this sense, the administrative authorization enables the undertaking to offer and contract insurance contracts in the lines of business and jurisdictions indicated in the said authorization.

Such material scope coincides with the authorized lines of business and its respective accessorial risks according to the authorization granted.[34]

*43.* The TRLOSSP is based on the general principle that the authorization is given for certain lines of business, including coverage of ancillary or complementary risks located in other lines. Nevertheless, the application and its respective authorization can be limited to covering part of the risks corresponding to certain line of business. In the case of cooperatives, variable premium mutual societies and social mutual societies have a limited material scope within which they can pursue the insurance business according to Article 10 of the TRLOSSP.

As far as territorial scope is concerned, the 1995 LOSSP introduced, as it is known, an important and new 'single license' or 'community passport'. Once granted the authorization is recognized by the different administrative authorities in the European Union (Article 5.5 of the TRLOSSP), except in cases when the application is limited to doing business within certain articles of a national jurisdiction, within a national jurisdiction or within the geographically limited scope established for mutual societies and cooperatives with variable premiums and social mutual societies according to the TRLOSSP.

---

agriculture who do not employ more than five workers); and (c) harvest of fields directly and personally cultivated by the farmer only if they are not included in the annual plan of crop and combined insurance and the integrated cattle in the family exploitation unit.

34. See in Art. 6 TRLOSSP the classification of the different insurance lines of business according to the classic classification derived from the Communitarian Law, direct non-life insurance and direct life insurance.

It is important to warn that undertakings that obtained the European passport are still subject to rules, general and specific provisions, with regard to the right of establishment and freedom to provide services in another Member State (Articles 49–56 and 78–86 of the TRLOSSP).

Authorized undertakings that are willing to expand their material or territorial scope of operation must obtain a new administrative authorization.

*44.* Regarding the procedure to obtain an administrative authorization to accede to the insurance market, undertakings must be publicly incorporated and registered in the commercial registry. With this registration they will acquire a legal personality as (insurance) a public limited company, a mutual society or a social mutual society. Insurance cooperatives must also be registered in the cooperatives registry. Only upon having acquired legal personality will they be able to apply for the administrative authorization and take up the business of insurance.

Once the undertaking obtains a legal personality, it can apply for the authorization. The proceeding requires the submission to the DGSFP documents that prove the compliance with the TRLOSSP conditions. At the end of the administrative procedure, the Ministry of Economy has the power to grant or reject the application for authorization by motivated Ministerial Order. The decision must be taken within six months of the application date and under no circumstance may administrative silence be interpreted as granting the authorization (Article 5 of the TRLOSSP).

Because of the existence of this administrative authorization and its legal effects as such, insurance contracts underwritten by non-authorized undertakings, or by undertakings whose authorization was repealed or who act outside the limits of the granted authorization, will be considered as void and have the consequences specified in Article 4.2 of the TRLOSSP.

## §2. Conditions of Access

*45.* The TRLOSSP establishes the following requirements that an undertaking must fulfil in order to obtain and keep the mentioned authorization (the unique passport for the EEE):[35]

- Be incorporated as an insurance limited public company, insurance cooperative, mutual society or social mutual society.[36]
- Comply with the required conditions with regard to the corporate name[37] and the corporate domicile.[38]

35. See Art. 5.2 of the TRLOSSP.
36. See Part I, Ch. 2.
37. The corporate name of insurance undertakings must include the words *insurances*, or *reinsurances*, or both at the same time, according to its corporate purpose. They cannot use a name that may cause confusion, may be related to another activity or use words that may be interpreted as public or official nature of undertaking except in cases when they actually share that nature. The words *insurances* or *reinsurances* are exclusively reserved for insurance undertakings. In the case of the mutual

- Comply with the conditions regarding the undertaking's close links with other persons or undertakings.
- Comply with the provisions regarding the purpose of the company.[39]
- Comply with the business plan (a sort of planning) that must be followed by the applicant.[40]
- Comply with the regulations relating to the capital or mutual funds to be met by the applicant.[41]
- Comply with the conditions concerning the information that must be provided with regard to the monetary and in-kind contributions of the partners to the corporate capital or mutual funds, and also with the conditions that they must meet in order to be considered as partners in an insurance undertaking.[42]
- Comply with the requirements to be met by persons who are to be managers or directors of the applicant entity.[43]

---

societies, cooperatives and social mutual societies, they will include also its nature and indicate whether they have 'a variable premium' or 'a fixed premium' (Art. 7 of the TRLOSSP and Art. 9 of the ROSSP).

38. Insurance undertakings must be located within the Spanish territory in the place where the centre of management and direction is effectively performed or the centre where the main establishment or place of main exploitation is located (Art. 10 of the ROSSP). The corporate domicile determines the authority of the control agency, which will grant the administrative authorization and will also control the undertaking during the development of the business.
39. The legislator limits the corporate purpose of insurers using double criteria indicating that the corporate purpose of insurers must comprise insurance transactions, capitalization operations, preparatory or complementary transactions and preventive activities (Art. 3 of the TRLOSSP). It also forbids performing the following activities under sanction to be declared void (Art. 4 of the TRLOSSP): operations that lack accounting technical foundations, any other type of commercial activity and mediation of private insurance. The corporate purpose of insurers is exclusive and 'excludes'. It 'excludes' because only authorized insurers may develop private insurance transactions. It is exclusive because insurers may pursue only private insurance business and cannot dedicate to other type of business. It is a matter of guaranteeing the solvency to impede that losses from other activities might be assumed by the reserves made for insurance transactions. Also the corporate name of insurers is characterized by its specialization. Insurers that intend to operate in life insurance must have a corporate purpose 'only' for transactions of that type of insurance. Insurers that intend to provide insurance services in any other lines of direct non-life insurance must have a corporate purpose accordingly.
40. Article 12 of the TRLOSSP.
41. See Art. 13 of the TRLOSSP.
42. Those physical persons and legal entities that directly or indirectly participate in the incorporation of the insurer though a significant participation must be appropriate for a healthy and prudent management.
43. Legislation for the organization and control of insurance business explains that there are 'necessary conditions of honourability and qualification or professional experience'. It is assumed they are professionally qualified, persons that have a university degree in law, economics, accounting and finance, management and direction of enterprises or in specific courses of private insurance. Also it is considered that as persons with professional experience the ones who at least for five years have performed functions of high management, direction, control and consultancy of financial undertakings subject to organization and solvency control by public administration or have performed functions of similar responsibilities in other public or private undertakings with similar size and requirements to the undertaking that is intended to incorporate. Honourability must be referred to commercial and professional scope and is considered as such when persons have complied with commerce regulations and others that regulate the economic activity and business life as well as good commercial, financial and insurance practices.

Also, the application may be rejected when the undertaking does not have the appropriate corporate legal forms as stipulated by law, when its by-laws do not comply with the TRLOSSP requirement when the undertaking lacks any other legal requirement for the validity of its legal form, according to Article 5.6(a) of the TRLOSSP.

§3. Conditions for Pursuit of Insurance Business

*46.* Once the administrative authorization to access the insurance market is granted, the legislation demands the compliance of determined conditions that include 'conditions of admission' and also 'conditions for the exercise of business'.

As specific conditions to pursue insurance business, the legislation distinguishes among capital requirements and requirements related to varied aspects or operations of insurance undertakings and to their business.

## I. Financial Requirements

*47.* The financial requirements imposed on insurance undertakings are to compose technical provisions and to keep up a margin of solvency that in no case shall be lower than a determined amount (the 'guarantee fund').

These requirements are in response to the need for a double solvency. First, a static solvency defined as the technical and financial capacity to face commitments that at a given moment were incurred with the subscribed insurance policies, and requiring the calculation, establishment and investment of sufficient technical provisions. Second, a dynamic solvency defined as the existence of a certain relationship between non-affected patrimonies and the amount of insurance business: this is the solvency margin and part of it will be the 'guarantee fund'.

Insurance undertakings must establish adequate technical provisions in respect to their entire business. To that end, provisions should be properly calculated, accounted for and invested in marketing assets.

*48.* In addition, undertakings must establish an adequate solvency margin in respect to their entire business. The solvency margin corresponds to the assets of the undertaking free of any foreseeable commitments less any tangible items.

The purpose of the surety guarantee fund is to make sure that the solvency margin, which, as has just been mentioned, depends on the volume of business, is never lower than determined amounts.[44]

44. As a general provision, legislation requires that undertakings always have non-compromised patrimony so they can access the insurance market and engage in business. This surety fund must be incorporated by the third portion of the minimum amount of solvency margin correspondent to the insurance undertaking either at the time of the application or along its business life for determined amounts established by the TRLOSSP according to the lines of business. In the case of mutual societies with passive revenue regime, there are specified minimum amounts.

*49.* With regard to distribution of profits, the legislator establishes an initial and temporal limitation, and a permanent prohibition. The first refers to the profits or surpluses gained during the first three full financial years of activity and also during the initial financial year if it is not completed. In these cases the profits cannot be distributed and must be integrally included as legal reserves in limited public companies, as legal reserve with identical regimen in mutual societies and as compulsory reserves in the capital of cooperatives. The (second) permanent prohibition refers to undertakings that have not entirely covered their technical provisions by matching assets or undertakings whose solvency margin or guarantee fund do not reach the legal minimum, in which case they are forbidden to distribute any dividends or apportionments.[45]

## II. Other Conditions to Engage in Insurance Business (By-Laws, Policies, Fees and Framework for Significant Participations)

### *A. Statutes, Policies and Fees*

*50.* The undertakings' by-laws form part of their incorporation act and must accompany the application for authorization. The legislator reminds that the by-laws of insurance undertakings must comply with the TRLOSSP, its complementary dispositions and also with the applicable legislation according to their legal nature.[46]

The contents of insurance policies must be in accordance with the TRLOSSP and 'also' with Title IV of the 1980 LCS on the conflict of law rules.[47]

Premium tariffs must respond to the principles of adequacy and freedom of competition in the insurance market. They also have to be in accordance with the principles of indivisibility, invariability, adequacy and equity.

45. Also insurers that face these situations will not be able to expand its operations to other insurance lines of business they will neither be able to expand its territorial scope nor its business under the right of establishment or freedom to provide services, and finally they cannot expand its commercial network.
46. Consequently, any modification of the undertaking's statutes must be notified to the DGSFP. If the modification determines that the insurer will not comply with some of the requirements or conditions to obtain the administrative authorization (such as in the case when the statutes do not comply with the regulations derived from the mentioned framework), an administrative procedure of revocation will be started without prejudice that can previously be rectified.
47. The ROSSP require: (a) that they should be written 'in a way that they are easily understandable'; (b) that, in the case of proposals and policies of life insurance with benefit participation, there are not numerical calculations of values based on future benefits of the insurer; and (c) that, in collective life insurance, besides the policy, adhesion contracts are used with the adhesion form subscribed by the policyholder and the insured. The ROSSP regulates (it is not really clear) the insurer obligation to provide copy and duplicate of these documents in case they get lost and the policyholder, insured or beneficiary demand them.

As far as the control of policy conditions is concerned, premium tariffs and their technical provisions, which must be based on statistical data, are not subjected to prior administrative authorization to the DGSFP[48] in a separate way, or do they have to be submitted.

*B. Regulatory Framework for Significant Participations*

*51.* One of the conditions for obtaining authorization to have access to business is that the partners, who possess significant participations, must be qualified in view of a healthy and prudent management of the undertaking. To this end, the DGSFP must be informed in the following cases: if, once the authorization is granted, any physical person or legal entities pretend to acquire directly or indirectly a significant participation of the undertaking, even in the case of increase or reduction of capital, mergers and spin-offs; when an increase in capital equals or surpasses the limits of 20%, 30% or 50% or when the undertaking comes to be controlled by those persons or legal entities.

The DGSFP will have three months from the date the information is submitted to make an opposition, which must be grounded on the lack of the acquirer to meet the appropriate conditions that assure a healthy and prudent management of the undertaking.[49]

## §4. Freedom to Provide Services and Right of Establishment Within the European Union and the European Economic Area

### I. Insurance Activities of Spanish Insurers in Other Countries of the European Economic Area

*52.* The TRLOSSP dedicates Chapter IV (Articles 49–56) to the regulation of the activity of Spanish insurers in accordance with the right of establishment and freedom to provide services within the European Economic Area. The general principle included in Article 49.1 of the TRLOSSP authorizes insurers having obtained the prescribed authorization to exercise their activities in the entire territory of the European Economic Area,[50] under their right of establishment or by virtue of the freedom to provide services.

48. It is only required 'to be available' to the DGSFP at the corporate domicile of the insurer: (a) the models of insurance policies of compulsory subscription; and (b) in life insurance contracts, technical foundations used for calculating the fees and for technical provisions, in order to control the compliance of accounting principles. Also if the DGSFP considers necessary, it can require the presentation of policy models, premium fees and technical foundations to control the compliance of technical provisions and regulations for insurance contracts. These requirements are not considered as previous conditions to engage in the insurance business.
49. The duty to previously inform the DGSFP is imposed also on those who intend to end, directly or indirectly, their significant participation, or decrease their participation below the limits mentioned before. In any case, the DGSFP cannot move to oppose but will impose an administrative sanction in case of failure to comply with the duty to inform.
50. See Art. 49.2 of the TRLOSSP about exceptions.

In case of cross-border activities, insurers should separately inform the DGSFP of the transactions performed in each Member State (Article 52 of the TRLOSSP).

### A. *Right of Establishment*

*53.* Article 55.1 of the TRLOSSP describes the information to be sent in advance to the DGSFP by the insurers who intend to open a branch in another State of the European Economic Area. Such information together with the certificate of their having satisfied the solvency requirement shall be sent within three months by the DGSFP to the competent authorities of the State where the Spanish insurer intends to open a branch. The insurer must also be informed of the moment when the information is sent.

When, upon receipt of such information, the DGSFP has reason to doubt the insurer's ability to establish a branch in another State of the European Economic Area, it may refuse to make the mentioned communication. The competent authority of the country where the branch is to be installed may indicate the conditions relating to the general good under which the insurance business must be carried on. Spanish insurance undertakings may be established and may begin their activities when the competent authority of the country of the branch gives notice of its decision, or on expiry of a period of two months upon the notification of the DGSFP that confirms the sending of the information to the supervisory authority.

### B. *Freedom to Provide Services*

*54.* The pursuit of insurance business by Spanish undertakings in other States of the European Economic Area under the right of freedom to provide services also requires an exchange of information process, which, in this case, is simplified because information is greatly reduced and deadlines are shortened (Article 56 of the LOSSP). Indeed, the DGSFP provides for a one-month deadline to send the information to the control authority, and the insurer may begin its activities from the date it is notified the information was sent by the DGSFP.

## II. Insurance Business of Insurers Domiciled in Other Member States of the European Economic Area within the Spanish Territory

*55.* The issue is governed by Articles 78–86 of the TRLOSSP, which prescribes a regime that is in accordance with the requirements imposed on Spanish insurers, be it this time approached from the opposite view. In this way, Spain recognizes as general principles the right of establishment and the freedom to provide services for undertakings domiciled in other Member Status of the European Economic Area who obtained authorization to operate in their Member State of origin (Article 78.1 of the TRLOSSP).

These undertakings must submit to the rules that are dictated by reason of general good and also to the organization and control regulations for undertakings that provide insurance services, including those that protect the insured. In addition, they must submit the information that is required by the Ministry of Economy to prove that they comply with the law (Article 78.2 of the TRLOSSP). At the same time, Article 78.3 describes the DGSFP's powers in case of non-compliance with the regulations: first, it will require the insurer to behave according to the legal system, and second, it will inform the supervisory authority of the undertaking's state of origin. Only in extreme cases it will directly act against the insurer.

Finally, these undertakings will be subject to charges from the Insurance Compensation Consortium, and if they deal with motor vehicle liability insurance they must participate in the Spanish office for vehicle insurers (OFESAUTO).

### *A. Right of Establishment*

*56.* The DGSFP will have to inform the supervisory authority of the country of origin of the undertaking that intends to open a branch in Spain of the conditions under which, for reasons of general good, the activity must be carried on. The mentioned undertaking may begin its operations from the date the DGSFP notifies its approval or after two months from the date the supervisory authority notifies that it sent the application to the DGSFP and did not receive such notification (Article 83.1 of the TRLOSSP).

### *B. Freedom to Provide Services*

*57.* Undertakings domiciled in other Member States of the European Economic Area may start their activity upon receiving notification from the supervisory agency of the country of origin informing that it sent the application to the DGSFP (Article 85 of the TRLOSSP).

These undertakings must appoint a representative for tax purposes. If they operate with motor vehicle liability insurance, they must also appoint a representative who will take care of the complaints presented by injured third parties and will represent the insurer before the judiciary and administrative agencies (Article 86 of the TRLOSSP).

# Chapter 4. Supervision

## §1. Control and Administration: Supervision of the Private Insurance Business

*58.* After having studied the organization of the insurance business and the setting up of insurance undertakings in previous chapters, let us now turn our attention to the legal framework of the system of supervision of the private insurance market by the public administration (DGSFP).

The legal framework of organization and supervision is based on the 'system of administrative authorization with permanent link'. This is the area of operative authorizations. The administrative system not only has to supervise the business of insurance but is also expected to submit the insurance undertaking to a status that implies constant surveillance – permanent link – by the administration in such a way that the insurance business is constantly performed in accordance with the legal framework. It also enables the administration to adopt diverse measures of intervention including the withdrawal of the granted administrative authorization.

*59.* As it was indicated by the preliminary recitals of the 1995 LOSSP the 'system of administrative authorization of permanent link' gives a legal basis for:

(a) Examining the financial, technical and professional requirements of the insurance undertakings to take up and pursue business in the insurance market.
(b) Controlling the financial safety and the compliance with regulations for insurance contracts and its statistics during the undertaking's activity in such market.
(c) Determining intervention measures with respect to undertakings that have not behaved in accordance with the mentioned regulations and taking 'special control measures' and even measures of withdrawing the administrative authorization or ordering the dissolution of the undertaking when it does not comply with the minimum requirements to operate in the market.

*60.* And all this operates through an information system that implies:

(a) The imposition of special information obligations upon undertakings wanting to take up and pursue activities in the private insurance market.
(b) The power of the administration to require undertakings to provide information.
(c) The existence of insurance inspection with extensive powers.

As it has been remarked by the doctrine, we are in front of a supervision activity based on information and data about the situation and evolution that must be provided for by the supervised undertakings themselves or eventually obtained by inspectors.

The information and data will be evaluated by the supervisory authority, which reacts in different ways and may consist of:

- A petition for complementary information or the ordering of further inspection with sufficient powers to obtain such information.
- A mandate ordering the undertaking to stop its operations because of the increase of solvency risks or lack of liquidity and proceed to redress the situation.
- The setting up of sanctioning procedures and the levy of correspondent administrative penalties.
- The adoption of specific measures called 'special control measures' (before 'provisional remedies') that include temporary replacement of management bodies, intervention and withdrawal of the administrative authorization that may lead to the undertaking's dissolution as previously mentioned.
- The withdrawal of the authorization either as an administrative sanction or as a consequence of the undertaking's dissolution.
- The dissolution of the undertaking.
- The intervention during the liquidation process of the supervised undertaking.
- The intervention during bankruptcy proceedings of undertakings.

*61.* By way of summary, supervision is carried out in two ways: surveillance and correction, and with the goal of preventing and thus avoiding incorrect behaviour.

The decisions are made after evaluating the information. These decisions aim at preventing and, in any case, correcting irregular situations appearing from that information.

Our legal system has chosen the model by which the functions of control and supervision of the insurance market are carried out by the general administration of the State, specifically from the DGSFP that hierarchically depends on the Ministry of Economy.

## §2. The Obligations of Providing Information to the General Direction of Insurance and Pension Funds, and the Insurance Inspection Agency

*62.* As was mentioned previously, information is one of the essential elements of the system. Besides the TRLOSSP, which establishes requirements for access to and pursuing of the insurance business, the legislator charges undertakings with special and concrete obligations to inform and also provides for extensive powers of the authorities to demand information. Article 71 of the TRLOSSP states that insurance undertakings 'will provide the DGSFP with the necessary documents and information, periodically and in the form lawfully determined by individual mandate of the General Direction'. In this way the Ministry of Economy complies with its financial control duty laid down in Article 25 of the TRLOSSP (policies, fees and premiums). The first of them consists 'in the verification of the state of solvency, technical provisions and assets that represent them'.

The information system is completed with the existence of the insurance inspection agency vested with extensive powers. According to Article 72.4 of the TRLOSSP, inspectors can control the legal, economic and technical situation as well as the conditions under which insurance operations are carried out. It also vests the

Ministry of Economy with powers to supervise the insurance business with general powers and also to carry out control on an individual basis.

*63.* For carrying out of its inspection functions correctly, the Ministry of Economy may examine all documents relating to the transactions that are performed by the undertakings and to require the originals on a temporary basis or copies of the incorporation act, so that they can be included in the inspection report. The undertaking has the duty to provide all of them and to give the administration all the facilities so it can accomplish its goal. If the person or inspected undertaking would have grounded reasons, it can refuse to give the copies alleging such reasons by writing. This document will also be incorporated in the act.

Inspection can be performed in the corporate domicile of the undertaking, in any of its branches where insurance transactions are carried out partially or totally or in the DGSFP offices when the elements can be examined there.

Insurance inspectors have access to the corporate domicile and branches, offices and locations where the inspected person or undertakings carry out insurance business; in case the undertaking refuses to provide documents, a judicial authorization, or in the case of inspection of other entities (‘*dependencias*’) an authorization of the General Insurance Direction.

Inspections reports are considered to be official documents and constitute evidence of the acts described and verified by the involved inspector, unless otherwise proved.

*64.* In addition to organizing the information system in this way, the TRLOSSP establishes specific mechanisms of forced intervention with respect to certain specific legal requirements by law (e.g., Article 22 concerning significant participations or Article 24 concerning assignment of portfolio, mergers, acquisitions, conglomerates and spin-off operations). Chapter III of the Royal Legislative Decree 6/2004 (TRLOSPP) enumerates five typical mechanisms of interventions: withdrawal of the administrative authorization, administrative dissolution of the undertaking, intervention during the liquidation proceeding, imposition of ‘special control measures’ and sanctions.

## §3. Special Control Measures

*65.* The rules on technical provisions, on the solvency margin and the guarantee fund, constitute a fundamental element of the supervision of insurance undertakings and an efficient way to assure their solvency.[51] When the current or future solvency of an undertaking might be affected, the legislation enables the supervisor to take a group of measures called, since 1995, special control measures, ‘provisional measures’ in the 1984 law. These laws have the purpose of preventing the danger of an insolvency.

51. Preliminary recitals of the TRLOSSP.

These special control measures have been qualified as 'the most genuine elements for supervision of insurance undertakings'. Situations that allow the supervisor to impose special control measures function as traffic lights because they give signals of current or future solvency problems and demonstrate the need to adopt specific measures to solve them. The nature of the administrative measures will depend on the seriousness of the detected situation.

*66.* Articles 38 and 39 of the TRLOSSP establishes as 'special control measures':

(a) Measures to guarantee future solvency of the insurer (Article 38 of the TRLOSSP).
(b) 'Special control measures' (Article 39 of the TRLOSSP) whereby it shall be noticed that the legislator uses for this second subcategory of 'special control measures' the same term as for the title of the entire group.

## §4. Administrative Sanction Framework

*67.* Violation of the regulation on the organization and supervision of the private insurance industry gives a lead to administrative sanctions. The legal framework for these sanctions is basically found in Articles 40–48 of the TRLOSSP and in Articles 93–96 of the ROSSP.

The rules for sanctions included in the 1995 law and currently in the 2004 TRLOSSP constitute a detailed and extensive system of sanctions, until then unknown in the insurance sector. They identify those that are subject to such regime and the rules they infringed; they categorize sanctions, regulate criteria for sanctions and also prescribe the particular measures for their implementation;[52] they regulate infringements and sanctions and determine the administrative agencies in charge of the infringement process.

Nevertheless, the TRLOSSP sanctions system must be supplemented (as a subsidiary system) with Law 30/1992 of 26 November concerning the legal framework for public administrations and common administrative procedures,[53] and with the Royal Decree 2119/1993 of 2 December concerning the procedures for sanctioning subjects that operate in financial markets and the procedure for the carrying out of the sanctioning power (Royal Decree 1398/1993).

*68.* As stipulated by Articles 46(a) of the TRLOSSP and 96 of the ROSSP, the different Sub Directions General of the General Direction for Insurance will be responsible for carrying out the proceedings according to the type of insurance that is involved. The imposition of sanctions for serious and light infringements is the responsibility of the GDSFP. Very serious sanctions are imposed by the Ministry of

52. Order of 'reposition' of the altered situation, the provisional appointment of administrators of the undertakings and publicity of the sanctions.
53. See Art. 70. 3 of the TRLOSSP.

Economy, on proposal of the GDSFP, except for the revocation of the authorization that can only be imposed by the Council of Ministers.

*69.* Chapter III titled 'Intervention of Insurance Undertakings' of the TRLOSSP includes, as has been stated before, the sanctions system. Notwithstanding its place in the legislation, sanctions and the sanctioning procedure are a separate set of measures contained in the TRLOSSP. Indeed, for example, the procedure for imposing special control measures might occur prior to the sanctions procedure, simultaneously with or consequently to the time of the revocation, dissolution or liquidation proceedings, which are established in the mentioned chapter of the Statute.

Doctrine has warned about the lack of coordination among the procedures of intervention and the need to analyse their compatibility when applied simultaneously.

Analysis of the different types of infringements stipulated in Article 40 of the TRLOSSP shows that certain types of behaviour may trigger the launching of a sanctioning procedure, a supervision proceeding or any other legally provided for intervention procedure.

### §5. Termination of the Insurance Undertaking

*70.* The termination of an undertaking is not an instant event but the result of a complex process in which the double aspect of the undertaking (obligational and institutional) is taken into account: indeed, not only does the corporate contract have to be cancelled but also the legal entity that was born as a result of that contract. Due to dependency of the insurance activity upon the obtaining and maintenance of the administrative authorization, its revocation adds a new element to this moment of the corporate life.

## I. Withdrawal of the Administrative Authorization

*71.* The withdrawal of the administrative authorization occurs when the same agency that granted the authorization decides through an administrative act to deprive the undertaking of the right to pursue activities within the insurance field. It is not a matter of considering null the administrative act that granted the authorization due to the discovering of lack of requirements, but rather a decision that is due to change of circumstances and public interest. Withdrawal must be understood as a formal act because it can only be adopted once the mentioned requirements in the TRLOSSP have been followed.

Furthermore, given their importance, the conditions stipulated by the legislator must be applied in a restrictive manner. Nevertheless, the prolific use of undetermined legal concepts allows a great margin of administrative discretion.

*72.* Article 26 of the TRLOSSP establishes the following causes for withdrawal: express resignation of the undertaking; failure of the undertaking to begin its operations for at least a year or interruption of operations for a period of six months; non-compliance of the undertaking with all conditions that are required by this law for the granting of administrative authorization or that are incurred in cause for dissolution; non-compliance of the undertaking with established measures under a financial plan to be complied within a fixed delay; or, finally, imposition the administrative sanction of withdrawal.

The TRLOSSP does not state a specific procedure to withdraw the administrative authorization but designates the Ministry of Economy as the responsible agency for doing so.

*73.* The withdrawal of the administrative authorization entails, in all cases, the immediate prohibition to underwrite new insurance, to accept reinsurance or to liquidate insurance transactions in the affected branches by the withdrawal. It is established then that the withdrawal does not extinguish the legal entity. It only impedes the practice of the insurance business.

In addition, if the withdrawal affects all operating branches of the undertaking, its administrative dissolution will follow without the dissolution procedure stipulated by the TRLOSSP, which requires a call for a general assembly. In contrast, if the revocation affects only one or some of the undertaking's branches, but not all of them, the undertaking must interrupt its operations in respect to those revoked branches but may continue with the rest.

## II. Dissolution of the Insurance Undertaking

*74.* Dissolution supposes the opening of the process that will extinguish the undertaking. That is to say, whereas the administrative revocation is an administrative act to prohibit the legal exercise of the insurance business, the dissolution opens the liquidation process of the corporation. It is the beginning of the process to cancel the corporate contract.

Normally, the revocation of the administrative authorization is related to the dissolution of the corporation, but it does not always happen this way. After ending the insurance business as a result of total withdrawal, the corporation continues performing other activities through the modification of its corporate purpose.

The TRLOSSP does not establish a time sequence between the revocation of the administrative authorization and the dissolution. Occasionally, withdrawal will lead to the corporation's dissolution; in other instances, revocation will occur during the liquidation of an already dissolved corporation.

*75.* Article 27 of the TRLOSSP establishes the following causes of dissolution:

(a) Administrative withdrawal that affects all branches of the undertaking's operations.

(b) The general assignment of the insurance contracts portfolio when it affects all operative branches of the undertaking.[54]
(c) When the number of partners has decreased under the legal minimum required in the case of the mutual societies, insurance cooperatives and social mutual societies.
(d) When there have been no passive apportionment (*derramas*).
(e) Causes of dissolution cited by the Articles.[55]

*76.* The causes of dissolution enumerated operate in different ways. Dissolution due to simple agreement of the general assembly – that is to say, without the need to allege any cause – must be adopted with the same majority that is needed for modification of by-laws. In this case, dissolution occurs at the time the agreement is reached.

Dissolution due to expiration of the fixed term established by the company by-laws will be automatically indicated by the commercial registrar without agreement of the board or general assembly. In such case, the undertaking may only avoid automatic dissolution if it has a corporate agreement to extend the deadline registered before the deadline expires. Dissolution in other cases will require agreement of the board meeting or of the general assembly. To this goal, its management bodies have to call for an assembly within two months upon the occurrence of the cause for dissolution. Any partner may require the managers to call for a board meeting or a general assembly when any legitimate cause for dissolution exists.

*77.* If there is legal cause for dissolution and the board meeting or the general assembly is not called, or even in the case it is called but not successful and an agreement is not reached, or if the agreement is against the dissolution, the management board must apply for administrative dissolution of the undertaking within ten calendar days from the date on which the call for the board meeting or general assembly should have occurred, or on the date agreed for its meeting or on the date of the meeting when an agreement for dissolution could not be reached or the agreement was against its dissolution.

Once the Ministry of Economy takes notice of the presence of a cause for dissolution or breach of duty of the corporate bodies mentioned previously, they will proceed to the administrative dissolution of the undertaking.

The agreement for administrative dissolution will withdraw the authorization for all operating branches of the undertaking.

Finally, it is also possible that the withdrawal of the administrative authorization may imply the administrative dissolution of the undertaking, in which case it will not be necessary to follow the procedure previously explained. The revocation by itself directly leads to the administrative dissolution.

---

54. Nevertheless, the assignment of the portfolio and the revocation of the administrative authorization are not cause of dissolution when there is a modification of the corporate purpose in order to develop an activity different from insurance.
55. Nowadays is regulated in Arts 360–363 of Capital Companies Act,

## III. Liquidation of an Insurance Undertaking

*78.* Liquidation is conformed by acts leading to liquidate the liabilities (satisfy credits) as well as the assets (charge debts and convert them into liquid amount) to finally distribute the remainder between the partners before cancelling the registration of the undertaking in the registry of insurance undertakings and the commercial registry.

The legal framework set out by the legislator establishes important exceptions to the general framework for commercial undertakings. They have the purpose of preserving the interests of the insured, the beneficiaries and injured third parties, so as to avoid that their expectations of receiving the right sums from the insurers could be damaged.

The opening of the liquidation phase not only reinforces the administrative authorities to organize and supervise but also enlarges the group of measures that the supervisory authority may adopt. Consequently, in order to save the interests of the insured, beneficiaries or injured and other insurers, liquidation will imply the appointment of liquidators or entrusting the liquidation to the CCS, stipulating officially or by petition of the liquidators the general or partial cession of the insurance contract portfolio of the undertaking and in this way facilitating its liquidation; and determining the date of the anticipated deadline of duration of the insurance contracts that form part of the portfolio of the undertaking in liquidation and avoiding major damages to the insured, the beneficiary and the injured third parties under those contracts.

*79.* The extensive powers of the supervisory authority lead the legislator to set out four ways to liquidate the insurance undertaking: liquidation according to corporations law, which assumes the adequacy of the assets to face all pending credits; liquidation in case of insolvency of the undertaking; liquidation set up by the administration, either through the appointment of an intervention official; or liquidation set up by the CCS, which will try to avoid a liquidation by insolvency and the ensuring potential damage to the interests of insured, beneficiary and injured third parties.

These types can be reclassified into three types because the way in which the liquidation takes place depends on the body that deals with the liquidation: the liquidators, the CCS or the administrator for solvency within the procedure of insolvency.

# Chapter 5. Accounting, Duty to Consolidate Debts and Auditing

*80.* The same reasons that give grounds for administrative supervision of insurers justify the establishment of a specific accounting system and the imposition of special obligations to provide mixed information derived from accounting and from other sources. This information also benefits the interests of the insurer, insured and the financial system as a whole because it allows the analysis of the degree of static and dynamic solvency of the insurers for a rational exploitation of the insurance activity and the adequate supervision by the administrative authorities.

This specific accounting system (Articles 20 and 21 of the TRLOSSP) considers undertakings individually. It also establishes the obligation to consolidate the accounts of the consolidated groups of undertakings that provide insurance services. This last obligation is different from the obligation to provide an annual balance sheet as established by the Commercial Code, the rules of which must be complied with by the group of corporations that form part of insurance undertakings.

The accounting and presentation of accounts by consolidated groups of undertakings are regulated first by the respective specific laws (TRLOSSP, ROSSP, regulations included in the Scheme of Accounts for Insurance Undertakings enacted by RD 2014/1997 of 26 December and complementary regulations) and in lack of that by the Commercial Code, the general scheme of accounts and by other commercial regulations for accounting. Specific regulations for accounting of insurance undertakings include accounting principles that are regulations for annual accounting statements; criteria to be used to evaluate these statements; and the framework for approval, verification, deposition and publication of such accounts.

The financial year will, in any case, coincide with the calendar year. Those undertakings authorized to operate simultaneously in life, accident and sickness insurance must organize their accounting separately and per type of insurance.

*81.* The legislation establishes special obligations to transmit accounting information to the DGSFP. On the one hand, it establishes that insurance undertakings, groups and subgroups of consolidated insurance undertakings or groups of corporations controlled by insurance undertakings must provide accounting information annually, quarterly or half-yearly. On the other hand, the law invests the DGSFP with powers to require useful information from these undertakings and other physical persons and legal entities related to insurers with a view to complying with its duty to supervise the insurance business.

Law 19/1988 of 12 July, about accounts auditing states that corporations or any undertaking with the corporate purpose to provide services regulated by the TRLOSSP should be subject to accounts auditing within the limits laid out by the regulations[56] except undertakings that may present an abridged group balance sheet according to Article 181.1 of the consolidated text of the limited public companies. Undertakings providing business lines of life, caution, credit, civil liability or the ones that are subject to special control or in a liquidation process will not be

56. Ad. Disp. 1a., 1, d). Reglamentarial Ad Disp. 5a., 1 of the ROSSP.

exempted from the auditing obligation. The DGSFP may also require accounts auditing when it considers it to be convenient to obtain information on the accounts.

# Chapter 6. Assignment of an Insurance Portfolio and Structural Modifications of Undertakings That Provide Insurance Services

## §1. Assignment of Insurance Portfolio

*82.* Spanish insurance undertakings are able to assign different types of insurance contracts between each other, except in the case of mutual societies, variable premium cooperatives and the social mutual societies, but they can only acquire the same type of portfolio.

The general assignment of one or more types of insurance portfolio has to follow the below rules:

(a) It cannot be the cause for cancellation of insurance contracts that have been assigned provided that the assignee is subrogated in all the rights and duties of the assignor and only if the involved companies are not mutual societies, variable premium cooperatives or social mutual societies.
(b) After the assignment, the assignee must have sufficient technical provisions and surpass the margin of solvency established by the legislation.
(c) The assignment must be authorized by the Ministry of Economy.

Once authorized, the assignment must be formalized by a public record that has to be registered in the commercial registry.

Partial assignment of an insurance portfolio is also admissible if it is provided for by regulation; in that case, policyholders are allowed to cancel the insurance contracts.

## §2. Spin-Off, Merger and Acquisitions of Undertakings That Provide Insurance Services

*83.* The social mutual societies, mutual societies and variable premium cooperatives can be transformed into fixed premium social mutual societies, fixed premium mutual societies and fixed premium cooperatives, and these can be converted into public limited companies. Any transformation of insurance undertakings into another legal form that is not included in the forms mentioned, even in the case of insurers, will be considered void.

The rules that govern assignments of portfolios in general are applied to the transformation of insurance undertakings except when policyholders can cancel the contracts.

Any insurance undertaking can merge into a public limited company, and public limited companies can absorb insurance undertakings in any legal form. Mutual societies and fixed premium cooperatives can merge into corporations of the same legal nature and form but may only absorb other insurance undertakings that are incorporated under a legal form other than that of the public limited company.

Mutual societies, variable premium cooperatives and the social mutual societies may merge in corporations of same nature and legal form but may only absorb insurance undertaking with the same legal form.

*84.* Insurance undertakings cannot merge with non-insurance undertakings or absorb non-insurance undertakings or be absorbed by them.

Regulations for general assignments of portfolios must be applied to mergers and absorptions of insurance undertakings. Spin-off of insurance undertakings is submitted to the same limitations and requirements required to mergers of insurers.

Mergers, spin-offs and acquisitions of insurance undertakings are regulated by the TRLOSSP and, in any aspect not expressly regulated by the TRLOSSP, by the consolidated text of the public limited company law only if it does not contradict the first.

# Part II. The Insurance Contract

## Chapter 1. Generalities

### §1. Definition of Insurance

*85.* From an economic perspective, insurance can be defined as reciprocal coverage of a future fortuitous quantifiable need. Insurance has a historical justification because it was born in the maritime business with a purpose of covering shipping risks. Starting from there, the concept of insurance was extended to cover losses to property and assets located on firm ground. During this first phase, the need arose to clearly distinguish the branches of insurance, and although the concept of insurance later extended to cover other risks, the purpose remained restricted to indemnification. Already then, a number of principles were developed, which still hold today.[57]

Later, in the middle of the nineteenth century, life insurance would develop. At first, the lawfulness of this branch of insurance was denied in most European countries, but the connection between insurance and savings, and the motivation to see workers' compensation insurance as an element of solidarity and as a social tool, would stimulate the development of the modern concept of life insurance. The initial reluctance against life insurance was responsible for the fact that after the change of attitude with respect to its lawfulness, the concept of life insurance remained separate from traditional insurance, which was seen strictly as a contract of indemnity. It so happened that a controversy about the nature of the insurance contract arose.

*86.* There are two theses at hand.[58] On the one hand, there is the indemnity thesis that aims at formulating a unitary concept of insurance, which includes diverse types and subtypes offered by the reality of practice. Its justification relies on the thesis that every insurance contract has the same cause: the function to indemnify.

57. Prohibition for double insurance, prohibition for unjust enrichment, and so on.
58. A summary may be found in A. Menéndez Menéndez, 'Preliminary. Articles 1 to 4', in *Comentarios a la Ley de contrato de seguro*, AA.VV. (Ed. E. Verdera) (Madrid: CUNEF, 1982), 84ff.

It can be either an objective indemnification – which is established after the occurrence of an insured event, and the valuation of which is done on the basis of objective criteria – or subjective, as happens in life insurance, in which case the sum to be paid is fixed a priori.[59]

On the other hand, there are those who defend the dualistic theory, claiming that every insurance contract is presumed to face a potential economic need, but that, strictly speaking, there is indemnification only in property insurance. In life insurance, the patrimonial need is abstract; the insurer has the obligation to pay a previously fixed sum in accordance with the premium and not related to the damage that is effectively suffered. Therefore, there is a distinction between one kind of insurance that covers an actual need (property insurance), where the insurer's obligation is subject to the existence and valuation of the damage, and the function of which is to indemnify; and a type of insurance that covers an abstract need (personal insurance), where the insurer's obligation is to pay a sum regardless of the damage occurred. When it does not have the purpose to cover an actual need, insurance has the sole function to save money.[60]

*87.* Contrary to what is the case in other legal systems, the Spanish legislator has chosen to give a definition of the contract of insurance. The reason for defining the concept of insurance was found in need to overcome the distinction between civil insurance and commercial insurance, that at one time was made in our codes, and also in the utility that a positive definition of the institution[61] could offer. The authors of the draft bill, who were inspired by the definition in Article 1882 of the Italian Civil Code, tried to avoid every preference between the existing doctrinal positions and intend to include all the basic branches of insurance.

Article 1 of the LCS defines the insurance contract as a contract by which the insurer is obliged, against payment of a premium, to indemnify or to pay a fixed sum or replace an income or to carry any other agreed-on obligation in case of occurrence of the insured event. Contrary to the intentions of the drafters of the text of the bill,[62] it is still showing some distrust against the 'unitarian' doctrine. The debate about the definition of the insurance contract thus remains open.

---

59. M. Traviesas, *Sobre contrato de seguro terrestre* (Madrid: Revista de Derecho Privado, 1933) R. Uría, 'Orientaciones modernas sobre el concepto jurídico del seguro del seguro', *RDM*, 1962, 263ff; M. Broseta Pont, *El contrato de reaseguro* (Madrid: Aguilar, 1961), 94ff; F. Sánchez Calero, 'Artículo 1. Definición', in *Ley de contrato de seguro. Comentarios a la Ley 50/1980, de 8 de octubre y sus modificaciones*, AA.VV. (Dir F. Sánchez Calero), 3th edn (Pamplona: Aranzadi, 2005), 39ff.

60. J. Garrigues, *Contrato de seguro terrestre*, 2th edn (Madrid, 1982), 28ff and 481ff; M. Broseta Pont, *Manual de Derecho mercantil*, 10th edn (Madrid: Tecnos, 1994), 560–562; F. Vicent Chuliá, 'Concepto y caracteres del contrato de seguro en la nueva Ley', in *Comentarios a la Ley de contrato de seguro*, AA.VV. ed. E. Verdera (Madrid: CUNEF, 1982), 137ff; STS 15-6-1987 (Civil). RAJ 1987/4468.

61. The STS 26-6-2001 (Social). RAJ 2001/6836 requires the intervention of an insurer undertaking in order to be qualified as an insurance contract.

62. A summary of the case law and procedures in the insurance contract law may be found in F. Sánchez Calero, n. 2, 86, 20ff *supra*.

## §2. CATEGORIES OF INSURANCE

*88.* Among the most important branches of private insurance are marine insurance, which is currently governed by the Commercial Code; aviation insurance, which is subject to a special regulation; and ground transport insurance, which is basically governed by the insurance contract law. There are also special laws that relate to some particular types of insurance.

The basic feature that differentiates them lies in the distinction between indemnity insurance and personal insurance. This is reflected in the insurance contract law that establishes general provisions applicable to all types of insurance contracts[63] and then covers indemnity insurance[64] separately from personal insurance.[65] Both types have their respective general provisions.

Furthermore, between indemnity insurance contracts it is possible to further differentiate between insurance that covers interest in goods,[66] or liability insurance that covers an interest in particular rights[67] or that covers patrimony as a whole.[68]

Personal insurance can be subdivided into insurance in which the interest covered is life[69] and those in which the interest covered is the physical integrity.[70]

## §3. CHARACTERISTICS OF INSURANCE CONTRACT LAW

*89.* Insurance doctrine states that an insurance contract is a contract under onerous title, an aleatory contract, contract of adhesion and of a contract of the utmost good faith. Insurance is 'under onerous title' because the insurer will pay the agreed-on compensation if the contingency occurs in consideration of a premium or mutual contribution paid by the insured. This characteristic is present in the definition of insurance where the obligations of the parties are expressly described.[71] The existence of reciprocal obligations establishes that an insurance contract is bilateral.

The insurance contract is aleatory because at the time of the conclusion of the contract the insurer does not know whether its consideration will be paid or, in the case of indemnity insurance, how much will be paid.[72]

*90.* Insurance is a contract of continuous duration. Against the policyholder's consideration, which consists in the payment of the premium, the insurer offers to cover the insured risk during the entire period of the coverage. Also, the insurance

63. Títle I, Arts 1–24.
64. Títle II.
65. Títle III.
66. For example fire, theft, ground transport.
67. For example credit and caution.
68. For example civil liability and reinsurance.
69. Life insurance for death, insurance for survival, mixed insurance.
70. Accident insurance, health assistance and sickness.
71. See the SSTS 20-3-1991 (Civil). RAJ 1991/2267 and 7-3-1997 (Civil). RAJ 1997/1645.
72. See the SSTS 22-10-1986 (Social). RAJ 1986/5881; 21-5-1990 (Social) RAJ 1990/4484; and 26-11-1991 (Social). RAJ 1991/8274.

contract does not end when the loss-producing hazard occurs, but it continues as long as the risk and the insurable interest exist.

The insurance contract terms are normally stipulated in a collective manner for which reason insurance is considered to be an adhesion contract.[73] Therefore, insurance is considered to be a business contract (*'contrato de empresa'*) and is assumed to be so in the LCS, which establishes control over the general and particular provisions.

*91.* Finally, insurance is a contract of the utmost good faith. This characteristic is based on the fact that insurance implies a relationship that is durable or of successive periods of duration, which generates obligations and very special duties for the parties. On the one hand, the insurer is a businessperson who normally has qualifications that are very superior to those possessed by the insured. On the other hand, the insured has an immediate insurable interest that makes her or his loyal collaboration an essential element at the time of conclusion and also during the lifetime of the contract. The concept of good faith should not be understood in its subjective sense (ignorance or wrongful belief) but as an objective standard of behaviour, prescribed by ethical requirements and current social consciousness.

*92.* Nevertheless, when legal doctrine mentions the utmost good faith element it intends to underline that besides the regular effects of any contract of adhesion, the insurance contract also generates other ones. There is a series of duties and obligations weighing on the parties not only during the life of the contract but also already at the time before its conclusion.

Good faith has bad faith as its correlate. Bad faith is not synonymous with malice but always implies fault. Without entering into a detailed analysis of the concepts of bad faith and malice, let it be noted that the LCS states that malicious behaviour of the insured is a cause for cancellation of the contract.[74]

## §4. Mandatory Provisions

*93.* The provisions of the LCS are mandatory.[75] They were intended by the legislator to protect the insured. It should be clarified that the terms *insured* and *consumer* in accordance with the LGDCU are not synonymous. The protection granted by the mandatory character of the LCS is acquired by the sole fact of being insured. This legislative choice was made in view of the weak position of the insured within a contract of adhesion. Insurance companies are invested with particular technical expertise, which gives them a superior position compared to regular contracting parties.

---

73. See among many others, the SSTS 10-6-1991 (Penal). RAJ 1991/4582; 5-9-1991 (Civil). RAJ 1991/6043; 27-11-1991 (Civil). RAJ 1991/8496; and 29-1-1996 (Civil). RAJ 1996/738.
74. Samples of this are Art. 19 of the LCS where the impossibility to insure the incurred event caused by the bad faith of the insured is established, and Art. 31 of the LCS where bad faith insurance is regulated.
75. See the SSTS 8-11-1989 (Penal). RAJ 1989/8592; 28-7-1990 (Civil). RAJ 1990/6185; 20-3-1991 (Civil). RAJ 1991/2267; and 5-6-1997 (Civil). RAJ 1997/4607.

*94.* The obligatory compliance with the LCS is not absolute, though. There are three exceptions: when the law itself stipulates the contrary, when a more favourable clause for the insured is agreed on or when large risks are involved.

First, in the LCS some specific provisions expressly state that they are not mandatory.[76] Consequently, the parties may agree whatever is convenient for them with the sole limitation of their own free will. They are 'dispositive' provisions that lead, *a contrario*, to consider the rest of the provisions as being mandatory.

*95.* Second, the parties may agree on a different regime whenever it is more favourable to the insured. The LCS is, therefore, a minimum law.[77] Nevertheless, the possibilities for agreement in favour of the insured are not unlimited because a more favourable agreement cannot violate the nature of the insurance contract by inserting a clause that infringes on the fundamentals of insurance. For that reason, the rights of the insured may arise from an extension of rights and prerogatives recognized by the legal framework in the form of charges, duties and obligations.

*96.* Finally, the insurance of the so-called large risks (Articles 44.2 and 107.2 of the LCS) and reinsurance (Article 79 of the LCS) are not subject to mandatory rules as stated in Article 2 of the LCS. The parties who stipulate these insurance contracts have the same qualification and sometimes even the same economic power as insurance companies. This is why the regulator has considered it preferable not to put constraints on the parties that are able to establish minimum capital requirements.

## §5. Insurance Policy and Interpretation[78]

*97.* An insurance contract is a contract of adhesion. In the insurance market, the use of general clauses has been imposed, up to a certain extent, as a technical requirement for homogenizing the risks and for determining the technical bases of the diverse types of insurance contracts.

This contracting system is not exempted from problems because it may lead to the use of not very transparent clauses that make it difficult to understand the rights and duties of the parties; therefore, the contract may also be used as a channel to include unfair terms to the detriment of the weakest contracting party: the adherent party.

*98.* Being aware of the problems with contracts of adhesion, the European Union enacted the Directive of the Council of the European Union 93/13/CEE, dated 5 April 1993, on unfair terms in consumer contracts. The directive has been implemented in the Spanish legal system by Law 7/1998 on general contract conditions in the scope of application, of which general clauses for insurance contracts are

76. See Arts 32, 52, 58 of the LCS.
77. SSTS 28-11-1985 (Social). RAJ 1985/5880; 3-2-1989 (Civil). RAJ 1989/659; and 25-10-1990 (Civil). RAJ 1990/8046.
78. Epigraph drafted in collaboration with Prof. Rafael Marimón Durá.

included. These rules are applicable not only to contracts with consumers but also to every type of contract (Article 2 of the Law for General Provisions for Contracts (LCGC)).

The following sections follow a systematic order used by the legislation contained in the LCGC and also comment on particular topics of the LCS. The three sections, in accordance with the types of control established by the LCGC are as follows: control on the inclusion of clauses, on their interpretation and on their content.

## I. Control on the Inclusion of Insurance Clauses

*99.* The law compels the insurer to include general clauses in the insurance proposal if there is one, or mandatorily in the insurance policy or in the complementary document (Article 3 of the LCS).[79] In addition, Article 5 of the LCS prescribes that the insurer must deliver the policy or at least a document with provisional coverage.

It is also necessary that the general clauses are accepted by the adherent party and signed by both parties. The specific provisions might include a clause that makes reference to the general clauses. In this case the acceptance of the general clauses is made by reference. With this purpose the insurer is compelled to inform the adherent party of the existence of general clauses.

Among the general clauses, it is important to specially point out those clauses that restrict the insured's rights. In that respect, the DGSFP requires graphic proof of the mentioned clauses in the policy, in such a way that the restrictive clauses stand out from the regular writing of the policy, either because a special typography is used or because they are presented in a separate paragraph within the contents of the policy.

*100.* Moreover, according to Article 3 of the LCS, restrictive clauses must be accepted in writing. As far as the form of this acceptance is concerned, case law considers the use of the words 'I accept' in the vicinity of the restrictive clause to be adequate as much as the subscription of a separate and complementary document to the policy where the clauses are written.

However, restrictive clauses that appear in the general conditions section are considered to be of doubtful legality. For this reason, the distinction between restrictive clauses and clauses that delimit the risks is controversial. Case law does not provide clear guidance for interpretation.

*101.* Occasionally, both types have been used indistinctively and the classification becomes irrelevant because both must be underlined and expressly accepted. According to another view, clauses that delimit the risk imply limitation of the coverage and are not subject to additional requirements, whereas restrictive clauses do

79. See the SSTS 16-2-1987 (Penal). RAJ 1987/1257; 19-6-1989 (Penal). RAJ 1989/5156; 30-6-1989 (Penal). RAJ 1989/5936; 16-11-1989 (Penal). RAJ 1989/8657; 28-10-1991 (Penal). RAJ 1991/7405; and 4-11-1991 (Civil). RAJ 1991/7932.

exclude from coverage certain aleatory events that are usually included in the coverage, and, therefore, the protection regime laid out by Article 3 must be complied with.

The next element that is subject to control follows from the requirement prescribed by the LCGC that the general provisions must be drafted in such a way as to comply with the principles of transparency, clarity and conciseness. The LCS requires that contract clauses (general and specific clauses) be drafted in a clear and precise way.

*102.* Next to the use of an understandable drafting, another requirement is that the policy uses language that is perfectly known by the insured. In this regard, Article 8 of the LCS sets out that the policy must be drafted, depending on the choice of the policyholder, in any of the official Spanish languages spoken in the place of the performance of the contract. If the policyholder so decides, the policy can be drafted in another language, in accordance with Directive 92/96.

The sanction of these requirements is the non-inclusion of the general provisions. In short, the contract will still be valid but its general provisions will not be part of the contract, and, therefore, the parties will not be bound by them.

## II. The Interpretation of the Insurance Contract

*103.* Once the clauses are included in the body of the contract, this meaning must be established through rules of interpretation provided for by the LCS and the rules of interpretation for contracts of adhesion, laid down in Article 6 of the LCGC.

The first hermeneutic rule uses the 'prevailing criteria' according to the most benefit rule; specific provisions prevail over general provisions except when the general provision is more beneficial for the adherent party, in which case the general provision will apply.[80]

Second, there is the case law rule 'in *dubio pro insecuritato'*, which is similar to the general principle that 'dark' clauses cannot benefit the contracting party who has drafted them.[81] Generally, 'darkness' occurs when a clause is ambiguous because it has two different meanings, in which case the clause must be interpreted in favour of the client.

This interpretation rule also applies when the ambiguity is caused by the existence of two different clauses that contradict each other. One of them contains the normal risk, and the other delimits the risk in such a way that it excludes certain situations from the understanding of the average policyholder or from the regular use of language. In these circumstances, the natural content should prevail.

Generally, the insurance contract is also subject to the general rules of interpretation for contracts as stipulated by the Civil Code (Articles 1281–1289).

80. See Art. 6.1 LCGC; SSTS 14-2-2002 (Civil). RAJ 2002/1444 and 11-11-2004 (Civil). RAJ 2004/6898.
81. See, among others, the SSTS 22-2-1989 (Civil). RAJ 1989/1245; 27-11-1991 (Civil). RAJ 1991/8496; 5-9-1991 (Civil). RAJ 1991/6043; 30-12-1996 (Civil). RAJ 1996/9512; 21-4-1998 (Civil). RAJ 1998/2510; and 22-1-1999 (Civil). RAJ 1999/4.

## III. Control of the Contents of Insurance Clauses

*104.* Once the problem of inclusion of general provisions is solved and once the clauses have been interpreted, the next step is to analyse their legality. For this purpose, the law distinguishes among (Article 8 of the LCGC):

(a) General clauses in contracts between professionals. Such clauses are void when they violate the law or any mandatory or prohibitive rule to the detriment of the adherent party, except if the infringing regulation establishes a different effect.
(b) General clause in a contract between a professional and a consumer. Here Article 8.2 of the LCGC applies. This rule is based on regulations for consumer protection with respect to unfair terms (Article 82 and ff. of the LGDCU). Terms that have not been individually negotiated and to which the parties have not expressly consented shall be regarded as unfair if, contrary to the requirements of good faith, they cause a significant imbalance in the parties' rights and obligations arising under the contract.

*105.* At this point, the 'harmfulness' rule laid out in Article 3 LCS must be mentioned because it is a rule against which the contents of a clause must be checked. Indeed, Article 3 of the LCS begins by mentioning that general clauses cannot have a harmful character. Although the LCS does not expressly mention it, it would appear that special clauses cannot be unlawful either. The sanction is the nullity of the clause, without invalidating the contract that contains the clause ('partial nullity').

The importance of the matter makes it necessary to raise the question about what is a harmful clause. Some authors define harmful clause as that which puts the insured in a special onerous situation; others identify harmful clause as an unfair term in the sense of consumer legislation. It has also been stated that harmfulness proceeds from a situation of disproportion or imbalance produced by general contract terms, independently from their exact content or from the mere fact of being contrary to the defined criteria of good faith.

The debate remains open and awaits case law decisions. Clearly, contrary to the multitude of decisions about the limitative character of clauses, case law has given little attention to the 'harmfulness' issue.

# Chapter 2. Insurable Risk

## §1. Risk

*106.* In every insurance contract, the insurer provides coverage because of the existence of a risk that the insured may face. The risk may be defined as 'the possibility of the occurrence of an event or situation that generates damage or need'.[82]

Risk is the cause of an insurance contract. There is no insurance without risk because otherwise the contract would be lacking its cause.[83] Accordingly, Article 4 of the LCS prescribes that the contract will be void 'if there was not risk at the time of the conclusion'.[84] The same applies to the situation where a risk that existed before the conclusion of the contract ceases to exist. Moreover, if the insurance relationship already exists and the risk disappears, the contract takes an end.

*107.* Now, what is really relevant is not that the risk exists at the time of the conclusion but that the risk arises from that moment onward.[85] Consequently, contracts where the exposure of the interest to the risk arises after the conclusion of the contracts, will be void.[86] However, the parties may fix a temporary delimitation of the risk that begins after the conclusion of the contract. In these cases, the contract will only be void if the risk is never born.[87]

In addition, not every risk can be covered by an insurance contract. Illegal risks or risks caused by bad faith of the insured are not insurable (Article 1275 of the Civil Code (CC)).

There are multiple risks that may be faced by persons, goods, rights or patrimonies; therefore, obtaining insurance coverage of them may take place through two proceedings. First, the insurance covers all legal and ordinary risks, in which case the principle of the universality of the risk is applied.[88] Second, the insurance covers one or many risks defined in the contract, in which case the principle of the speciality of the risk applies.[89] In both cases the contract must specify which proceeding has been followed. For this reason Article 8 of the LCS requires that the policy mention the nature of the risk.

82. M. Broseta Pont, *Manual de Derecho mercantil*, 10th edn (Madrid: Tecnos, 1994), 564.
83. The STS 3-11-1987 (Civil). RAJ 1987/8132 declared that the risk must be future and uncertain.
84. The SSTS 20-2-1989 (Civil). RAJ 1989/1212; 9-7-1994 (Civil). RAJ 1994/6383; and 22-12-2001 (Civil). RAJ 2001/1036 declared the contract void due inexistence of risk.
85. F. Sánchez Calero, 'Article 4. Existencia del riesgo', in *Ley de contrato de seguro. Comentarios a la Ley 50/1980, de 8 de octubre y sus modificaciones*, AA.VV. (Dir F. Sánchez Calero), 3th edn (Pamplona: Aranzadi, 2005), 86, 119.
86. For example, a ground transport insurance contract for merchandise that is intended to perform next month.
87. For example when merchandise is not transported.
88. For example ground transport insurance of merchandise.
89. For example fire or theft insurance.

§2. INSURABLE INTEREST

## I. Insurable Interest in Indemnity Insurance

*108.* In insurance of damages (*seguros de daños*) the concept of interest is essential because these contracts have the purpose to insure interests. Thus, the coverage does not directly concern the insured object itself but the interest. Interest can be defined as the relationship between a person (insured) and a good, right or patrimony (insured object), which is susceptible to pecuniary evaluation, where this relationship may suffer damage as a consequence of a certain event.[90]

Identifying the person who is entitled to the interest allows us to identify the insured. It is not important to identify who stipulated the contract. The relevant criterion to identify the insured lies in finding who is entitled to the interest.

This matter gets fundamental significance in insurance contracts stipulated for the benefit of a third party or in contracts where the title of the insured has changed in the course of the contract because the insured (entitled to the interest) will only receive the indemnization when the insured event occurs.[91]

*109.* The existence of the risk is essential for the existence of the insurance contract. Article 25 of the LCS prescribes that the insurance contract is void if, at the moment of conclusion, the insured does not have insurable interest in indemnization. The interest must not exist at the moment of its conclusion, but it must exist at the time when the contract begins to have legal effect. Also, the interest should survive during the lifetime of the contract; otherwise, a cause for resolution will occur.[92]

The development of the interest concept allows us to analyse jointly or separately the diverse relationships with respect to a good, a right or a patrimony that can be done separately or together as a whole.[93]

It is appropriate to mention already that the value of the insured interest implies the selling of limits for the indemnification. The value of the insured interest represents the maximum amount fixed before the occurrence of the event to be paid by the insurer. If the interest is insured, the indemnity can never surpass its value; the contrary would lead to the enrichment of the insured, which has been expressly forbidden since the origin of the insurance contract.

Finally, although risk and interest are concepts that are studied separately, it is important to remember that the insurable interest is threatened by the risk. For this reason the two concepts are contractually tied to each other.

---

90. M. Broseta Pont, *Manual de Derecho mercantil*, 10th edn (Madrid: Tecnos, 1994), 564.
91. The STS 21-12-1992 (Civil). RAJ 1992/10707 considered that the insurer did not have to indemnify the insured for loss of goods that did not belong to the insured.
92. F. Sánchez Calero, 'Article 25. Existencia del interés asegurado', in *Ley de contrato de seguro. Comentarios a la Ley 50/1980, de 8 de octubre y sus modificaciones*, AA.VV. (Dir F. Sánchez Calero), 3th edn (Pamplona: Aranzadi, 2005), 86, 475ff.
93. This occurs, for example, with the landlord and tenant, owner and easement beneficiary, and so on.

# Chapter 3. Formation of the Insurance Contract

## §1. Insurance Advertisements

*110.* Article 71 of the TRLOSSP, as explained by Article 111 of the ROSSP, contains the rules applicable to advertisements made by insurer undertakings. First, advertisement is not subject to previous supervision of the DGSFP, which nevertheless may require the rectification or suspension of advertisement that infringes on the current legislation.

Second, the insurer must give true, efficient and sufficient information about the characteristics of the insurance, including at least the identification of the insurer and the contract that is offered. For other matters the mentioned regulations refer to Law 34/1988 of 11 November about general advertisement and according to us to Law 3/1991 of 10 January on unfair competition. Together these two laws contain the general legal framework on advertisement.

## §2. Pre-contractual Phase

*111.* According to Spanish private law, the conclusion of the contract occurs when offer and acceptance meet (Article 1.262 of the CC). This mechanism implies that each of the parties may take the initiative to conclude the contract.

Nevertheless, in order to better protect the policyholder and to give her or him sufficient time for reflection about the definitive conditions of the contract, the LCS has not followed this model. On the one hand, Article 6 of the LCS establishes that the application does not bind the applicant. Therefore, the policyholder cannot make a real proposal or contract offer but only an application that invites the insurer to submit an offer.[94] On the other hand, the same Article 6 of the LCS declares that the insurer's proposal binds the proposal for a period of fifteen days, which means that the insurer's offer is not revocable during that period. Such a period is in favour of the policyholder and can be extended but not reduced. After the deadline expires, the offer will not be valid anymore unless the insurer decides to extend it. It is assumed that the proposal has to be written and must contain the basic elements of the contract, especially the general conditions (Article 3 of the LCS) and the premium.[95]

94. An important special case represents the compulsory motor vehicle insurance. Article 9 of its regulation establishes that the insurance application, upon the date it is introduced by the insurer or authorized representative, or the insurance proposal upon the date of acceptance by the policyholder, produce legal effects providing coverage to risks during the period of twenty days.

95. Qualifies as a proposal that the document have relevant requirements even though the word *application* may appear in the same document as it is laid out by the STS 26-2-1997 (Civil). RAJ 1997/709, contrary to STS 12-11-2004 (Civil). RAJ 2004/7229.

§3. FORMATION OF THE CONTRACT

*112.* The conclusion of an insurance contract is a controversial topic because of the difficulties to interpret Article 5 of the LCS. Here, with respect, states 'insurance contract and its amendments and annexes must be formalized in writing. The insurer is compelled to deliver the insurance policy or at least a document containing provisional coverage'. Spanish authors may be gathered around two theses.[96] On the one side, there are the ones who support the 'formal' thesis, stating that the contract is concluded when both parties subscribe to the policy. In support of this view they advance the following arguments:

(a) if the text of Article 5 of the LCS is linked to Article 52 of the Commercial Code (Ccom), the conclusion must be that the policy is essential for the existence of the contract;
(b) if the effects of the contract can be retroacted to the time of the application or the proposal (Article 6.2 of the LCS), it is because this generates effects upon the issue of the policy;
(c) the rule's preparatory antecedents induce to conclude to a formal requirement because the consensual expression 'to prove' was substituted by the current 'to formalize';
(d) maritime insurance is formal; therefore, there are no reasons to justify a different solution;
(e) to require a written document benefits the insured because time for reflection is given from the consent date until the date where the policy is received.

*113.* On the other side, the thesis has been supported that insurance solely requires the meeting of wills. Supporters of the 'consensual' thesis rely on the following arguments:

(a) The section's title distinguishes between 'conclusion' and 'documentation', from which it must be deduced that the two words referred to different concepts.
(b) If it is possible to give retroactive effects to the contract up to the time of the proposal or the application, it must be understood that already at that time there was an agreement between the parties about the conclusion of the contract.
(c) Article 8 of the LCS states that the contents of the agreed clauses of the policy prevail; *ergo* if a verbal pact may prevail over the policy, it is because the contract already exists upon the existence of such pact.

---

96. For deeper discussion consult M.L. González APARICIO, 'Consideraciones sobre la naturaleza jurídica de la póliza en el contrato de seguro', in *Estudios homenaje Menéndez*, AA.VV. (Madrid: Civitas, 1996), 2727ff; C. Salinas Adelantado, 'Article 5. Conclusión y documentación del contrato', in *Comentarios a la Ley de contrato de seguro*, AA.VV. (Coords J. Boquera, J. Bataller & J. Olavarría) (Valencia: Tirant lo Blanch, 2001), 92–104; and F. Sánchez Calero, 'Article 5. Obligación de entrega de la póliza', in *Ley de contrato de seguro. Comentarios a la Ley 50/1980, de 8 de octubre y sus modificaciones*, AA.VV. (Dir F. Sánchez Calero), 3th edn (Pamplona: Aranzadi, 2005), 86, 129ff.

(d) The insurer's obligation to deliver the policy is coherent with its *ad probationem* character. The objective is to compel the insurer to draft the previous agreement in writing. Such obligation only makes sense as generated from an already existing agreement.
(e) In Spain, the principle of the free form prevails. Therefore, when there is no actual declaration in favour of the formal characteristic of the insurance contract, the general principle must prevail.
(f) The consensual thesis benefits the insured because what the insured really wants is to be covered for the longest possible time, whereas formalism delays the beginning of the coverage.

In that respect, case law is not unanimous and decisions may be cited in the one and the other direction.[97] Nevertheless, it currently would seem that the consensual thesis is getting more acceptance as some authors who first opted for the formal thesis with respect to insurance contracts have moved recently to the consensual thesis.

Finally, the legislator has also foreseen the possibility to conclude 'distance' contracts.[98]

## §4. Effects of Insurance

*114*. The legislator is aware of the importance of the matter and decides that one of the obligatory items of the policy contents is precisely 'the contract duration indicating day and time when its effects begin and end' (Article 8.8 of the LCS). Normally, although not always, the insurer provides coverage as from the time of the conclusion of the contract. Nothing prevents the parties from agreeing on a later start of the coverage.[99] In the same manner, it is possible that the coverage may be given retroactive effect up until the time the application was presented or the proposal was formulated as authorized by Article 6.2 of the LCS. Nevertheless, this last option can only be used when none of the parties knows whether the insured event

97. It is sufficient to compare the SSTS 15-7-1988 (Civil). RAJ 1988/5694 and 24-5-1988 (Civil). RAJ 1989/4330, which follow the formal thesis with the SSTS 19-9-1988 (Civil). RAJ 1988/6836 and 25-5-1996 (Civil). RAJ 1996/3918, which follow the consensual thesis. Nevertheless, the STS 27-12-2000 (Cont.-adm.). RAJ. 2000/9725 confirms the resolution of the general office for insurance by which the use of related documentation in temporary life insurance and where the formal character of the contract is declared suspended. It is not possible to forget either the STS 30-11-2004 (Civil). RAJ 2004/7902, which has decided for the consensual character of insurance.
98. Commerce of distance contracts of financial services for consumers law.
99. Let us think, for example, in transport insurance when the trip will begin afterwards or in a multirisk insurance to cover a property which acquisition has not been occurred.

occurred.[100] In the opposite case, the insurer would be the owner of a premium without assuming the correspondent if not there would be violation of Article 4 of the LCS.[101]

Finally, there is a matter of great practical importance that is appropriate to mention here. It is the breach of the duty to pay the premium. In that respect it must be said, that in case of the faulty shortcoming of the policyholder, non-payment of the first premium implies that the insurer is released from her or his obligation.[102]

## §5. Right of Withdrawal

*115.* The Spanish legislator has introduced, by way of implementing community directives, the policyholder's right to withdraw in non-life and life insurance (Article 10 of the law on distant selling of financial services to consumers).[103] In the first place, this right is granted to any policyholder of a distance insurance contract,[104] performed by a physical person and with non-commercial or professional purposes.[105] This unilateral capacity to resolve the contract does not require a motivation, and it cannot be penalized. It can be exercised only when the insured event, the object of the coverage, has not occurred within the period of fourteen days – thirty days if it is a life insurance – upon the conclusion of the contract, or the date the policyholder received contracting obligations and information required by Article 7 of law on distant selling of financial services to consumers, when this came later.

The unilateral capacity to withdraw the contract must be carried out by the policyholder by informing the insurer according to the terms of the contract before the expiration of the deadline. Upon the issue date of this communication, the coverage of the risk assumed by the insurer will cease and the policyholder will have the right to reimbursement of the premium except for the portion corresponding to the period in which the contract would have been valid. The insurer will have a maximum period of thirty days upon reception of the notice of withdrawal (Article 11 of the law on distant selling of financial services to consumers).

---

100. This possibility comes from maritime insurance: formerly, the policy used to be subscribed when the ship would have been departed, but as communication with the ship was impossible, it was unknown whether it had suffered an incident. The current telecommunication development seriously restrains this possibility, even more in the case of ground insurance.
101. This article forbids the closing of the incident when this has already occurred. See Part II, Ch. 2.
102. See more about obligation to pay the premium (Part II, Ch. 4).
103. See Part V, Ch. 4, epigraph 4.
104. Article 4 of the commerce of distance contracts of financial services for consumers' law defines distance contract as the one that exclusively uses distance communication techniques including contract subscription.
105. Article 5 of the commerce of distance contracts of financial services for consumers' law.

## §6. Cover Notes

*116.* A document of provisional coverage is a provisional document that refers to the definitive insurance contract while the policyholder awaits receipt of the policy. Both the document of provisional coverage and the definitive document refer to the same contract; they are different ways of documenting the same contract. This document, which differs from the policy, must have neither a 'fixed' content nor a precise denomination. It is any document that refers to the essential elements of the contract, which is temporary and which provides evidence of the contract before the delivery of the policy.

## §7. Insurance Policies

*117.* The policy is a private document subscribed by the policyholder and insurer that contains the insurance contract. It has three functions: a probatory function, a normative function and one of legitimation. The insurance policy has enormous importance because it not only serves to prove the existence of the contract but also its contents. It contains the rules that govern the legal relationship arising from the insurance contract. In complex contracts, such as insurance contracts, the validity of which may extend over a long period of time and in which conflicts may arise long after the conclusion of the contract, the written proof of the general and specific conditions is fundamental. Apart from providing evidence and norm, the policy may function as a legitimation document in which the beneficiary can be designed nominatively, payable to the order of a person or to the bearer. Nevertheless, in liability insurance, the indemnity can only be effectively received by the person who is entitled to the interest. The policy simply establishes a presumption.

Contract modifications can also be formalized in writing either in the policy or in an appendix or a complementary document.

In this matter it is important to take into account that the DA 1ª (the general supplementary provision) of the LCS considers as equivalent to the traditional written form (i.e., is to say, on paper) any durable medium that enables keeping, easily recovering and reproducing the contract or information without changes.

*118.* The policy must contain at least the contents enumerated by Article 8 of the LCS:

(1) Name and last names or corporate name of contracting parties and their domicile, as well as the insured or beneficiary as the case may be.
(2) The nature of insurable interest.
(3) Nature of the covered risk.
(4) Identification of insured objects and their situation.
(5) Insured amount or coverage limit.
(6) Amount of premium, charges and taxes.
(7) Expiry dates for payment of premium payment, place and form of payment.
(8) Duration of contract, beginning and ending date and time.
(9) Name and class of the insurance intermediary who intervened in the contract.

(10) In case of a floating policy, it must be specified the form to be used in the bonus declaration.

1 (1) The lack of any of these elements does not make the document lose its quality as the main document of the contract but it may lessen its probatory value.

*119.* Article 5 of the LCS and Article 76.2 of the ROSSP prescribe the insurer's duty to deliver the policy to the policyholder at the time of the conclusion of the contract and afterwards in the case of loss.

Currently, policy models are not subject to previous administrative authorization or to systematic remittance to the DGSFP. Nevertheless, the supervision authority may forbid the use of policy documents if their contents appear not to be in conformity with the provisions of the TRLOSSP and LCS after the required administrative procedure.[106]

## §8. Agreement on Material Terms

*120.* Article 8 of the LCS *in fine* solves potential differences between the policy and the insurance proposal. Actually, it establishes that if the content of the policy differs from the insurance proposal or agreed clauses, the policyholder can claim the insurer to solve the existing difference within a month upon the delivery of the policy. After the deadline has expired, it is the terms of the policy that will govern the problem.

106. See Arts 2.4 TRLOSSP and 76 ROSSP.

# Chapter 4. Obligations and Duties of the Insured

*121.* When the insured is also the policyholder who negotiated the contract, there is no doubt about the question as to who is compelled to comply with the obligations and duties arising out of the insurance contract. Nevertheless, when they are different persons, the policyholder is the one responsible for such compliance, except when given the nature of those duties and obligations they have to be complied with by the insured. Nevertheless, the insurer should not refuse the compliance by the insured of obligations and duties that belong to the policyholder (Article 7 of the LCS).

As can be deduced from the legal definition of insurance, the main obligation of the policyholder is the payment of the premium, in exchange for the assumption of the risk by the insurance undertaking. On this matter, the doctrinal debate concentrates on determining whether the secondary duties of the policyholder (declaration of the risk and its aggravations, declaration of the insured event, etc.) constitute real obligations or charges in the technical-legal sense (*oneri*). This discussion is based on the fact that their legal treatment is different from the one given to mere obligations because the secondary duties of the policyholder are neither properly legal tasks nor susceptible to forced performance,[107] nor are they subject to rules on synallagmatic relationships.[108] This second opinion should prevail.

## §1. Description of Risk

### I. Pre-contractual Description of Risk

*122.* Its current legal framework is found in Article 10 paragraph 1° of the LCS, the original draft of which was completed by Law 21/1990. As was explained previously, declaration of risk is not an obligation but a duty that arises from the acts preparatory to the conclusion of the contract; in other words, it is a pre-contractual duty that is not found in the contract but, in our opinion, in the law.

According to the literal text of Article 10 of the LCS,[109] it is the duty of the policyholder. However, even when the policyholder and the insured are not the same person, the duty should be complied with by the policyholder except when circumstances are only known by the insured (Article 7 of the LCS).[110] It is the insurer[111] who will receive the information, but the communication will have the same effects if it is received by the insurance agent who acted as an intermediary in the insurance contract.[112]

107. As opposed to what occurs with the payment of the premium.
108. J. Garrigues, *Contrato de seguro terrestre*, 2a.ed. (Madrid, 1982), 151.
109. It would be better to refer to the applicant because this is the phase previous to the closing of the contract.
110. For example the STS 8-7-1996 (Social). RAJ 1996/5764.
111. When referring to the insurer, we are referring to its employees or authorized persons as it happens with doctors who perform medical examinations in personal insurance contracts.
112. Article 12.2 of the LMSRP.

The declarations of the risk by the policyholder are declarations about science or knowledge. It is not a declaration of intention. As a consequence, there is a difference between the declaration of the risk by the policyholder – which is a science declaration – and the declaration of intentions given by both parties to conclude the insurance contract. Even though both declarations are obviously related, there is a distinction between the breach of the duty to describe the risk and fraudulent declaration because both have different regimes: Article 10 of the LCS applies to the first; Articles 1265 and the following CC to the second.[113]

*123.* Despite some initial doctrinal discussion[114] after the 1990 reform, the dominant opinion is the one according to which Article 10 of the LCS limits the duty to declare the risk to the questionnaire prepared by the insurer.[115] This implies that if the insurer does not formulate appropriate questions, the policyholder will be released from the consequences of this duty.[116] This limitation is in accordance with the principle of utmost good faith,[117] which implies that the insurer has a professional duty to inform[118] the policyholder about the relevant circumstances that may influence the value of the risk.

The questionnaire must be drafted by the insurer in clear terms and it is not necessary to use a separate document from the insurance application. Neither is it necessary to include well-known facts or those that the insurer must know given the nature of the risk.

The duty to declare the risk concerns those circumstances that might influence the calculation of the risk.[119] Such is deemed to be reflected in the questionnaire, evidence to the contrary set aside. The breach of such duty, which is a 'declaration of science', requires at least negligence by the policyholder. The text of the law is clear about this issue: the policyholder should declare all known circumstances or, as doctrinal writing adds, circumstances that the policyholder should have reasonably

113. See the SSTS 6-2-2001 (Civil). RAJ 2001/1005; 22-2-2001 (Civil). RAJ 2001/2609 y 14-6-2002 (Civil). RAJ 2002/4901, where the taker's malice in insurance contracting was accepted as argument for releasing the insurer from the payment of the indemnity.
114. Before the 1990 reform, it was used to support a broader scope of the duty to declare which is why it was not circumscribed to the previous questionnaire.
115. For deeper doctrinal debate, the following texts may be consulted: Ruiz M. Muñoz, 'Deber de declaración del riesgo del tomador en el contrato de seguro y facultad rescisoria del asegurador', *RES*, 1991, núm. 65, 13ff.; J. Bataller Grau, *El deber de declaración del riesgo en el contrato de seguro* (Madrid: Tecnos, 1997); N. Latorre Chiner, 'Article 10 LCS. Deber de declaración del riesgo', in *Comentarios a la Ley de contrato de seguro*, AA.VV. (Coords J. Boquera, J. Bataller & J. Olavarría) (Valencia: Tirant lo Blanch, 2001), 164ff; F. Sánchez Calero, 'Article 10. Deber de declaración del riesgo', in *Ley de contrato de seguro. Comentarios a la Ley 50/1980, de 8 de octubre y sus modificaciones*, AA.VV. (Dir F. Sánchez Calero), 3th edn (Pamplona: Aranzadi, 2005), 86, 228ff; P.J. Rubio Vicente, *El deber precontractual de declaración del riesgo en el contrato de seguro* (Madrid: Mapfre, 2003).
116. See, among others, the SSTS 19-10-1989 (Civil). RAJ 1989/6939, 18-5-1993 (Civil). RAJ 1993/3567; 23-6-1993 (Civil). RAJ 1993/4781; 29-9-1998 (Civil). RAJ 1998/6802 and 7-2-2001 (Civil). RAJ 2001/1164.
117. SSTS 4-4-1988 (Civil). RAJ 1988/2650 and 8-2-1989 (Civil). RAJ 1989/761.
118. The SSTS 24-4-1986 (Civil). RAJ 1986/1872; 1-2-1991 (Civil). RAJ 1991/696; 18-5-1993 (Civil). RAJ 1993/3567; and 23-6-1993 (Civil). RAJ 1993/4781 considered as not imputable to the insurer the lack of medical exam, which controls declarations about health conditions.
119. See the SSTS 12-11-1987 (Civil). RAJ 1987/8376 and 2-12-1997 (Civil). RAJ 1997/8773.

known (canon of the ordinary diligence). However, the text also makes it difficult to define breach without a reference to guilt: there is breach only when there is a relevant difference between what is declared and reality.[120] As a result, an insignificant lack of similarity should not be taken into account.[121] In addition, to judge such differences, one should evaluate the questionnaire as a whole because omitted information in certain matters can be inferred from the rest of the answers to the questionnaire.

### A. *The Insurer Is Aware of the Breach of Duty Before the Occurrence of the Event*

*124.* The insurer who knows about the breach of duty to declare the risk is entitled to rescind the contract. Such rescission should be modified to the policyholder within a month after the date of obtaining such knowledge (Article 10.2 of the LCS).[122] Once the deadline for such modification has elapsed, the right to rescind the contract extinguishes. The assumption is that the insurer does not attach any relevance to such breach. However, in order to lose the right of rescission, the insurer had to know the scope of the policyholder's breach. Once the insurance contract is rescinded, the insurer is responsible for the premium corresponding to the current period at the time of declaration except in case of malice or gross negligence of the insurer (Article 10.2 *in fine*).

### B. *The Insurer Becomes Aware of the Breach of Duty after the Insured Event Has Occurred or, Knowing It Previously, the Contract Has Not Been Rescinded and the One-Month Deadline Has Not Yet Passed since the Insured Became Aware*

*125.* The legislator attaches different consequences according to the policyholder's behaviour. In the absence of malice or gross negligence from the policyholder, the equity rule will apply. In other words, the benefit is proportionally reduced to the difference between the agreed-on premium and the one that would have been applied if the insurer would have known the real scope of the risk. In the case of malice or gross negligence of the policyholder, the insurer is released of her or his liabilities under the contract (Article 10.3 LCS).

120. Compare some recent sentences, the SSTS 23-11-2005 (Civil). RAJ 2005/7643 and 21-12-2005 (Civil). RAJ 2006/284 with the STS 15-12-2005 (Civil). RAJ 2005/10154.
121. See the STS 8-2-1986 (Civil). RAJ 1986/450, which understood as not relevant that one machine had different brand but with similar characteristics.
122. Furthermore, an analogue interpretation of Art. 12 of the LCS would allow the insurer to propose the policyholder to amend the contract.

## II. Increase of Risk

*126.* The pre-contractual duty to declare the risk tries to ensure the adequate formation of the consent, whereas the legal framework for aggravation of risk intends to preserve the balance of the parties' obligations when an aggravating circumstance, not foreseen at the perfect time of the contract, has appeared.

The duty to communicate aggravated risks is governed by two rules, Article 11 of the LCS, which lays out the duty to communicate, and Article 12 of the LCS, which stipulates the right to denounce the contract as well as the legal effects of breaching such duty.[123] The declaration of aggravated risk as described in Article 10 of the LCS is a duty in a technical sense. The difference is that here the duty to communicate the aggravations applies during the validity of the contract.

*127.* Aggravation of risk has to meet the following requirements:

(1) Novelty: it did not exist at the time of the closing.
(2) Lack of prevision: it was neither foreseen nor envisaged by the insurer.
(3) Durability: the aggravation cannot be a contingent variation of short duration but aggravation implies a new state of affairs.
(4) Relevancy: new circumstances imply an increase of probability of the occurrence of the insured event or of the size of potential damages.

Finally, notice that the evolution of legislation overcomes the traditional distinction between voluntary and non-voluntary aggravation and that, therefore, it cannot be upheld that the insured has a duty not to aggravate the risk.

*128.* According to Article 11 of the LCS, both the policyholder and the insured are under obligation.[124] The communication performed by one of them releases the other from his or her liabilities. The insurer or the insurance agent who was the intermediary in the contract must receive the communication about the aggravation of the risk.[125]

However, this obligation does not make sense when the aggravation is evident or when the insurer has become aware of it through other means before the occurrence of the insured event. Neither will communication be necessary when the insurer should have known of the aggravated risk on the basis of the professional efforts that can be expected from the insurer.[126]

*129.* Article 11 of the LCS does not stipulate any deadline for this communication. It simply states that it should be informed 'as soon as possible', which is why it is necessary to analyse the circumstances in each case.

---

123. For deeper study on the regime of risk aggravation, see N. Latorre Chiner, *La agravación del riesgo en el Derecho de seguros* (Granada: Comares, 2000).
124. See the STS 20-7-2000 (Civil). RAJ 2000/6187.
125. Article 12.2 of the LMSRP.
126. STS 22-12-1992 (Civil). RAJ 1992/10690.

The aggravation of the risk, explains Article 11 of the LCS, will only be relevant when the circumstances 'are of such nature that if they had been known by the insurer at the time of conclusion of the contract, he would not have concluded it or would only have done so under other, more burdensome conditions'. Whereas the legal norm emphasizes the subjective aspect of the insurer,[127] nevertheless, Article 11 of the LCS cannot be interpreted without taking into account Article 10 of the LCS, which describes the duty to declare aggravated risks by answering the questionnaire. Therefore, only the issues included in the questionnaire are relevant.[128] However, not all of them are relevant simply because they appear in the questionnaire. To overcome these difficulties, it is desirable that the insurer warn the policyholder that any change of the facts referred to by the questionnaire has to be communicated.

### A. *Effects of the Compliance with Duty to Communicate Aggravations of Risk*

*130.* Article 12 of the LCS vests the insurer with two rights from the moment that she or he received communication of aggravation of risk: ask for amendments of the insurance contract or for its resolution. For this purpose, it is not only required that the insurer was informed about the new circumstances but also that such circumstances imply a true aggravation of the risk.

The insurer has the right to resolve the contract within one month from the date the aggravation of the risk became known to him or her. Such knowledge must not necessarily come from the policyholder or the insured. After the one-month deadline has expired, the right to resolve the contract will have expired also.[129] When the insurer obtained knowledge of the aggravation by other means (i.e., it has not been communicated to him or her by the policyholder or insured), it will be difficult for the insured to prove the date when the insurer got notice of such circumstances, and, therefore, it will be complicated to prove that the rescission right has expired because of the expiration of the deadline.

This right has to be exercised against the 'insured', states Article 12 of the LCS. However, there is discussion as to whether the legal rule has to be strictly understood or whether it can include the policyholder. Also, notice must be given in writing, but because there are no further requirements, any written form will be valid.

*131.* Once the insurer has exercised the right to resolve, the contract will terminate immediately unless the parties agree to continue until the end of the current period. The legislator does not decide what will happen with the non-used part of the premium. We share the view of an automatic application of the principle of indivisibility of the premium. Thus, the insurer must return the premium when the insured has fulfilled her or his duty of notification or when the lack of notification

---

127. See the STS 8-2-1986 (Civil). RAJ 1986/450.

128. In opposition N. Latorre Chiner, 'Article 10 LCS. Deber de declaración del riesgo', in *Comentarios a la Ley de contrato de seguro*, AA.VV. (Coords J. Boquera, J. Bataller & J. Olavarría) (Valencia: Tirant lo Blanch, 2001), 133ff.

129. See the STS of 15-12-1989 (Civil). RAJ 1989/8831.

was not imputable to him. Otherwise, the insurer can appropriate the premium except in cases of malice or gross negligence from his part.

To amend the contract, the insurer has two months from the date in which he or she was informed of the aggravation or from the date he or she became aware of its existence. Once this period has expired, the insurer will lose such right. Accordingly, after having learnt about the aggravation of risk, the insurer has two options: to propose the resolution within one month or to amend the contract within two months. Once both deadlines have passed, the insurer will lose every right; the aggravation of the risk will be assumed and, from that moment onward, will be qualified as irrelevant.

*132.* The proposed amendment should be addressed to the policyholder starting from the date of notification; the policyholder has fifteen days to either accept or reject it. If she or he accepts it, the amendment to the contract should come into effect. If not, in case of rejection or silence of the policyholder during those fifteen days, the insurer will have the right to resolve the contract. If the insurer does not exercise such right, it will be considered as acceptance of the aggravation and the contract will continue its course. Nevertheless, the resolution will be effective when the insurer informs the policyholder about this circumstance. The resolution will be provisional and will become definitive when:[130]

(1) The policyholder is warned that if she or he does not accept the amended contract, the insurance contract will be resolved.
(2) The second period of fifteen days from the date the policyholder received notice of this new communication has expired.
(3) The policyholder rejects again the proposal of the insurer or is silent again.

Only after the mentioned requirements are complied with, will the insurer be able to definitely resolve the insurance through a new modification of the resolution addressed to the policyholder within an eight-day deadline.

In short, three modifications addressed to the policyholder are necessary to resolve the contract. The first one in which the amendment is proposed, the second with a warning about the consequences if there is no acceptance and the third one giving notice of the definite resolution.

### *B. Effects of the Breach of Duty to Communicate the Aggravation of the Risk*

*133.* The consequences that arise from the breach of duty to notify not only require that neither the policyholder nor the insured had complied with this duty but also that such circumstances were unknown to the insurer. The problem lies then in proving that the insurer was aware of them although not because of a modification from the policyholder or insured. In our opinion, the problem leads us to the diligence of the insurer, who, as a professional, is supposed to know certain facts.

130. The following are expiration deadlines, which is why, after due date, insurer's rights will also end. See the STS 16-3-1996 (Civil). RAJ 1996/2183.

In case of breach, two scenarios must be distinguished. First, if the policyholder or the insured acted in bad faith, the insurer is released from liability. Second, in other cases, the rule of equity should apply and the insurer's obligation will be proportionally reduced to the existing difference between the agreed premium and the premium that would have been asked if the true magnitude of the risk had been known (Article 12.2 *in fine* of the LCS).

## §2. Payment of Premium

*134.* In exchange for the obligation assumed by the insurer, the obligation to pay the premium arises.[131] Premium is an essential element in the insurance contract from the technical-economic perspective as well as from the legal perspective.[132]

Focusing on its legal dimension, premium is an object of concern both from the viewpoint of contract law and from the viewpoint of the legal framework of the insurance sector. With respect to the second item, Article 25 of the TRLOSSP prescribes that the premiums used by insurance undertakings are not subject to previous administrative authorization. However, the premium must be sufficient in accordance with reasonable actuarial hypotheses so that insurance undertakings can live up to all their obligations derived from insurance contracts and, in particular, be able to constitute adequate technical provisions.

*135.* The general contract law regime is found in Articles 14 and 15 of the LCS, which apply to every type of insurance, regardless of whether the contract is made with a public limited society or a mutual.[133] In addition, they apply to indemnity insurance as well as for personal insurance, without forgetting the important specifications contained in Articles 94 and following of the LCS.[134]

The debtor of the obligation is the policyholder even when the insured complies. The creditor is the insurer who will demand payment either directly or through an authorized person.[135]

*136.* The obligation is the payment of a sum of money; therefore, it is a pecuniary debt and because of its importance must be included in the policy (Article 8.6 of the LCS).

The premium is invariable because once it is included in the contract it cannot be unilaterally amended. However, when the contract foresees its renewal, the policy includes objective criteria in order to increase the premium. It is also usual that the amendment is done tacitly through the mere notice addressed to the policyholder informing of the premium increase, which he or she accepts in the form of payment.[136]

---

131. See the SSTS 21-5-1990 (Social). RAJ 1990/4484 and 10-6-1990 (Social). RAJ 1990/5046.
132. See the STS 30-3-1989 (Civil). RAJ 1989/2284.
133. Mutualists quotas are subject to this regulation, even in these cases also special rules will have to be taken into account.
134. See epigraph 5 of Part V, Ch. 4.
135. See Part VIII for existing differences on this matter between agents and brokers.
136. See the important STS 1/10/2010.

## I. Compliance with the Obligation

*137.* The place of payment is stipulated in the policy (Article 8.7 of the LCS). In the absence of a contracting provision, Article 14 of the LCS in accordance with Article 1171.3 of the CC fixes as payment place the domicile of the policyholder.

The time for payment will be included in the policy (Article 8.7 of the LCS). The obligation to pay can be one payment at once in cases of a unique premium or periodic payment when the duration of the insurance comprises several periods (Article 22 of the LCS). The unique premium is used in short duration insurance[137] and also in some types of life insurance. Also the unique and periodic premiums may be deferred, in which case the obligation will not be affected but its compliance. The obligation is unique in relation to the period of the insurance, even when the execution is paid in instalments. Different is the case of premium in fractions, which are premiums for periods shorter than one year.

The payment of premium is made as a precondition to the coverage of the risk by the insurer.[138] Such payment in the case of a unique premium is compelled after the conclusion of the contract.[139] Obviously, it is also possible to agree about deferring the payment.

*138.* The payment of the premium is made with the transfer of the agreed sum of money. It can also be paid with a check[140] or even with a credit card, wire transfer or bank.[141] Other methods of payment need to be accepted by both insurer and policyholder. Finally, one should remember that after the payment is made a receipt is delivered to the policyholder.[142] For this reason, the receipt is in the hands of the policyholder will constitute proof of payment, which will be considered valid when done in good faith.

## II. Breach of Obligation

*139.* The legal regime for breach of the obligation to pay the premium is found in Article 15 of the LCS. A distinction is made between lack of payment of the first premium or unique premium and the lack of payment of a subsequent premium.

137. A characteristic example is transport insurance.
138. See the STS 1-4-1987 (Civil). RAJ 1987/2482.
139. The debate on contract closing affects the beginning of coverage by the insurer but also the enforceability of the premium. Only after the closing of the insurance contract, will the insurer be able to claim the payment to the taker.
140. It is also regular practice that the policyholder draws a check whose drawee is the insurer. The general applicable regime described by Art. 1170 of the CC helps to understand when the obligation is considered fully complied.
141. Currently, the most practical assumption is the payment of the premium by direct deposit, which is agreed in the policy together with the information about the credit undertaking, the designated checking account and the taker's authorization so the insurer can collect the premiums.
142. When the payment of the premium is done through direct debit. It is proved with the correspondent bank statement, which substitutes the traditional receipts.

### *A. Breach of Payment of the First or Unique Premium*

*140.* Because this is the general regime, it will apply to all insurance contracts, even life insurance.[143]

Breach presumes the non-payment of the premium on the expiry date. In the case of the first premium, unless the contrary is agreed, the breach occurs at the time of the conclusion. Apart from an objective element – the non-payment of the amount due – the existence of a subjective element, the policyholder's fault, is also required. The drastic consequences require two conditions: (1) that the premium has not been paid, (2) a cause of the policyholder's fault.[144]

If both conditions are effectively fulfilled, the insurer may choose between resolving the contract or continuing it and claiming the amount due from the policyholder. The resolution of the contract does not need judicial declaration. To exercise the right to denounce, the simple insurer's declaration is sufficient. Moreover, Article 1124 of the CC[145] is not applicable so that the insurer will not be able to claim indemnity for damages. However, if the parties agreed to continue with the contract, the payment may be claimed.

Most importantly, if the premium has not been paid before the occurrence of the insured event, the insurer will be released from her or his liability.[146]

### *B. Breach of Payment of Successive Premiums*

*141.* Article 15.2 of the LCS sets out the consequences of non-payment of one of the subsequent premiums, and here the consequence is that the insurance coverage is suspended one day after the premium expires. Thus, the insurer will not have to face the payment of insurance money. At first glance, the law seems to establish that the policyholder will be in default without the need of the insurer's request. Nevertheless, the joint interpretation of Articles 14 and 15 of the LCS makes us conclude to prudently interpret the regulator's mandate. We support the position that the suspension of coverage will not occur if the receipt of the premium was not presented at a timely moment,[147] or if the payment expiry date of the premium was not notified with an indication of the place where payment could be made.

Given the policyholder's breach, the insurer may choose between claiming the payment of premium and resolving the contract. If the insurer does not claim the

---

143. The types of insurance in regards to this last modality are presented in the breach of successive premiums, not in respect to the first premium or unique premium.
144. The insurer had to pay the indemnity despite the lack of payment of the premium in the SSTS 26-2-1985 (Social). RAJ 1985/702; 22-11-1985 (Civil). RAJ 1985/5631; 19-9-1988 (Civil). RAJ 1988/6836; 1-12-1989 (Penal). RAJ 1990/790; and 25-5-1996 (Civil). RAJ 1996/3918.
145. Article 1124 of the CC contains the general regime for breach of reciprocal obligations.
146. In this manner it was understood by the SSTS 27-9-1999 (Civil). RAJ 1999/7236 and 6-6-2000 (Civil). RAJ 2000/2564.
147. Interesting decisions are the SSTS 27-5-1981 (Penal). RAJ 1981/2286; 14-12-1985 (Civil). RAJ 1985/6441.

payment within six months after the payment expiry date of the premium, it is presumed that the contract will be extinguished.[148] If the contract would not have been resolved or extinguished, the coverage will be valid twenty-four hours after payment of premium by the policyholder.

Although the legal framework contained in Article 15.2 of the LCS is of general application, important types of life insurance are mentioned in Article 94 and following of the LCS where the policyholder's right to advanced payment, or to a reduction of premium and to the surrender of the policy, are recognized.

## §3. Duty to Mitigate the Consequences of the Occurrence of the Insured Event

*142.* The duty to mitigate the consequences of the occurrence of the insured event, also called in practice duty to salvage, is governed by Article 17 of the LCS. This duty is related to other duties of the policyholder and the insured before the occurrence of the insured event: one negative duty not to provoke the insured events and another positive duty to avoid it when the circumstance depends on either the policyholder or the insured.

The mentioned provision begins by stating that 'the insured and the policyholder should use any means at hand to mitigate the consequences of the insured event'. The policyholder and the insured are the persons obliged to comply with this provision.[149] In practice, whoever is in immediate contact with the insured object at the moment of occurrence of the insured event is obliged to mitigate its consequences.

There is a double duty to mitigate, limit the scope of the insured event[150] and diminish its economic consequences.[151]

*143.* Finally, the question of the appropriate means at hand that may be used to mitigate the consequences is a matter of debate. If there are insurer's instructions and they have been followed, then the duty has been complied with. However, when there are no such instructions, the insurer will have to prove that the policyholder or the insured could have mitigated the consequences but did not do it, and even state the degree of guilt. However, the compliance of the duty cannot imply more than reasonable actions.[152]

The consequences of the breach revolve around two parameters, the importance of damage resulting from the breach of duty and the degree of guilt. Therefore, the clear intention to damage or mislead the insurer implies that the insurer will be released from liabilities that arise from the insured event.

148. See the STS 18-6-1998 (Civil). RAJ 1998/5062.
149. As described in STS 1-10-1994 (Civil). RAJ 1994/7440, the evaluation of the duty compliance has also to include the behaviour of persons who are at the service of the insured and the policyholder.
150. For example, prevent fire spread.
151. For example, identify who caused the insured event to facilitate insurer's subrogation.
152. The STS 1-2-1991 (Civil). RAJ 1991/696 declared that the salvage duty does not oblige a person who suffers from cardiac disease to undergo surgery that 'would' decrease the significance of sequels caused by an accident.

But apart from this hypothesis, the breach will give the right to proportionally reduce the insurer's obligation taking into account the importance of the damage and the insured's guilt. Thus, in order to reduce the obligation, it will be necessary that there has been damage. In the face of the compensation of damages prescribed by the legislator resulting from the breach of other duties, the insurer has the right to reduce the obligation. In short, the prejudice is compensated with the reduction of the indemnity and this calculation will depend on the amount of the damage caused by the breach and the degree of guilt. 'In an adequate proportion', says the provision, without explaining the concept.

*144.* As a counterpart of the duty, salvage costs will be at the insurer's expense, but under certain conditions and within certain limits.[153] In the first place, they cannot be inopportune or disproportionate compared to the assets saved. Second, the amount to be covered by the insurer may be limited in the contract.[154] If nothing has been foreseen in this regard, the LCS prescribes that salvage costs cannot exceed the insured sum. It does not mean they are subsumed into the insured sum but that the insurer should pay these expenses next to the insured amount. Furthermore, the LCS stipulates that salvage costs will have to be borne by the insurer even when they did not have effective or positive results.

Finally, in case of underinsurance, the insurer only has to face a proportional part of the salvage costs, unless the insured had acted following the insurer's instructions, in which case, the insurer will pay a larger amount in function of the given instructions.

## §4. Duty to Notify the Insured Event

*145.* Once the insured event occurs, it is necessary that the insurer knows about it; otherwise, it would be difficult to comply with the obligation to indemnify. Accordingly, the first two paragraphs of Article 16 of the LCS establish the duty to declare the insured event.

The conditions required for the existence of the duty to notify the insured event are:[155]

---

153. The STS 28-1-1995 (Civil). RAJ 1995/178 sets up that the insured has the burden of proof of salvage costs.

154. In Spanish contracting practice, it is used to include an amount for salvage costs, which is frequently a percentage of the insured amount.

155. J. Olavarría Iglesia, 'Article 16 LCS. Los deberes de comunicar el siniestro y de dar toda clase de informaciбn sobre sus circunstancias y consecuencias', in *Comentarios a la Ley de contrato de seguro*, AA.VV. (Coords J. Boquera, J. Bataller & J. Olavarría) (Valencia: Tirant lo Blanch, 2001), 231–235.

(1) Occurrence of the insured event: the insured event must be covered by the policy. Furthermore, in insured events with a prolonged duration, the duty does not arise when the event has already occurred but already while it 'is occurring'.[156]
(2) The occurrence of the insured event must be known to the policyholder, the insured or beneficiary.
(3) Absence of knowledge of the occurrence of the insured event by the insurer.[157]

*146.* The persons who are under the obligation to comply with this duty are the policyholder, the insured and the beneficiary if there is one. A duty to communicate arises independently in each of the persons, even though the compliance performed by one of them releases the others. Also, the insured event can be notified by third persons who have a right to indemnification. If they do, the other obliged subjects will be released from their duty. Third parties, though, are not subject to such duty.[158]

The addressee of the notification is the insurer. Because it is performed between legal persons, the communication should be done through employees or assistants. It may also be addressed to their agents, which will have the same legal effects.[159]

The LCS sets up a seven-day deadline from the date of knowledge of the insured event, even though it is possible to extend the delay by previous agreement, which has to be included in the policy.[160] Such term applies independently to each subject if they took notice of the insured event on different dates.

*147.* The communication is not subject to any form, although the written form is recommended in order to facilitate proof, mainly of the occurrence date.

With respect to its contents, it is a declaration of knowledge and not of will. The declarant will refer to what she or he considers is an insured event regardless of whether it is really an insured event.

Breach of the notification duty does not result in losing the right to the insurer's benefits.[161] But the insurer will receive indemnity for damages caused by the delay in the communication. Therefore, the insurer cannot refuse the payment of the owed insurance money and will have to comply first and claim compensation for late compliance through judicial or extra-judicial proceeding. The insurer must submit evidence of the breach and of the actual damages caused by the delay, in addition to the casual relationship between damages and the delayed communication.

---

156. In liability insurance, case law interprets that an insured event, for declaration matters, is neither an injured third-party claim nor the acknowledgment of the responsibility but the event that causes damage.
157. The burden of proof lies on the person who alleges knowledge from the part of the insurer.
158. For example, mortgage creditors.
159. Article 12.2 of the LMSRP.
160. In Spanish contracting practice, it is not common to agree to an extension of this deadline.
161. See the SSTS 19-2-1988 (Civil). RAJ 1988/1118; 10-4-199 (Social). RAJ 1990/3457; 21-5-1990 (Social). RAJ 1990/4484; 10-6-1990 (Social). RAJ 1990/5046; and 30-1-1991 (Social). RAJ 1991/198.

## §5. Duty to Provide the Insurer with Complementary Information Related to the Insured Event

*148.* After the occurrence of the insured event, the insurer must receive information about the circumstances, consequences and relevant data regarding the insured event that can be useful to reduce damages and, therefore, to liquidate them. Ultimately, it is a duty that results from the principle of utmost good faith.

This duty is described in Article 16.3 of the LCS. It has been added to the duty to notify the insured event for which the legislator provides a different regime. Obliged subjects are the policyholder, insured and beneficiary.[162] The LCS does not set up any term for its compliance because it is a duty of permanent compliance. Moreover, it is a duty that is not subject to formalities and is contained in any type of information about the circumstances and consequences of the insured event.

Nevertheless, Article 38.1 LCS sets up this duty in the case of indemnity insurance where the communication addressed to the insurer must be in writing and should contain the list of existing objects, the ones that were saved and an estimation of damages at the time of the occurrence of the event.

*149.* The consequences of the event depend on the behaviour of the obliged subjects. In case of malice or gross negligence, the right of indemnity is lost. Therefore, given the importance of the behaviour, these concepts should be interpreted in a restrictive way.[163] In other words, the evaluation should take into consideration the non-communicated relevant information and its correspondent consequences along with the insurer's behaviour in the absence of information. However, when there is only ordinary negligence, the party who violated the contract will incur contractual liability, which will generate the consequent indemnity for damages. Finally, when the absence of information is caused by force majeure, or where the information could not possibly be obtained, neither the policyholder nor the insured nor the beneficiary will be responsible.

## §6. Duty to Communicate Cumulative Insurance

*150.* Articles 32 and 101 of the LCS regulate indemnity insurance and accident insurance, respectively, and are also applicable to sickness and health insurance. These provisions establish the duty to communicate to the insurer the existence of other insurance contracts that apply when the insured incurs a situation of cumulative insurance.[164]

162. Although the beneficiary had not been expressly mentioned by Art. 16.3 of the LCS as obliged subject, it can be concluded through a systematic interpretation and the rule's logic.
163. For example the SSTS 5-7-1990 (Civil). RAJ 1990/5776 and 4-9-1995 (Civil). RAJ 1995/6491.
164. On cumulative or multiple insurance, see epigraph 4, Part III, Ch. 1.

# Chapter 5. Obligations and Duties of the Insurer

## §1. Duty to Inform the Policyholder

*151.* In the increasingly more integrated European insurance market, the duty to inform the policyholder has great importance. This duty imposed by Community Directives has been implemented in the Spanish law through Article 60 of the TRLOSSP, compared with Articles 53 and 81 of the TRLOSSP and developed by Articles 104–107 of the ROSSP.

In the first place, Article 60 of the TRLOSSP catches our attention because it establishes that the person who will receive the information is the policyholder, when the chapter is dedicated to the insured. It is known that policyholder and insured may not be the same person (Article 7 of the LCS) and also that the policyholder is the person who has subscribed to the contract. However, it cannot be forgotten that, in certain hypotheses, it is the insured who, among all those who may appear in an insurance contract (policyholder, insured and beneficiary), needs to be more protected. The problem that must be raised is whether the term *insured* in certain provisions must be broadly interpreted to include also the policyholder and beneficiary, as is done in the LCS. Maybe it is possible to follow the inverse path and understand the concept policyholder in a 'broader way', including also the insured. This has been the interpretation chosen by Article 106 of the ROSSP with respect to collective insurance.

*152.* However, to determine whether the person who contracts non-life insurance should be protected causes a certain perplexity; the criterion is that the policyholder must be a physical person. This criterion adopted literally by Article 31 Directive 92/49/CEE is completely strange to our legislative tradition and it is unlikely to be justified. Perhaps it would have been more convenient to use the concept of consumer if the intention was to exclude businesspeople from the scope of protection.

The duty to inform is regulated with varying intensity. Before the conclusion of any contract, the following information should be provided: the Member State and the authority in charge of supervising the insurance undertaking; the applicable legislation; correspondent instances in case of legal disputes and proceedings; and, if one is not dealing with a large risk, the corporate domicile, address or if that is the case, branch address, corporate name and corporate form (Article 104 of the ROSSP). Moreover, Article 105 of the ROSSP prescribes a specific duty for life insurance and 105bis ROSSP for burial insurance with broader scope than the general rule established by Article 104 ROSSP.[165]

*153.* Furthermore, if the contract will be subscribed under the context of distance service contracts and the policyholder is a physical person who acts for non-corporate or professional purposes, the consumer must be informed of the contents

165. It should be informed this way, among other mentions, on offered guarantees and options, during the contract, conditions for rescission, calculation and allocation of benefit participations and indication of values of rescue and reduction.

of Article 7 of the law for distant selling of financial services to consumers within sufficient time and before the consumer assumes any obligation.

From the perspective of the supervision legislation, it seems clear that breach of its regulations is an administrative infringement that will cause the correspondent penalty. The problem lies in determining whether the breach of the duty to inform influences the insurance contract. Its omission (unfortunately, too frequent in contracting practice) enables the policyholder to apply for the cancellation of the contract on the basis of the error in the formation of the consent (Articles 1265–1266 of the CC).

## §2. Duty to Deliver the Policy

*154.* Article 5 of the LCS sets up the insurer's duty to deliver the policy, or at least the document for provisional coverage. Such duty exists both at the time of conclusion of the contract and later on in case of loss (Article 76.2 of the ROSSP). The document may be on paper or on a durable supporter (DA 1$^{a}$ of the LCS).[166]

This way the insurer is compelled to provide the insured with fundamental proof both of the existence of the insurance contract and of its contents.

## §3. Duty to Perform the Agreed Obligation

*155.* Once the insured event occurs, the main obligation of the insurer arises: to perform the agreed obligation. This is the counterpart of the obligation to pay the premium by the policyholder. Its regulation is found in Articles 18–20 of the LCS.

The insurer's obligation requires:[167]

(1) The existence of a valid and binding contract.[168]
(2) The occurrence of an event that is covered by the insurance contract.[169]
(3) The insurer is released when any circumstance extinguishes the insured's right. This is the case with malicious and grossly negligent behaviours that are penalized with loss of indemnity. It occurs when the insured causes the insured

166. Lasting means enables to keep, easily recover and reproduce without changes the contract or the information.

167. L. De Angulo Rodríguez, *La liquidación del siniestro en los seguros contra daño en las cosas* (*Barcelona: Escuela del Seguro*, 1989), 73–75; F. Sánchez Calero, 'Article 18. Pago de la indemnización', in *Ley de contrato de seguro. Comentarios a la Ley 50/1980, de 8 de octubre y sus modificaciones*, AA.VV. (Dir F. Sánchez Calero), 3th edn (Pamplona: Aranzadi, 2005), 86, 340ff.

168. An ineffective contract or even a valid contract the coverage of which is suspended does not generate a payment obligation from the insurer (see Art. 15 of the LCS).

169. The insured interest may suffer damage or the insured person may see affected his or her existence, corporal integrity or health. But these circumstances are not relevant for the contractual relationship if the occurred event is not covered by the policy.

event with bad faith (Article 19 of the LCS) or, citing an already cited hypothesis, when at the insured event occurrence, the existence of malice or gross negligence at the time of the pre-contractual declaration of the risk (Article 10 of the LCS) is discovered.

*156.* The insurer's obligation is normally the payment of an amount of money. Nevertheless, Article 18.2 of the LCS expressly recognizes the possibility that the insurer's obligation can be complied with through an *in natura* obligation ('compensation or replacement of insured goods').[170] The legislator stipulates two conditions: the insurance nature will allow it and the insured will have to consent to it.

The occurrence of the insured event triggers the arising of the insurer's obligation. Nevertheless, this is not immediately settled and enforceable. The insurer must carry out his or her obligation after the investigations and necessary expert evaluation. A time period is granted to decide if he or she owes (*an debeatur*) and, in those insurance contracts where the insurer's obligation is not pre-determined by the contract, to quantify the obligation (*quantum*).

This does not mean that the insurer can postpone carrying out the main obligation. On the contrary, the legislator chooses the fastest possible liquidation, and this is why it provides for mechanisms that should dissuade the insurer who is reluctant to pay (advance payment on account and accrued interest). The occurrence of multiple insured events in practice makes it impossible to fix in advance a term that is not too long for some insured events or too short for others. Nevertheless, this lack of precision cannot cover arbitrary behaviours by the insurer. The deadline will depend on the concurrent circumstances of each insured event.

*157.* In order to alleviate this lack of precision, Article 18 of the LCS establishes the insurer's obligation to pay a minimum amount if the liquidation has not been done within forty days after the notification of the insured event. The legislator recognizes that there may be a need to extend liquidation of the insured event in time, but he or she is also aware of the fact that after the occurrence of the insured event the insured will have to face numerous debts that do not admit delays. The insurance was precisely concluded to cover needs caused by the insured event, and that is why the delay in payment would frustrate the insurance's function.

Minimum payment requires the concurrence of two conditions. The first is temporary: forty days must have passed from the reception of the declaration of the

170. The rule is also applied to personal insurance. In those, the insurer can commit to performing certain services, such as providing health assistance.

insured event or from the date the insurer had notice of it through other means.[171] The second requirement is material: the debt is admitted even if its amount is disputed.[172],[173]

*158.* The amount that will satisfy the insurer is the 'payment of minimum amount of what the insurer owes according to the circumstances known by him'. In practice, the multiplicity of the possible situations led the legislator to use a vague legal concept to specify the amount owed by the insurer. However, the fixing of the amount depends exclusively on objective criteria: the concurrent circumstances in each insured event that in any case will be determined by a jurisdictional body.[174]

*159.* Article 20 of the LCS finalizes the system with the regulation of the insured's arrears.[175] The provision is applicable to arrears of the insured, injured third party in liability insurance, beneficiary of personal insurance and to special policyholder's rights in life insurance. The legislator, aware that the liquidation of the insured event may be extended, has fixed maximum deadlines:

(1) After the occurrence of the insured event and once it is notified within the prescribed deadline, the forty-day period minimum known amount of payment described by Article 18 of the LCS and explained previously, begins. Lack of payment causes default and the accrual of arrears will begin.
(2) If the indemnity for indemnity insurance or the insured amount in personal insurance is not paid three months after the insured event was communicated

---

171. F. Sánchez Calero, 'Article 16. Comunicación del siniestro', in *Ley de contrato de seguro. Comentarios a la Ley 50/1980, de 8 de octubre y sus modificaciones*, AA.VV. (Dir F. Sánchez Calero), 3th edn (Pamplona: Aranzadi, 2005), para. 86, 319ff; nevertheless, they demand the communication of the insured event; J.A. Gómez Segade, 'La declaración del siniestro y la información complementaria', in *Comentarios a la Ley de contrato de seguro*, AA.VV. (Ed. E. Verdera) (Madrid: CUNEF, 1982), 436–437, L. De Angulo Rodríguez, *La liquidación del siniestro en los seguros contra daño en las cosas*, 84.
172. SSTS de 4-9-1995 (Civil) RAJ 1995/6491, 19-6-1997 (Civil) RAJ 1997/5425 y 3-11-1997 (Civil) RAJ 1997/7923; M.A. Calzada Conde, *El seguro de responsabilidad civil* (Pamplona: Aranzadi, 2005); F. Sánchez Calero, 'Article 18. Pago de la indemnización', in *Ley de contrato de seguro. Comentarios a la Ley 50/1980, de 8 de octubre y sus modificaciones*, AA.VV. (Dir F. Sánchez Calero), 3th edn (Pamplona: Aranzadi, 2005), 86, 345; por el contrario, L. De Angulo Rodríguez, *La liquidación del siniestro en los seguros contra daño en las cosas*, 82 considers that this duty arises yet without certainty about the obligation of payment.
173. To the contrary, if the debt is already completely determined, its total payment can be required to be paid by the insurer due to the loss of mandate. Also in the assumption the insurer denies the existence of her or his obligation, the only solution is the resolution of controversies method.
174. For this matter, very interesting are SSTS 2-2-1993 (Civil). RAJ 1993/797 y 22-7-1994 (Civil). RAJ 1994/6584, which fixed this amount as equivalent to the indemnity fixed by the insurer's experts.
175. There has been abundant literature about Art. 20 of the LCS, among them we cite, besides comments: LCS, V. Cuñat Edo, 'El nuevo artículo 20 LCS', in *Estudios en homenaje al Prof. Justino F. Duque* (Valladolid, 1998), 1221ff; R. La Casa García, *La mora del asegurador en la Ley de contrato de seguro* (Madrid-Barcelona: Marcial Pons, 2000); R. Saraza Jimena, 'Algunas reflexiones sobre el nuevo Article 20 LCS', Actualidad Civil, 1997-3 (n° 33), 773ff, F. Vega Perez, 'El interés especial del seguro como cláusula penal', in *Estudios homenaje al Prof. Aurelio Menéndez*, T. 3° (Madrid: Civitas, 1996), 3019ff.

within the foreseen period, the insurer will be in default unless she or he proves that the lack of payment is due to justified cause not imputable to the insured.

*160.* These interests will be imposed ex officio by the court. The applicable type of interest is the legal interest plus 50% or the contractually agreed higher amount for the period between the start of the calculation and two years. After the expiration of this deadline a minimum charge of 20% or the contractually agreed higher payment will be applied to the rest of computable period.[176] The calculation of deadlines, when the insured event was not modified in the agreed term, will be computed either from the communication date or from the date of the direct action claim by the injured, but only if the company proves that it did not know about the insured event before. If it did know, the calculation will start from the date it took notice. Nevertheless, the accrued interests will start from the date of occurrence of the insured event when it is notified within the foreseen term, and from the date of notice or claim according to the terms previously described, when the notification was not made within the deadline. When the arrears are produced in relation to the indemnity that has become indisputable, the accrual calculation will begin from the date the debt acquired that condition.

*161.* It is important to mention rules that contradict general rules for arrears:

(a) The imposition in which the surcharge interests will start not from the date of the fact's occurrence that causes arrears (lack of payment within the deadline) but from before (date of the insurance event or from the date it is modified). This is related to 'penalty' and not simply to indemnity.
(b) The substitution of habitual causes of excuse in contracting such as force majeure or fortuitous case for concepts still to develop, such as 'justified cause' or 'imputability to a third person'.
(c) 'Imposition ex office' regime of indemnity, which is not new but comes from the fact of lack of payment once the due date has passed.
(d) The interest rate after two-year increases at a minimum of 20%.

## §4. Duty to Reduce Premium in Case of Risk Decrease During the Validity of the Contract

*162.* Article 13 of the LCS, as a counterpart to the duty to declare the risk, contains the regime of decrease of the declared risk. In the course of the contract, the policyholder and insured may give notice to the insurer about all circumstances that decrease the risk and that are of such nature that if they would have been known by the insurer at the time of the conclusion of the contract would have changed to more favourable conditions. In such case, finalizing the period covered by the premium, the future premium must be proportionally reduced. Otherwise, the policyholder has

176. STS 1-3-2007 (Civil). RAJ 2007/798 establish the thesis of double period, derogating some cases that defence the unique period theory.

the right to resolve the contract and get reimbursement of the difference between the satisfied premium and the one that would have corresponded to pay from the time of notice of the risk decrease.

## Chapter 6. Insurance and Third Parties

*163.* The focus of our attention in this chapter goes to Article 7 of the LCS because it shows the difference between the policyholder, the person who subscribes to the contract, and the insured, the person exposed to the risk.

Policyholder and insured may be the same person when the policyholder contracts on his or her own behalf. In this case there are no problems establishing who is obliged to perform and who is entitled to the rights.

Instead, policyholder and insured are different subjects when the contract is subscribed on behalf of another. The policyholder takes care of and protects the interest of the insured through the contract.[177] Subscribing a contract on behalf of another may result from the policyholder's free will or from a contractual duty, binding both policyholder and insured.[178] Article 7 of the LCS states that in case of doubt it is assumed the insurance contract had been subscribed on one's own behalf.

*164.* This presumption implies that there is a contract on behalf of another only when it is clear that the policyholder is acting in that capacity. Moreover, the third party will only be the insured party when facing a risk. In indemnity insurance the risk falls on the interest of the insured.

Likewise, Article 7 of the LCS mentions that the third party may be a concrete person or a person susceptible to be determined. Therefore, an insurance contract is legal even when the insured has not been determined at the conclusion of the contract (insurance on behalf of whom it may concern) because it is not known who will be the person entitled to the insured interest afterwards. The purpose is to leave the possibility of many successive insured parties during the existence of the contract. The insured will be determined whenever she or he acquires the interest subject to risk. Note that the issue is not the existence of the insured but the possibility that they have to be determined.

*165.* The insured may be determined according to the rules contained in the contract or the rules laid out by law or customs. In contrast if the insured is determined by the contract, the assignment of the insurance when the interest is transferred is subject to the regime described by Articles 34 and 35 of the LCS.[179]

The figure of the beneficiary[180] is characteristic of personal insurance contracts, especially when its purpose is to cover death because the essence of that type of insurance makes it impossible for the insured to directly receive the indemnity. A third person appears then on the contract who will be entitled to the rights derived

177. A different problem of insurance on behalf of another is the insured contracted in name of the other. As it happened with any contract, the insurance may be terminated by the taker through a representative. In this case, the representative does not contract on her or his own name but on behalf of another, that is to say in representation of the policyholder.
178. For example, a CIF sale.
179. See epigraph 5, Part III, Ch. 1.
180. More information found in epigraph 2, Part V, Ch. 4.

from the insurance contract and to whom the legislator has also given autonomous right, as opposed to heirs and creditors of the policyholder (Article 88.1 of the LCS).[181]

*166.* Nevertheless, in indemnity insurance it is also common to mention the beneficiary within the general provisions together with the policyholder and insured. The parties designate the beneficiary, who is not the insured, to receive the indemnity. However, the regulation for this 'beneficiary' is not the same as mentioned previously. The specific regime for the beneficiary of life insurance in accordance to the LCS does not prescribe any rule for the 'beneficiary' of the indemnity insurance.[182] Basically, this is one and not more than an assignee of the right to indemnification.

The appropriate regime to use is, therefore, the assignment of rights and not the one that is proper to the beneficiary of life insurance. Although it is not convenient to include the assignment of right in the insurance policy, the legal transaction will keep its own substance.[183]

Different is the case of the system that covers third-party damages in liability insurance. The LCS has recognized the third party's right to file a direct action. Consequently, when a debt arises out of liability insurance and it is covered by a policy, the third party who suffered the damages may directly claim against the insurer through the mentioned direct action.[184]

181. See the STS 1-12-1987 (Social). RAJ 1987/8804.
182. See the STS 17-12-1994 (Civil). RAJ 1994/9428.
183. We should not confuse the mentioned legal entity of the beneficiary with the one of the contract on behalf of others. In order to assign the indemnity, it is necessary the assignor is the insured. This is to say the person entitled to the interest (entitled to the credit) must assign the indemnity to a third party. In the contrary, in insurance on behalf of others the taker is not entitled to the interest. In these events, it is the insured who receives the indemnity and not the assignee because the insured will be entitled to the interest.
184. For more information see epigraphs dedicated to explain direct action in liability and motor vehicle insurance.

## Chapter 7. Termination of the Insurance Contract

*167.* The first possibility of contract termination occurs when the risk or insurable interest[185] disappears[186] because the contract cannot continue to exist without the presence of essential elements. Furthermore, as has been analysed before, the contract can be rescinded or resolved in certain cases when the policyholder or insured violates the contract.[187] Likewise, the insurer may rescind the contract when the insured transfers the insurable interest.[188]

However, at this point, our main interest is to focus on the duration period.[189]

Given the fact that insurance is a duration contract, it is extremely important to know exactly the coverage period. Following this trend, Article 8 of the LCS stipulates that the contents of the policy must include the time when the coverage starts and ends.

However, Article 22.1 of the LCS stipulates that the duration of the contract will not be more than ten years, without prejudice of successive deferrals. If a longer duration is agreed on, the clause would not be valid and it would be necessary to assume that the parties agreed to the maximum period (ten years).[190]

*168.* The parties may agree to prolong one or more times for no longer than one year each time. The conditions for prolongation are:[191]

(1) the contract should be for a fixed period;
(2) the final deadline foreseen by the contract has passed;
(3) The prolongation has been foreseen in the contract.[192]

Even when the prolongation has been foreseen in the contract, it requires lack of action from the contracting parties, that is to say, none of them has practised the right to denounce the contract making opposition to the prolongation. Indeed, the

185. Article 25 of the LCS.
186. Article 4 of the LCS.
187. Pre-contractual duty to declare the risk (Art. 10 of the LCS), duty to declare aggravated risks (Arts 11–12 of the LCS), duty to pay the premium (Arts 14–15 of the LCS).
188. Article 35 of the LCS.
189. Doctrine distinguishes among:
   (a) Formal duration: it starts with the closing of the contract. Although the parties are already obliged, the obligations' effects can be postponed up until a certain moment.
   (b) Material duration: time during which the insurer assumes the coverage of the risk.
   (c) Technical duration: time calculation considered for the premium (e.g., an annual premium can have a material and formal period of ten years).
190. Contracting practice in Spain is usual, besides the case of some specific insurance types (e.g., life insurance) that the duration period is one year, with possible annual deferrals.
191. F. Sánchez Calero, 'Article 22 of the LCS. Duraciόn del contrato', in *Ley de contrato de seguro. Comentarios a la Ley 50/1980, de 8 de octubre y sus modificaciones*, AA.VV. (Dir F. Sánchez Calero), 3th edn (Pamplona: Aranzadi, 2005), 86, 430ff.
192. The absence of the third requirement was acknowledged by the STS 14-12-1990 (Criminal). RAJ 1990/9509.

mentioned Article 22 of the LCS prescribes that the parties may oppose the prolongation by written notice to the other party[193] within a two-month period before the conclusion of the contract.[194] The burden of proof that the prolongation has not taken place lies on the one who invokes termination of the contract.[195]

*169.* Another important practical matter lies in the possibility that insurer and policyholder have to resolve the contract after the insured event has occurred. This clause is frequently figuring in insurance policies. It is convenient that the occurrence of the insured event does not terminate the insurance, except in cases where the insured event totally destroys the insurable interest. The clause stipulates that the contract will be resolved when a partial insured event occurs or even when the claim has been rejected by the insurer and the damage has not been indemnified. Policies lay out the proceeding to resolve contracts by which the parties are compelled to communicate such intention to the other party. After such notice, there will be a lapse of time before the contract is effectively resolved. Furthermore, usually the policyholder is reimbursed with the non-used part of the premium. This clause has been declared null and void by the Supreme Court because it was considered to be abusive since it breaks the fair balance between the parties and despite the fact that it is bilateral and mutual.[196]

*170.* Finally, it is necessary to point out that Article 57 of the LCS prescribes that ground transport insurance may be contracted for certain periods of time. Likewise, as life insurance contracts are divided into different types, it is not recommended to fully apply the general regime described previously. In other words, the regime laid out by Article 22 of the LCS applies to life insurance, except when it is incompatible with a specific regulation. By nature, life insurance contracts have an indefinite duration.[197] Consequently, the ten-year limitation introduced by Article 22 of the LCS does not apply. Nevertheless, the policyholder has the right to denounce the contract.

---

193. Oral opposition lacks legal effects according to the STS 30-4-1993 (Civil). RAJ 1993/2960. Much more flexible is the STS 9-12-1994 (Civil). RAJ 1994/9434.
194. STS 25-10-1991 (Civil). RAJ 1991/7251 declared an opposition unenforceable because it was presented late.
195. SSTS 25-6-1987 (Civil). RAJ 1987/4552 and 15-11-1991 (Civil). RAJ 1991/8118.
196. SSTS 4-3-2002 (Cont.-Adm.). RAJ 2002/1869; 4-3- 2002 (Cont.-Adm.). RAJ 2002/2612; 29-4-2002 (Cont.-Adm.). RAJ 2002/6098; 13-6-2002 (Cont.-Adm.). RAJ 2002/5921; 24-6-2002 (Cont.-Adm.). RAJ 2002/5857; 11-7-2002 (Cont.-Adm.). RAJ 2002/9416.
197. Nevertheless, temporary life insurance presents important peculiarities.

# Part III. Indemnity Insurance

*171.* The LCS divides insurance into two big categories: indemnity insurance and personal insurance,[198] and it establishes general provisions applicable to all types of insurance as well as a specific regime for property insurance and personal insurance. Regarding indemnity insurance, the LCS contains a group of general provisions designed for property insurance in addition to special rules referring to certain contractual modalities. Their importance is unquestionable because they are applied not only to property insurance typified in the LCS (e.g., fire insurance) but also to atypical property insurance (e.g., insurance against water damages).

198. More extensively see epigraph 1 in Part II.

# Chapter 1. General Provisions in Indemnity Insurance

## §1. Value of the Insured Interest

### I. Legal Concept and Legal Framework

*172.* The structure and functioning of property insurance are governed by the calculation of indemnification of the loss for which the insurer must pay. The indemnification is quantified in its functioning of three factors: interest value, insured amount and damage. The respect to the indemnity principle prevents the changing of these values in such a way that the insured event may cause an unjust enrichment in favour of the insured (Article 26 of the LCS).[199]

We have already defined insurable interest as the relationship between a person (insured) and a thing, right or patrimony (insured object) susceptible to pecuniary valuation, a relationship that may suffer damages as a consequence of certain events.[200] As a result, the interest value or insured value is the value that reflects the relationship between the insured and the insured's assets. It is a reality that is independent of the will of the insurance parties and it may suffer modifications during the lifetime of the contract. For this reason, we distinguish among the initial value (interest value at the time of the conclusion of the contract), subsequent value (the value any time during the life of the contract) and final value (interest value at the time immediately before to the occurrence of the insured event). The problem is to know which of all mentioned values is relevant to fix the indemnification. The answer is found in Article 26 of the LCS where it is established that the relevant value is the interest value at the time immediately before the occurrence of the insured event (final value).[201]

### II. Illegal Pacts for the Modification of the Legal Criteria

*173.* Nevertheless, the legal criterion is not immovable. First, Article 28 of the LCS regulates estimated or valued policies. They imply that the parties have fixed by mutual agreement the value of the insured interest, which has to be taken into account to calculate the indemnification after the occurrence of the insured event. Consequently, an agreement between both parties about the interest value is necessary. A simple declaration of the policyholder about the interest value should not be considered as a valued policy. What is required is that insurer and insured have

199. Respect to the indemnification principle was demanded in the SSTS 13-4-1983 (Civil). RAJ 1983/2111; 7-10-1986 (Civil). RAJ 1986/5331; 1-9-1994 (Civil). RAJ 1994/7243; and 3-12-1994 (Civil). RAJ 1994/9400.Doctrine may be consulted in P. Girgado Perandones, *El principio indemnizatorio en los seguros de daños. Una aproximación a su significado* (Granada: Comares, 2005).

200. See corresponding epigraph in Part II.

201. On that matter, it may be consulted the SSTS 7-10-1986 (Civil). RAJ 1986/5331; 1-12-1989 (Civil). RAJ 1989/8785; 3-2-1989 (Civil). RAJ 1989/659; and 5-10-1994 (Civil). RAJ 1994/7455.

expressly accepted the interest value,[202] an agreement that has to be formalized in writing, as is required for all other contract clauses. This pact may be made at the time of the subscription of the contract or afterwards but always before the occurrence of the insured event. The existence of valued policies does not eliminate the liquidation of the insured event[203] but facilitates it because it will not be necessary to discuss the interest value that has been previously established.[204] Furthermore, the estimated value may be challenged but the grounds for challenge are limited.[205] The insurer will be able to challenge the estimated value when his or her acceptance had been given under violence, intimidation or malice, or in case of errors the valuation is clearly superior to the real value at the time of the insured event as estimated by experts.[206]

*174.* Second, it is possible to agree to a 'new for old' policy.[207] This contractual modality arises from the dissatisfaction of the insured with the final value rule because it implies that the assets have to be valued taking into account the use and wear and tear suffered by the passage of time, while at the time of replacement no assets similar to the damaged ones can be found in the market. The difference between what is received as indemnification and the value of replacement or repair of affected assets will be borne by the insured. To avoid this, policies include the so-called new value clause in which the insurer agrees to indemnify the insured without any deduction due to change of the old value to a new value but by taking into account the value of the damaged interest at the time of the insured event. In principle, real property and personal property may be the object of new value coverage insurance. Nevertheless, certain personal property is excluded because of its nature: fungibles, durable goods of excessively fast depreciation, non-depreciable durable goods. However, in order to avoid an excessive difference between real value and insured amount, it is common in this type of insurance to exclude certain goods with a high degree of depreciation and fix barriers to the depreciation that may have as a result that the compensation for the loss of certain goods with new value insurance may be reduced to real value or another inferior value. Furthermore, it is applied to any type of risk that may affect insured goods. Overinsurance and underinsurance may occur in new value insurance with the same consequences

202. Despite the fact, case law has applied a flexible interpretation of this requirement in the SSTS 28-2-1990 (Civil). RAJ 1990/724 and 30-11-1990 (Civil). RAJ 1990/9218. Nevertheless, in the SSTS 1-12-1989 (Civil). RAJ 1989/8785 y 11-2-2002 (Civil). RAJ 2002/3108 the existence of estimated policy was not considered.
203. For example, the STS 9-4-1999 (Civil). RAJ 1999/3139.
204. They considered that the estimated policy assumes conventional derogation of the proportional rule in the SSTS 28-2-1990 (Civil). RAJ 1990/724 and 30-11-1990 (Civil). RAJ 1990/9218.
205. See the STS 28-2-1990 (Civil). RAJ 1990/724.
206. For deeper study of the challenging of the estimated policies, consult F. Sánchez Calero, 'Art. 28. Fijación convencional de la indemnización', in *Ley de contrato de seguro. Comentarios a la Ley 50/1980, de 8 de octubre y sus modificaciones*, AA.VV. (Dir F. Sánchez Calero), 3th edn (Pamplona: Aranzadi, 2005), 86, 509ff and J.M. Embid Irujo, 'Art. 28 of the LCS. Las pólizas estimadas' in *Comentarios a la Ley de contrato de seguro*, AA.VV. (Coords J. Boquera, J. Bataller & J. Olavarría) (Valencia: Tirant lo Blanch, 2001), 366ff.
207. See Muñoz Paredes, M.L., *El seguro a valor nuevo* (Madrid: Civitas, 1998).

as in real value insurance. Finally, in contractual practice, it is frequent to make indemnification payments dependent on the reconstruction or repair of the good.

*175.* As insurance is a contract that generally lasts in time, it is usual to foresee stabilization clauses to adjust the value of insured objects during the lifetime of the contract. They are governed by Article 29 of the LCS in which the legislator orders to expressly include in the policy a clause that fixes the criteria and proceeding of adaptation of the insured amount and premiums. The agreement may take place at the time of conclusion of the contract or afterwards. In this last case an annexe or complementary document is required. Likewise, it is possible to a *posteriori* eliminate the clause that was originally included. In practice it is common to use consumer price indexes.

Stabilization clauses try to keep the initial proportion among the insured amount and the interest value intact, an objective that may only be reached when the chosen index is really adapted to the evolution of the interest value.[208] Consequently, and despite the incorrect literal text of the provision, underinsurance is not excluded.

## §2. The Damage

*176.* Just like the interest value, the damage (or loss) is a reality that is independent of the parties' will. Its valuation is made by finding the difference between the interest value before the occurrence of the insured event and after it. That is to say, damage equals the final value (interest insured value before the occurrence of the insured event) minus the residual value (interest value after the insured event) thus obtaining the damage value (damage = final value – residual value).

## §3. The Insured Amount

*177.* The insured amount in property insurance has the function of serving as a foundation for the premium calculation and represents maximum limits for the indemnification for which payment is assumed by the insurer in each insured event (Article 27 of the LCS).[209] This amount will be the result of the parties' will and may or may not coincide with the interest value.

The legislator does not define the insured amount as the maximum limit for each contract but for each insured event. During the insurance coverage, the insurer's liability is unlimited only if the interest is renewable and the insured carries out such renewal. In contrast, if the interest of the suffered damage is not reinstalled, the insured amount will be reduced to the indemnification amount. Otherwise, it would presume the disruption of the initial proportion agreed in the policy.

---

208. For example, if the Consumer Price Index (IPC) is used to adequate the continent value (that is to say real property), as it is common use in Spanish practice, maybe the evolution of both values is not parallel (the IPC does not include construction value among the parameters to be considered at the time of its calculation).

209. SSTS of 1-12-1989 (Civil). RAJ 1989/8785; de 17-3-1995 (Penal). RAJ 1995/2027; and of 27-10-1995 (Civil). RAJ 1995/7739.

§4. Relationship Between the Interest Value and the Insured Amount

*178.* There might be voluntary or non-voluntary quantitative divergences between interest value and insured amount at the contract time of conclusion or later on during the lifetime of the contract. These circumstances are not relevant because the effects are the same.

## I. Full Insurance

*179.* There is full insurance when the interest value and the insured amount coincide (SA = VI). In the absence of mutual agreement of the parties, this is the ideal situation for insurance. The premium has been correctly calculated and with the occurrence of the insured event, the insurer indemnifies the total loss suffered by the insured.

## II. Overinsurance

*180.* Overinsurance occurs when the interest value is inferior to the insured amount (SA > VI), and this situation is governed by Article 31 of the LCS. Traditionally, overinsurance was considered with distrust because it was feared that the insured might provoke the insurance event or simply apply less care due to the expectation of an insured event that will report benefits. But it is convenient to remember that, in the LCS, overinsurance does not have other consequences for the insured besides payment of a more expensive premium than the one due because indemnification can never be greater than the damage sum. Before the occurrence of the insured event, any party may demand premium reduction and the insurer will have to reimburse the excess premiums received. After the insured event, the damage will be effectively indemnified. However, when overinsurance is the result of bad faith from the insured, the contract becomes ineffective.[210] In such case, the insurer may in good faith retain due unpaid premiums together with those corresponding to the current period.

## III. Underinsurance

*181.* There is underinsurance when the interest value is greater than the insured sum (SA < VI). The legislator has treated this situation in Article 30 of the LCS obliging the insured, consequently, to follow the so-called proportional rule: the

210. About good faith and bad faith of the insured in over-insurance, it may be consulted the SSTS 14-7-1987 (Civil). RAJ 1987/5492; 1-12-1989 (Civil). RAJ 1989/8785; 31-3-1992 (Civil). RAJ 1992/2317; 9-7-1994 (Civil). RAJ 1994/6383; and 11-7-1995 (Civil). RAJ 1995/5955.

insurer will indemnify damages in the same proportion as the one in which the insured sum covers the insured (indemnification = insured sum × damage / interest value).[211]

The same Article 30 of the LCS authorizes the parties to eliminate the application of the proportional rule, either at the time of conclusion of the contract or afterwards. This is the way it occurs in practice with first risk insurance, with tolerance clauses and capital compensation clauses.

*182.* First, it is frequent to agree to certain guarantees at first risk.[212] Its purpose is to cover the existence of different insured objects that are unlikely to suffer a total loss so that the coverage offered takes care of the first one, the results of which affect fixing an insured sum that coincides with the most valuable insurable interest.

At the same time, the insurer completely renounces applying the proportional rule. We have to point out though that the first risk clause is generally linked with an indemnification that is limited to a maximum amount. In contrast, the derogation of the proportional rule is commonly agreed on and once the insurer has paid the totality of the insured sum, the policy is cancelled.[213]

*183.* Frequently, policies also contain tolerance clauses in which the exclusion of the proportional rule is agreed to when the discrepancy between the insured sum and the interest value is not very important or the amount of the damage does not exceed a certain amount. This provision is valid according to Article 30.2 of the LCS and involves partial derogation from the proportional rule, so that the insured will collect in the mentioned cases the entire value on the damage and not on a proportional basis. The purpose is to solve problems arising from valuation of goods because frequently, when the insured event occurs, a small deviation from the value of the goods prevents full satisfaction of the insured whose intention was to contract a full insurance regime.[214] On the contrary, when the deviation is important and the amount of the damage is significant the proportional rule recovers its effect.

*184.* Also, capital compensation clauses are characteristic of multi-risk insurance. When there are many insured interests in one policy, an excess of insured capital may be applied to other interests that are not sufficiently insured only if the resultant premium after applying premium fees to this new capital distribution does not exceed the satisfied premium. In other words, if, as a result of these clauses, overinsurance and underinsurance occur, the excess of one will be applied to compensate the other only if the paid premium was sufficient.

---

211. Detailed analysis of the proportional rule maybe consulted in A.L. Monge Gil, *La regla proporcional de la suma en los seguros de daños (Art. 30 LCS)* (Pamplona: Aranzadi, 2002).
212. Case law about the subject is rare and not clear: the following sentences observe this agreement SSTS 22-7-1991 (Civil). RAJ 1991/5411; 5-3-1986 (Civil). RAJ 1986/1101 and 5-11-1999 (Civil). RAJ 1999/8861. There is an extensive doctrinal study in M.L. Muñoz Paredes, *El seguro a primer riesgo* (Madrid: EDERSA, 2002).
213. See the STS 29-10-2004 (Civil). RAJ 2004/7216.
214. Frequently, tolerance clauses are linked to stabilization clauses in the policy (see *supra*).

## IV. Multiple or Cumulative Insurance

*185.* Finally, we must analyse multiple or cumulative insurance,[215] which is governed by Article 32 of the LCS for situations where one policyholder concludes various contracts with different insurers that cover the effects that one risk may cause to the same insured interest and during the same period of time. The motivation of the legal regulation is to preserve the indemnity principle, which is in danger when the total amount of the indemnifications due by different insurance contracts exceeds the value of the insured interest.[216] An interpretation of the provision, which is in accordance with this motivation, leads us to state that we face a situation of multiple insurance when one insured accumulates various insurance contracts that operate jointly, having been contracted with different insurers without the consent of these insurers to this plurality, lead to an at least partial coincidence of interest,[217] risk and coverage period between the mentioned contracts.[218]

The legislator has prescribed that the policyholder or insured must address two communications to every insurer; a first communication at the time of the conclusion of the contract and another after the occurrence of the insured event. After having referred to the communication duty at the time of conclusion of the contract, Article 32.1 of the LCS prescribes that insurers are not obliged to pay indemnification[219] if the communication was omitted intentionally and the insured event occurs in a situation of overinsurance.

*186.* Regarding the indemnification owed by the insurer, Article 32.3 of the LCS stipulates that the insurers will contribute to the indemnification payment proportionally to the insured sum but without ever exceeding the amount of the damage. Further on, it also states that within this limit the insured may claim from each insurer the payment of the indemnification according to the respective contracts. Therefore, it is clear that in no case the sum of the received indemnifications by the insured may be greater than the damage. But for the rest, the liability of every insurer towards the insured does not undergo any change because of the intervention of other insurers. Insurers are liable to the insured in accordance with the respective contracts, and their obligation to indemnify does not change except, as mentioned before, when the insured pretends to collect a greater sum than the one that corresponds to the damages.[220] When Article 32.3 of the LCS mentions the

---

215. More extensively J. Bataller Grau, *El seguro múltiple* (Valencia: Tirant lo Blanch, 1998).
216. This way it was stated by the SSTS 13-4-1983 (Civil). RAJ 1983/2111 and 16-5-1996 (Civil). RAJ 1996/3788.
217. The STS 22-7-2000 (Civil). RAJ 2000/6192 considered that there was not multiple insurance among two liability insurances, one subscribed by the undertaking where the insured event was caused and another by the professional body of the authorized employees of the undertaking.
218. Cumulative insurance should not be confused with co-insurance (Art. 33 of the LCS). The difference characteristic of cumulative insurance against co-insurance lies on the inexistence of agreement among concurring insurers. On the contrary, co-insurance assumes the existence of a previous agreement among different insurers with the purpose of distributing the risk. Its limitation in respect to co-insurance maybe also consulted in Part IX.
219. See the STS 31-7-1998 (Civil). RAJ 1998/6931.
220. The STS 16-5-1996 (Civil). RAJ 1996/3788 declared that the existence of cumulative insurance does not oblige one to sue all insurers only to communicate its existence.

insurers' contribution in proportion to the sum insured by each insurer, it is referring to the recovery right that the insurer who paid the indemnification has against other insurers. It is a limitation that only affects insurers and cannot be opposed against the insured that pays each insurer a premium for total coverage.[221]

As a counterpart to the insurers' liability regime in multiple insurance, the legislator authorizes the insurer who paid a sum greater than the corresponding proportional sum to recover against the rest of the insurers.

## §5. Transfer of Insured Interest

*187.* Articles 34–37 of the LCS are the prescriptions that the legislator intended to contain in the legal framework applicable to insurance contracts when the insured object is transferred.[222]

### I. Assignment of Insurance Contracts

*188.* Article 34 of the LCS establishes that mere transfer of the insured interest produces the acquirer's subrogation in the rights and obligations of the previously entitled person. Thus, the general regime of contract assignment in Spain requires as previous requirement to the subrogation, the consent of the assignee, the assignor and the debtor. However, as opposed to most of the LCS prescriptions, Article 34 of the LCS is a non-mandatory provision when it is included in the general conditions, and the risks are not compulsorily covered, which is the case in most contracts.

From the text of the provision, it is inferred that two conditions must be fulfilled for the assignment of the insurance contract to take place: first, the existence of an insurance contract valid at the time immediately previous to the transfer; second, transfer of the insured interest.[223] The interest must be transferred in its totality.[224] Nevertheless, the transfer of the insured interest does not have to coincide with the transfer of the property, and the type of business that causes the transfer is not relevant. It is presumed that the effect of the assignment is the transfer that is an independent fact from the specific business that causes it. Finally, automatic transfers of insurance contracts that cover liability of professional activity and liability arising from the use or ownership of an object are excluded.

---

221. J. Bataller Grau, *El seguro múltiple* (Valencia: Tirant lo Blanch, 1998), 73ff. Nevertheless, V. Cuñat Edo, 'Disposiciones generales referidas al seguro de daños', in *Comentarios a la Ley de contrato de seguro*, AA.VV. (Ed. E. Verdera) (Madrid: CUNEF, 1982), 540.
222. For deeper information about the subject, see A. Brel Pedreño, *La cesión del objeto asegurado* (Madrid: Mapfre, 1996); and M. Vérgez Sánchez, 'La continuación del contrato de seguro por transmisión de las cosas aseguradas (significado y fundamento)', in *Estudios de Derecho Mercantil en homenaje a Rodrigo Uría*, AA.VV. (Madrid: Civitas, 1978), 829ff.
223. Here there is a demonstration of the inadequacy of the rule when referring to the transfer of the object.
224. See the STS 13-6-1998 (Civil). RAJ 1998/4687 considered that the transfer of insured interest had occurred because in a lease contract there is only transfer of possession.

*189.* The effects described by Article 34 of the LCS take place when the acquirer becomes entitled to the same rights that the transferor had in relation to the insured interest. The subrogation of the acquirer in the contract occurs automatically with *ex nunc* effects without the need to comply with any other requirement and without any transitory term.

The modification of the interest transfer to the insurer is not a *conditio iuris* of the transfer and the aggravation of the risk does not prevent it either. On this matter, it is surprising that there is not specific sanction for the lack of notification. It appears that it should not be the suspension of the insurance effects nor the loss or reduction of the indemnification because it is the acquirer and not the one who committed the breach who will suffer damage. Once the transfer occurs, the acquirer fills the transferor's position.

In addition, Article 34 of the LCS establishes solidarity between the acquirer and the previously entitled payment of due premiums before the date of the transfer. This provision benefits the insurer.

## II. Right to Denounce the Insurance Contract

*190.* Article 35 of the LCS recognizes the right of the insurer and acquirer to denounce the contract. This right can be freely exercised by both parties and there is no need for any type of damage, aggravation of risk, increased insolvency risk or any other shortcoming.

The expiry terms for the exercise of this right starts to run for the interested parties when the insurer and acquirer are aware of the existence of the insurance and of the interest transfer, respectively, even when the communication does not come from the insured or it is not made in writing.

Communication of facts must have a minimum content so that the acquirer has an exact idea of the contract and the insurer knows details of the new subject who enters into the relationship.

*191.* The expiration term should not run until such information is known. There is no specific sanction in case the insured does not comply with the duty to communicate and for the violation of which she or he will be liable for damages.

The insurer may rescind the contract within fifteen days after acquiring knowledge of the interest transfer. Once this right is exercised and the acquirer is notified in writing, the insurer is bound during the month after the date of notification. In this case, the insurer is obliged to reimburse the non-consumed premium.

Likewise, the acquirer may rescind the insurance contract if this is communicated in writing to the insured in the period of fifteen days upon the knowledge of the contract existence. In this case, the insurer keeps the current premium.

## §6. Mortgage Creditors, Secure Loan Creditors or Privileged Creditors

*192.* Reality reveals it is relatively frequent that insured goods are encumbered with guarantees or privileges. The regulator has foreseen provisions for this hypothesis in Articles 40–42 of the LCS, in which the position of the entitled to property rights or privilege rights is reinforced. These provisions recognize certain measures of control over the indemnification and restrain the termination of the contract.[225]

### I. Scope of Application of Articles 40–42

*193.* Creditors who are protected by Articles 40–42 of the LCS include the mortgage creditor – mortgage on immovable or movable property – the secured loan creditor – with or without transfer of possession – and the creditor who has a privilege on the insured goods, which excludes creditors with general privilege.

These rules do not apply to credit insurance with mortgage, pledge or privilege – the insured is the creditor – or to loan amortization insurance – a life insurance that covers debtor's death. Neither do they govern those insurance contracts where the insured interest is the mortgage, pledge or privilege itself when they differ from the owner's interest. When they differ, the insured is the creditor and he or she will receive the indemnification directly from the insurer.

The mentioned provisions most frequently concern situations in which the interest of the guarantee or privilege is insured against damages caused by the insured, not by the creditor. However, it is irrelevant whether the insured – and consequently the entitled to the insured interest – is also the debtor of the guaranteed obligation.

### II. Requirements to Obtain Legal Protection

*194.* The protection described in Articles 40–42 of the LCS may be enjoyed by the creditor if the main obligation is already born, the guarantee has already been constituted and a property insurance contract covering the encumbered assets, and vis-à-vis which the creditor is a third party, has already been subscribed.

In addition, the legal framework includes the duty of the insured and policyholder to notify the insurer about the existence of encumbrances. This notification, which is frequently articulated through the inclusion in the policy of an identification of encumbrances or privileges and privilege holders, will not be considered as a necessary requirement for the extension of the guarantee to the indemnification. It simply facilitates its exercise although it is also true that the insurer cannot be compelled to inform the creditor about the lack of payment of the premiums. The insurer will not be bound by the loss of right of opposition against the creditor due to the extinction of the insurance.

225. More extensively, C. Vargas Vasserot, *El seguro de la finca hipotecada* (Madrid: Marcial Pons, 2003).

## III. Insurance Elements over Encumbered Assets

*195.* The debtor affected by the guarantee or privilege must only assume the insurance of the assets on which rest the encumbrances. Requiring a different obligation would constitute an abusive clause according to the LGDCU.

Also, it is not possible to impose the obligation to conclude the policy with a designated insurer. Such clause would be abusive and that action would be sanctioned as a mode of unfair competition.

*196.* The risks that are covered must be adapted to the nature of the assets that are encumbered with guarantee or privilege. Traditionally, assets were insured against fire but currently this coverage has been extended to multi-risk policies. However, in any case, it is impossible to require the coverage of risks that do not affect the interest; otherwise, we would be again in the face of an abusive clause. In practice, the insured sum is usually fixed based on three criteria:

(1) Insurance for the total amount of credit or for the portion of the credit amount that remains to be amortized. When the insured sum is fixed independently from the value of the interest – an asset is insured and not the credit – the possibility exists that there is underinsurance – credit was given for a lower value than the asset's value – and even overinsurance – that is, loans granted for 120% of the selling amount of real property. Apart from the danger that underinsurance causes to the creditor, the insured will also suffer for the part of the damage that is not covered by the insurer.
(2) Insurance for the amount of the insured asset. This offers satisfying results although in real property the value of the land must be excluded because it is not insurable. Nevertheless, it is important to remember that the idemnifiable damage will be calculated on the basis of the value of the asset as determined just before the occurrence of the insured event, and that, therefore, this amount may be insufficient if the intention is to replace or repair it.
(3) Insurance at new value and with reconstruction clause. This possibility is the most adequate one because the insured asset may be reconstructed, the guarantee will remain unharmed and the insured asset will be repaired or replaced. Furthermore, the reconstruction clause will minimize the risks that are created if the indemnification received to repair or replace the asset is paid in cash.

## IV. Creditor Rights Before the Occurrence of the Insured Event

*197.* The legislator grants the creditor two rights for a better defence of her or his guarantee or privilege in the course of the lifetime of the obligation and previously to the occurrence of the insured event. First, the insurer must notify the creditors about the unpaid premium and they will be able to pay it if they consider it convenient to do so, even if the policyholder and insured makes opposition to that.

Second, the extinction of the insurance contract cannot be opposed more than one month after the notification of the fact that caused the extinction.

### V. Creditor Rights After the Occurrence of the Insured Event

*198.* The most important protection measure for creditors included in Article 40 of the LCS is the recognition of the real subrogation that consists in substitution of the indemnification in the place of the asset as it was before the occurrence of the insured event. Hence, as there is a subrogation, we understand that the indemnification should reach just until the limits of the encumbrance or privilege so that if the indemnification is greater than the guaranteed obligation, the regime of Article 40 of the LCS will not be applicable to the surplus. Furthermore, the insurance event does not give the creditor the right to indemnification but right over the indemnification: the existing guarantee or privilege over an asset is extended now over indemnification.

*199.* To achieve effective real subrogation, the legislator has foreseen two measures in favour of the creditor:

(1) Once the insured event occurs, the insurer will not be able to pay the indemnification without the consent of the mentioned creditors. If there is no agreement between the creditor and insured, the LCS prescribes the insurer's obligation to constitute a deposit.
(2) When the indemnification is used for reconstruction, the insurer will not pay the indemnity as long as there is no agreement between creditors and the persons who are entitled to the guarantees that will be affected with the reconstruction (Article 42 of the LCS).

Finally, Article 40 of the LCS prescribes that if the insurer pays the indemnification she or he will be released of the obligation after three months from the date of notification of the insured event.

## §7. Subrogation

*200.* Once the insurer has paid the indemnification, he or she will be entitled to exercise the rights and bring the actions that because of the insured event belong to the insured against those who are responsible for the event and within indemnification limits (Article 43 LCS).[226]

226. About subrogación, besides the comments to the LCS, A. Tato Plaza, *La subrogación del asegurador en la Ley de contrato de seguro* (Valencia: Tirant lo Blanch, 2002) may be consulted. In maritime insurance but very interesting J.M. Ruiz Soroa, 'Fundamento de la subrogación legal del asegurador', *Anuario de Derecho Marítimo*, 1984-II, 45ff; J.L. Iglesias Padra, 'La subrogación del asegurador en el seguro marítimo', *RES*, 1981, n° 25, 19ff.

## I. The Justification of Subrogation

*201.* In general, according to Spanish doctrine, there are three arguments to justify subrogation. First, it prevents the enrichment of the insured that would result if she or he could collect from the insurer and from the one who caused the damages. Second, subrogation prevents the liable third party from getting released from the obligation to indemnify. Finally, the insurer obtains additional resources that allow her or him a better exploitation of the business (reduction of premiums due to the fact that the insured event costs less).

These theses have been recently questioned, arguing that, because the legal framework foresees subrogation, it establishes a mechanism for application of the indemnity principle.[227]

Specifically, the reasons that explain why it is applied only to property insurance and not to personal insurance are found in its justification. Subrogation is possible in personal insurance regarding health care expenses (Article 82 of the LCS).

## II. Limits

*202.* Subrogation occurs when the following requirements are met:

(1) The existence of a valid and efficacious insurance contract requirement, of which the absence may be alleged by a third party who causes damages.
(2) The carrying out of the obligation to indemnify,[228] which will be considered complied with according to the type of payment (money, commercial instrument or *in natura*). Likewise it determines the maximum amount that the insurer will receive by way of subrogation.[229]

---

227. A. Tato Plaza, *La subrogación del asegurador en la Ley de contrato de seguro* (Valencia: Tirant lo Blanch, 2002), 35ff. has criticized that the foundation of subrogation lies on preventing the third party who is liable of damages to get released of the obligation to compensate; also it is not consider the obtaining of additional resources from the insurer that enables him a better exploitation of the business.

228. The STS 7-5-1993 (Civil). RAJ 1993/3448 rejected the insurer's claim because the indemnification payment did not occur.

229. The SSTS 25-1-1990 (Penal). RAJ 1990/504; 31-3-1990 (Civil). RAJ 1990/1903; 20-4-1993 (Civil). RAJ 1993/3102; 9-11-1993 (Civil). RAJ 1993/8973; 29-1-1996 (Civil). RAJ 1996/6365; 22-10-1996 (Civil). RAJ 1996/7238; and 11-6-2002 (Civil). RAJ 2002/4885. In addition, the STS 28-5-1999 (Criminal). RAJ 1999/3563 considered relevant the insurer's subrogation against a third party who is liable for damages for an amount that is superior to the sale value of the vehicle because the indemnification agreed in the contract imposed the vehicle to be replaced by another with similar characteristics. On the contrary, the STS 7-3-2001 (Civil). RAJ 2001/2729 did not allow the insurer's subrogation because the indemnification was partially paid.

(3) The existence of a claim for compensation[230] of the insured against a third party[231] as consequence of the same damage that has caused the insurer indemnification.[232]
(4) The insurer must have the will to produce subrogation because it is not automatic but is conceived as a facultative right.

*203.* After prescribing the conditions of subrogations, Article 43 of the LCS also enumerates specific cases when there is no subrogation and it later mentions exceptions to these exclusions. Article 43 of the LCS prevents the occurrence of subrogation: (a) when he or she who caused damages is a person to whom the insured must respond and (b) when the liable person is a relative of the insured and they live together. Nevertheless, these exclusions will not be opposed against the insurer and thus subrogatory action will arise: (a) when the insured event is intentionally caused by these persons and (b) the person who is liable has covered his or her liability with a liability insurance.

## III. Exercise

*204.* Subrogation occurs from the moment that the insurer manifests to the insured her or his will to use subrogation. Notification made to a third liable party is not a presumption for the validity of subrogation but for its efficiency vis-à-vis the third party. Thus, if the third party pays the insured in good faith, she or he will be freed because there is an appearance of ownership. Nevertheless, the insurer may recover from the insured.

The insured may exercise her or his insurance claim not only before collecting the indemnification but also afterwards, till the moment the insurer gives notice of her or his intention to subrogate: until that moment she or he keeps the title of credit.

Subrogation rights expire after their exercise, after two years[233] and by renunciation.

## IV. Effects

*205.* The subrogation recognized in Article 43 of the LCS must be qualified as legal subrogation. Consequently, the insurer acquires claims that are identical to the insured's claims, up till the indemnification limit. Thus, the insurer will also keep the same privileges as are attached to the insured claim. Likewise, the expiration deadline of the action against liable third party is the same as the one that applies to the insured.

---

230. It is not relevant if the origin is contractual or tort.
231. Case law interprets that the insurance taker is also third party in order to claim the indemnification. For example, the SSTS 25-4-1986 (Civil). RAJ 1986/2002; 29-1-1996 (Civil). RAJ 1996/6365; and 19-7-1997 (Civil). RAJ 1997/5613.
232. The STS 20-11-1991 (Civil). RAJ 1991/7974.
233. The Art. 23 of the LCS establishes a two-year deadline for the extinction of actions arising from property insurance.

In those cases when totality of loss is not indemnified, there will be partial subrogation, in which case the insurer and insured will co-own the claim against the third party. Insurer and insured will share the compensation for losses and damages that are obtained from the person who caused damages, in proportion to their respective interest (Article 43.4 of the LCS).

Finally, the insured has the duty not to obstruct the subrogation (Article 43.2 of the LCS). The content of the duty has to be understood in the wide sense because the insured cannot engage in any behaviour or abstinence in a way that might cause damage to the claim against a third party.

## Chapter 2. Fire Insurance

*206.* Fire insurance has an extensive historical tradition that starts with the community statutes in the late Middle Ages and reaches its maximum expansion during the eighteenth and nineteenth centuries, especially in Germany and England. Nevertheless, in Spain it was regulated for the first time in the 1885 Ccom. It is currently regulated in section 2 Title II (Articles 45–49) of the LCS.[234]

### §1. Insured Risk

*207.* Risk is the defining element of this contract and distinguishes it from other types of property insurance, such as explosion, lightning, water damage, glass breaking and so on. Here the insured risk is fire, which is defined in Article 45.2 of the LCS: 'Fire is the combustion and flame scorch which is able to spread from an object or objects that were not intended to be burned in the place and time in which the fire occurs.' This concept finds support in the law and will not be modifiable by the parties except when the intention is to extend it to the benefit of the insured. It is customary to associate fire with the existence of flames. Nevertheless, the STS of 16-3-1988 (Civil) RAJ 1988/1972 stated that legally fire comprises flame scorch and combustion, that is to say, without flame.[235]

*208.* On the contrary, the following are not comprised in the concept of fire:

(1) Utilitarian fire, that is to say, voluntary combustion of assets in an appropriate place.
(2) Objects that are burned in a chimney, home or store that, according to its regular use, were not intended to be burned.
(3) Operation damages, that is to say, when voluntary fire is transformed to damaging fire due to its intensity or duration because the facilities and tools used operate were defective.
(4) The so-called *Bagatellshäde*, in which damages are the result of only one action from the heat, due to direct or indirect contact with heating devices, home lights, or due to a smoker or domestic accident or when insured objects fall into fire, qualified as non-fire in isolated cases.
(5) Slow combustion or oxidation.

234. About fire insurance J. Duque Domínguez, 'Seguros de incendio, contra el robo, de transportes terrestres y lucro cesante', in *Comentarios a la Ley de contrato de seguro*, AA.VV. (Ed. E. Verdera) (Madrid: CUNEF, 1982), 762 ss; A. Sotillo Martí, 'Arts. 45 a 49 LCS', in *Comentarios a la Ley de contrato de seguro*, AA.VV. (Coords J. Boquera, J. Bataller & J. Olavarría) (Valencia: Tirant lo Blanch, 2001), 559ff; and F.J. Tirado Suarez, *'Art. 45 and ff. Seguro de incendios'*, in *Ley de contrato de seguro. Comentarios a la Ley 50/1980, de 8 de octubre y sus modificaciones*, AA.VV. (Dir F. Sánchez Calero), 3th edn (Pamplona: Aranzadi, 2005), 807 and following articles.

235. The cited decision declared that the insured event did not occur due to cause or defect of the insured thing; or due to defect or accident of manufacturing. The cause of the insured event is not endogenous (there was not fermentation of the dough or the raw material that constitutes one of the insured object) but exogenous.

However, assumptions of spontaneous combustion and electrical damage are doubtful.

*209.* A clear distinction must be made between the risk of fire and the risks that are covered in the so-called extended risks because sometimes the distinction may lead to confusion.

We have seen how fire requires that damages come from combustion and flame scorch. However, among extended risks, damages arising from operation, lightning, electrical damage and so on are excluded. But it cannot be inferred that fire caused by lightning or from explosion must be included in the policy of these extended risks. Fire insurance covers damages caused by combustion and flame scorch originating in such physic-chemical phenomenon. Extended risks, and from here it takes its name, extend the insurance damage coverage to insured objects from which arise insured risks (explosion, lightning hit, etc.) that have not been caused by fire.

*210.* The causes of fire are mentioned in Article 48 of the LCS. According to this provision, the insurer's duty to indemnify will arise if the fire occurred as a result of acts of nature (force majeure), malicious mischief or negligence of the insured or of a person for whom the insured will be responsible. Acts of nature are unforeseeable and inevitable events. Malicious mischief implies direct action of third persons other than the insured and her or his legal surroundings that caused the fire. As far as the insured's negligence is concerned, this includes any type of negligence regardless of its qualification as penal or administrative. Conversely, wilful misconduct and gross negligence of the insured are excluded from insurance coverage.[236] The inclusion is the negligence of those for whom one is vicariously liable and finds its justification in the fact that this liability leads to what is traditionally known as culpa *in vigilando* or *in eligendo* of the insured. Hence, included are losses caused by minors in respect to their parents, by disabled persons in respect to their legal guardians, by employees in respect to their employers and the liability of teachers for their students.

## §2. Insured Interest

*211.* Assets can be the objects of insurance coverage if they are susceptible to damage by fire. However, the legal relationship with the asset is not relevant, although it has to be mentioned in the policy. Insurance coverage will be extended to include objects described in the policy (Article 46 of the LCS).[237] There are also

236. The SSTS 27-3-1992 (Civil). RAJ 1992/2340; 17-12-1994 (Civil). RAJ 1994/9428; 12-3-2001 (Civil). RAJ 2001/6634 remind that wilful mischief must come from the insured and the STS 30-5-1986 (Civil). RAJ 1986/2919 that the burden of proof is on the insurer. Furthermore, the SSTS 30-5-1986 (Civil). RAJ 1986/2919; 15-7-1988 (Civil). RAJ 1988/5694; and 25-7-1991 (Civil). RAJ 1991/5419 establish that the qualification of wilful mischief behaviour is exclusively of civil jurisdiction, not criminal. The STS 12-4-2000 (Civil). RAJ 2000/2564 stated that if in criminal jurisdiction it was declared that a person did not commit certain facts, then such declaration binds the civil jurisdiction.

237. See the SSTS 21-12-1992 (Civil). RAJ 1992/10707 y 28-11-1998 (Civil). RAJ 1998/8782.

rules for purposes of interpretation of the parties' intentions. In insurance of movable goods, the coverage will extend to objects of ordinary use for the insured, relatives, employees and persons who live with the insured, but apart from an agreement to the contrary, securities, commercial paper, paper money, art objects and valuable objects are excluded from fire insurance. Destruction or damages of objects that are not located in the place described in the policy will be excluded from the insurer's indemnification, unless its relocation was previously communicated in writing and the insurer did not notify her or his disagreement within fifteen days (Article 47 of the LCS).[238]

Fire insurance may cover any type of real property or construction (rural or urban property for living purposes, agrarian activities or commercial or industrial establishments). However, land cannot be the object of fire insurance, only construction.[239] Policies commonly refer to this type of insured real property by referring to building (and contents) or real property. Nevertheless, the concept of real property or building, expressed in policies, does not coincide with the concept of real property referred to in Article 334 of the CC.

## §3. Indemnification

*212.* The insurer will indemnify all material damages caused by the direct impact of the fire and also those caused by inevitable consequences of fire (Article 49 of the LCS).[240] According to this provision, we have to include:

(1) damages caused by necessary measures taken by the authorities or the insured to prevent, stop or extinguish the fire as well as expenses for application of such measures unless otherwise agreed;
(2) expenses made by the insured to transport insured objects or any other measures taken to save them from the fire;
(3) deterioration suffered by the objects saved due to circumstances described in items 1 and 2;
(4) the value of lost objects only if the insured can prove its pre-existence, unless the insurer proves they were stolen or robbed.

This legal list cannot be strict or be interpreted in a way that all inevitable consequence of fire should be under one of the enumerated cases of this provision.[241]

238. The STS 2-9-1997 (Civil). RAJ 1997/6380 considered that the insurer was released of the obligation to indemnify as the assets were not located in the place described in the policy.
239. J. Garrigues, *Contrato de seguro terrestre*, 2nd edn. (Madrid, 1982).
240. Thus, there must be causal relationship between fire and caused damages.
241. J. Duque Domínguez, 'Seguros de incendio, contra el robo, de transportes terrestres y lucro cesante', in *Comentarios a la Ley de contrato de seguro*, AA.VV. (Ed. E. Verdera) (Madrid: CUNEF, 1982), 762 ss, 791; A. Sotillo Martí, 'Arts. 45 a 49 LCS', in *Comentarios a la Ley de contrato de seguro*, AA.VV. (Coords J. Boquera, J. Bataller & J. Olavarría) (Valencia: Tirant lo Blanch, 2001), 570–571; and F.J. Tirado Suarez, 'Art. 49. Daños indemnizables por el seguro de incendio', in *Ley de contrato de seguro. Comentarios a la Ley 50/1980, de 8 de octubre y sus modificaciones*, AA.VV. (Dir F. Sánchez Calero), 3th edn (Pamplona: Aranzadi, 2005), 884ff.

The important element is the existence of causality connection between the insured event and damages, even when such damages are not directly caused by fire but are inevitable consequences of fire and should have a relationship with objects subject to fire insurance. At the same time, the policy may extend or add other damages to those that are susceptible to indemnification but may not repeal or eliminate this list of damages to the detriment of the insured. The other side of the coin is that fire insurance does not cover personal damage or loss of profits.[242]

242. Nevertheless, these risks may be the object of insurance through other coverages.

# Chapter 3. Loss of Profits Insurance

## §1. Concept and Legality

*213.* Loss of profits insurance is defined as the contract with the purpose of indemnifying the insured against the loss of economic return that would have been gained if the insured event had not occurred (Article 63 of the LCS).[243]

The legality of loss of profits insurance has not been easily admitted through time. Causes for this rejection find their origin in its relationship with the indemnification principle:[244]

> Insurance cannot be an object of enrichment (unjust) for the insured. Naturally, the confusion disappears if there is awareness that damages, as described by Article 1.106 of the CC, include emerging damages and loss of profits. Consequently, it is a reality that arises from the activity or the act affected by the insured event and, therefore, its insurance is lawful.

*214.* The legislator intended to clear up any doubt regarding its admissibility expressly by recognizing this contractual type and dedicating Articles 63–67 of the LCS to its regulation. However, there is also a certain level of distrust that is inferred from the introduction of two cautions:

(1) Establishment of a special duty to communicate to each of the insurers when the policyholder or the insured concludes a loss of profits insurance contract with the insurer and a property insurance with another insurer with respect to certain objects (Article 64 of the LCS).
(2) Valued policies are forbidden when the contract's exclusively purpose is to cover loss profits (Article 67) but not when this guarantee would have been agreed to as complementary insurance.[245]

## §2. Elements

*215.* The insurer's indemnification is due when two elements meet: verification of one of the events described in the contract (fire, malfunction, etc.) and that event

243. For deeper study on this contractual modality, consult F.J. Tirado Suarez, *El seguro de pérdida de beneficios por interrupción de la empresa*, Jerez de la Frontera: Caja de ahorros de Jerez de la Frontera y Universidad de Jerez, 1976; F.J. Tirado Suarez, *'Art. 63 and ff. Seguro de lucro cesante'*, in *Ley de contrato de seguro. Comentarios a la Ley 50/1980, de 8 de octubre y sus modificaciones*, AA.VV. (Dir F. Sánchez Calero), 3th edn (Pamplona: Aranzadi, 2005), 1099ff, and following articles; R. Verdera Server, 'Arts. 63 a 67 LCS', in *Comentarios a la Ley de contrato de seguro*, AA.VV. (Coords J. Boquera, J. Bataller & J. Olavarría) (Valencia: Tirant lo Blanch, 2001), 711 y ss; F. Blanco Giraldo, 'El seguro de lucro cesante en el derecho español', *RDM*, n° 198, 1990, 827ff.

244. Currently in Art. 26 of the LCS.

245. The option to agree loss profits insurance as complementary guarantee is the most frequent in the market, especially through multi-risk policies.

causes probable damages. Consequently, the interest is identified with benefit expectations from act or activity. And precisely, the fact to conceptualize loss of profits as mere expectation (that would have been materialized afterwards if the insured event would not have occurred) is the reason that underlies the difficulties of specifying the interest value and thus the insured sum. In practice, this difficulty is alleviated through different contractual mechanisms that facilitate the fixing of insured value.[246]

*216.* Damages that are susceptible to be indemnified as a result of loss of profits insurance are, unless the policy states otherwise:[247]

(1) Loss of benefits caused by the insured event during the period foreseen in the policy.
(2) General expenses that continue to be lumbering the insured after the occurrence of the insured event.
(3) Expenses that are the direct consequence of the insured event.

## §3. Modalities

*217.* In practice, loss of profits insurance is encountered under diverse modalities. We can cite insurance against hail; insurance of probable benefit in transport; insurance against business interruption of ship, aircraft or auto; rental loss damage insurance; rain insurance; event cancellation insurance, employment risk insurance, especially of high-level executives; insurance for a subsidy due to lack of driving license; and business interruption insurance. Given its importance acquired in the market, this last modality has been expressly recognized by the regulator in Article 66 of the LCS.[248]

246. Expert procedure ad hoc, through indexes of past valuation and future exploitation; valued policies with limitations indicated in Art. 67 of the LCS; fixing of value a *forfait* on the basis of certain value and easily provable and so on.
247. Article 65 of the LCS.
248. Article 66 of the LCS defines it as that contract by which 'the owner of a business may insure loss of benefits and general expenses suffered while the business is partially or totally interrupted as consequence of the events determined in the contract'.

# Chapter 4. Transport Insurance

*218.* Historically, as we know, insurance emerged with respect to maritime shipping risks; specifically, the first known regulations in the world are the 1435 Ordenanzas de Barcelona (Ordinances of Barcelona). However, it was necessary to wait until the 1829 Commercial Code for the introduction in Spain of the first regulation on ground insurance: ground transport insurance, transferring in this way maritime regulation to the ground scope. Chronologically, aviation insurance was the last to appear, which is logical. We will focus now on the first two insurance contracts leaving aviation insurance for a later chapter.

## §1. Maritime Insurance

### I. Concept and Legal Framework

*219.* Maritime insurance covers the insured against damages caused by maritime shipping risks.[249] It is property insurance.

In Spain, its current legal framework is found in Article 737 and following Articles of the Commercial Code.[250] Doubts arise concerning the question of the role of the LCS because it is a general law.[251] Case law study shows that the application of the LCS to maritime insurance has been restrictive[252] and it was applied to those cases where both regulations agree.[253]

249. Maritime insurance has an extensive bibliography among which the following stand out because of their general character R. González Hevia, *Manual de seguro marítimo*, 2° ed. (Madrid: Mapfre, 1980); J.M. Ruiz Soroa, A. Arranz de Diego, S. Zabaleta Sarasua, *Manual de Derecho del seguro marítimo* (Vitoria: Gobierno Vasco, 1993); J.L. Gabaldón García, J.M. Ruiz Soroa, *Manual de Derecho de la navegación marítima*, 2th edn (Madrid: Marcial Pons, 2002); J.L. Rodríguez Carrión, *Los seguros marítimos y aéreos*, in *Tratado de Derecho mercantil, Derecho de la Navegación*, AA.VV. (Dirs M. Olivencia, C. Fernández-Novoa & R. Jiménez de Parga), vol. 5 (Madrid: Marcial Pons, 2003), AA.VV., (Dirs. J.L. García-Pita); Estudios de Derecho marítimo, Thomson Reuters Aranzadi: Cizur Menor, 2012).

250. Despite initial doubts after the enactment of the LCS, case law has declared it this way many times. For example, the SSTS 19-10-1987 (Civil). RAJ 1987/7297, 10-12-1988 (Civil). RAJ 1988/9423, 21-7-1989 (Civil). RAJ 1989/5771, 22-4-1991 (Civil). RAJ 1991/3018, 2-12-1991 (Civil). RAJ 1991/8901, 22-6-1992 (Civil). RAJ 1992/5463, 16-2-1994 (Civil). RAJ 1994/1617, among others.

251. About doctrinal debate, it is sufficient to compare J. Bataller Grau, 'De nuevo sobre la aplicación de la Ley 50/1980, de 8 de octubre, de contrato de seguro al seguro marítimo', in *El contrato de seguro en la jurisprudencia del Tribunal Supremo*, AA.VV. (Coords J. Bataller, J. Boquera & J. Olavarría) (Valencia: Tirant lo Blanch, 1999) with the opinion stated in J.L. Rodríguez Carrión, *Los seguros marítimos y aéreos*, in *Tratado de Derecho mercantil, Derecho de la Navegación*, AA.VV. (Dirs M. Olivencia, C. Fernández-Novoa & R. Jiménez de Parga), vol. 5 (Madrid: Marcial Pons, 2003), 40 and ff.

252. SSTS 22-6-1992 (Civil). RAJ 1992/5463, 16-2-1994 (Civil). RAJ 1994/1617, 23-11-1996 (Civil). RAJ 1996/8644, 10-12-1988 (Civil). RAJ 1988/9423, 19-10-1987 (Civil). RAJ 1987/7927, 22-4-1991 (Civil). RAJ 1991/3018, 21-7-1989 (Civil). RAJ 1989/5771 and 20-2-1995 (Civil). RAJ. 1995/883, 2-12-1991 (Civil). RAJ 1991/8901, 26-4-1995 (Civil). RAJ 1995/3550, 23-1-1996 (Civil). RAJ 1996/638, 12-2-1996 (Civil). RAJ 1996/1247, 21-11-1996 (Civil). RAJ 1996/8282 and 31-12-1996 (Civil). RAJ 1996/9394. Nevertheless, the SSTS of 19-2-1988 (Civil). RAJ 1988/1118 and 2-12-1997 (Civil). RAJ 1997/8773.

253. SSTS 1-4-1987 (Civil). RAJ 1987/2482, 11-11-1991 (Civil). RAJ 1991/8152 and 23-12-1993 (Civil). RAJ 1993/10114.

*220.* Party autonomy is called to play a crucial role in maritime insurance because Ccom in its Article 738 declares the legal character of its rules. Likewise, in accordance with Community Directives, Article 107 of the LCS qualifies marine hull insurance, cargo insurance and shipowner's liability insurance as large risks, which implies the prevalence of freedom to contract.

The making of a maritime insurance contract goes through policies and standard clauses, in particular the 1934 Spanish policies and the clauses from the London Underwriters Institute that typify the international character of maritime insurance. The institute clauses are directly included without being translated, and frequently dispute resolution is submitted to arbitration. It is easy to predict the difficulty of interpreting these policies in practice because clauses drafted according to English law and English practice has to be combined with Spanish legal tradition.

*221.* Finally, we should point out that at the time of the writing of this monograph a new maritime shipping law is in preparation. This law project has the purpose of derogating from the nineteenth-century rules that are found in the still valid Commerce Code. The proposed new law of maritime shipping organizes the legislation of maritime insurance contracts in three chapters. The first contains general provisions, establishing its scope of application in only two rules: inherent risks to maritime shipping and the traditional freedom of contract in these matters. The second chapter, titled 'Of the Standard Provisions for Different Types of Maritime Insurance', contains six sections dedicated to the insured's interest, insured value and co-insurance, shipping risks, conclusion of the contract and duties of the contracting parties, indemnification and statute of limitations. The third and last chapter contains rules that address the three types of maritime insurance: marine hull insurance, cargo marine insurance and liability insurance.

## II. The Conclusion of the Contract: The Policy

*222.* One of the characteristics of marine insurance is its formality. The policy is an essential element for the validity of marine insurance. The policy must be issued in double (Article 737.2 of the Ccom), and it should contain the essential elements of a contract (Article 738 of the Ccom, although not all are essential) together with those agreements reached by the parties. They may be nominative, order or bearer policies (Article 742 of the Ccom).

## III. Insured Risk

*223.* The concept of sea risks used in our definition of marine insurance allows us to limit the scope – although some risks covered are not strictly due to the sea[254] – and it also connects with the principle of universality of the risk that rules maritime insurance. Indeed, unlike ground insurance, here, the principle of universality of the risk is applied, thus the insured simply needs to demonstrate that the insured

254. For example, damages during the loading to the vessel.

event occurred as a result of sea risk and there is no need to prove in a precise way the cause of the loss. However, this principle must be specified because usually policies mention the risks that are covered – do not forget that Article 755 of the Ccom contains a list of risks that are merely optional – and the excluded ones – with the possibility of extending or reducing the list of legal exclusions.

## IV. Insured Interest

*224.* The insured interest – as we know – is the relationship between a person and an asset, right or its patrimony susceptible to be economically valued. Therefore, in maritime insurance it is possible to distinguish between different insurable modalities according to the insured interest. From this perspective, we may discuss the following:

(1) Marine hull insurance (or vessel insurance):[255] the object of which is the economic interest that link any person (owner, lessor, freighter or charterer) to the vessel (Article 745.1 of the Ccom).
(2) Cargo insurance (or of 'facultades'):[256] this covers the interest on the merchandise that is the object of maritime transport (Article 745.2 of the Ccom).
(3) Expected benefits insurance: this guarantees profits that the insured expects to obtain on the arrival of merchandise to the harbour of destination (Article 748 of the Ccom).
(4) Freight insurance: this covers the carrier against loss of rights on the freight (Article 743.7° of the Ccom).
(5) Shipowner's liability insurance (*P & I*):[257] contract by which the shipowner covers his or her liability against third parties.

## V. Obligations and Duties of the Contracting Party

*225.* The main obligation of the policyholder is the payment of the premium. The policy must mention the price that is agreed on, plus time, place and form of payment (Article 738.13 of the Ccom). Furthermore, the policyholder and insured must comply with duties relating to communicating circumstances that affect the insured risk, the aggravation of the risk and the occurrence of the insured event.

---

255. Véase J. Hernández Martí, *Contrato de seguro marítimo: La póliza de buques* (Valencia, 1982).
256. J. Hernández Martí, 'Seguro de transporte marítimo de mercancías', in *Contratación internacional*, AA.VV. (Coord. C. Espulgues Mota), 2th edn (Valencia: Tirant lo Blanch, 1999), 776ff.
257. M. Clavero Ternero, *Clubs de P & I* (Madrid: Instituto Europeo de Estudios Marítimos, 1992); M.C. Hill Prados, *Los clubs de protección e indemnización en el campo del seguro marítimo* (Barcelona: Bosch, 1992).

## VI. Insurer's Obligation: Payment of the Indemnification

*226.* With the occurrence of the insured event, the insurer's obligation to indemnify the insured arises. This obligation does not automatically arise and it requires that it first be decided whether the risk is protected by the policy and what amount is to be paid. The legislator has prescribed two forms to liquidate the loss:

(1) Average adjustment is a common procedure, and the rest of insurance contracts consist in determining the exact suffered damage. The insured may choose this possibility regarding total or partial damage.
(2) Abandon adjustment is an adjustment method that is reserved for major losses. When declaring the abandonment, the insured transfers her or his rights on the insured interest in exchange for the indemnification of the total loss.

### §2. Ground Transport Insurance

## I. Concept and Legal Framework

*227.* Ground transport insurance is governed by Articles 54–62 of the LCS. These provisions must be completed with the Law of Cargo Ground Transport Contract; the Law for Organization of Ground Transport (LOTT), which regulates this activity in Spain and also international agreements on ground transport (CMR, CIM, ADR, ATP, COTIF).[258]

Ground transport insurance may be defined as the property insurance for material damages that arise because of or as a consequence of the contractual transport phenomenon.

On the one side, limitation of material damages excludes not only indemnification of losses, indirect damages and other cases of loss of profits but also liability. Furthermore, this insurance must not be confused with travellers' insurance, which is an accident insurance that covers corporal damages of the travelling persons. On the other side, this type of insurance is not conceived in function of a specific event or group of events but through the principle of universality of risks.

*228.* Ground transport insurance is linked to the transfer of movable goods from one place to another. A characteristic that differentiates it from other types of property insurance that cover goods is that the covered objects depart from a risk that has been determined in the policy. However, insurable coverage is not limited to the

258. For more exhaustive analysis of this insurance, see J. Boquera Matarredona, *El contrato de seguro de transporte de mercancías por carretera* (Valencia: Tirant lo Blanch, 2002); A.B., Viega Copo El contrato de seguro de transporte terrestre de mercancias, Thomson Reuters Civitas: Madrid, 2013; AA.VV (dirs A. Emparanza; J.M. Osante), Seguro de transporte terrestre de mercancías; Marcial Pons: Madrid-Barcelona-Buenos Aires, 2013; M.R. Isern. El derecho de subrogación en el seguro de transporte terrestre de mercancias por carretera, Marcial Pons: Madrid-Barcelona-Buenos Aires, 2013).

physical fact of transporting by ground but is also extended to the risks that threaten the insured interests during the time before the transport, during interruption times and after the transport.[259]

Ground transport insurance is a non-compulsory insurance contract because the ministry for traffic, which is the relevant body, has not yet imposed the obligatory character.

Finally, Article 54 of the LCS establishes the modalities of transport insurance: merchandise carried, means used or other insured objects.

## II. Cargo Insurance

*229.* The insured object of cargo insurance consists of portable corporal goods. They can have different nature but, in summary, all those goods that may be the object of contracts for ground transport are susceptible to be insured. Hence, there is a clear connection between transport contract and insurance. Consequently, administrative regulations or common commercial transport conditions also influence the validity and efficiency of the insurance contract.

This insurance covers damages that the merchandise suffers because of the transport, regardless of the carrier's liability.[260] Nevertheless, it is also true that Spanish practice is different from that in other countries because there is no clear separation between cargo insurance and the insurance that covers the carrier's liability.[261]

## III. Insurance for Means of Transport

*230.* After proclaiming its existence, the legislator has not established specific regulation for this modality and the only mention is in Article 61.2 of the LCS, which has dispositive character.

Spanish practice places motor vehicle hull insurance within the single insurance policy for motor vehicles. Thus, it is possible to insure damages that the vehicle may suffer as a consequence of an accident that occurred by an exterior, violent and instantaneous cause, or fire or explosion, that in any case is independent of the driver's will, and regardless of whether the vehicle was standing still or moving.

## IV. Other Insurances Related to Transport

*231.* First, we need to mention the compulsory travellers' insurance – governed by RD 1575/1989, of 22 December – which object is to indemnify travellers or their

---

259. See the STS 30-12-1993 (Civil). RAJ 1993/9899 about warehouse-to-warehouse clauses.
260. This insurance contract which object is merchandise, excludes accessory elements to the technical team indispensable to perform the transport (f. ex. packing material, pallets). Regarding the vehicle, used containers and cisterns are also excluded.
261. More extensively, see J.L. Pulido Bejines, *Seguro de mercancías y seguro de responsabilidad civil del porteador terrestre* (Barcelona: Bosch, 2001).

assignees when they suffer corporal damage as a result of an accident that took place at the occasion of the movement of public medium.

Second, it is possible to insure loss of profits, that is, patrimonial interests that go beyond the destroyed or deteriorated property. In Spanish practice, there is some spreading of an insurance that covers the temporary privation of the license to drive (*carné de conducir*). The insurer assumes the payment of a monthly subsidy for a fixed amount and within the limits established by the contract, when the driving license is temporarily withdrawn by judicial decision in the case of a traffic accident but only when caused by non-criminal negligence of the professional driver.

*232.* Third, there is liability transport insurance because the provision of a specific transport service may give rise to liability of the carrier and of other instances that work in the transport business (commission agent, transport agency, etc.). We must remember here that compulsory auto liability insurance does not cover liability for carried goods or for complementary modalities, which has led to the emergence of autonomous formulas of carrier liability insurance, regardless of the traffic liability insurance that exists. In the absence of express regulation, this insurance is subject to Article 73 and following Articles of the LCS on liability insurance. Its scope of coverage lacks sharp and typical delimitation of the insured risk, which has clearly a contractual origin.

# Chapter 5. Liability Insurance

## §1. Legal Framework

*233.* Liability insurance is governed by Articles 73–76 of the LCS. In principle and with certain exceptions, general rules for insurance contracts in general contained in the LCS and those for property insurance must be applied in liability insurance.

This set of rules is directly applicable to all non-compulsory liability insurance and compulsory insurance that do not have specific regulations and, in a subsidiary way, to compulsory contracts that have their own legal framework. Furthermore, these rules are applied to liability insurance of major risks in those matters that are considered not to be subject to the parties' will because they relate to the treatment of the position of third party, damaged or other essential elements of the contract.

Finally, it is convenient to remember that rules contained in LGDCU and LCGC, as well as regulation of liability in the Criminal Code also apply.

## §2. Notion

*234.* The notion of liability insurance is found in Article 73 of the LCS; leaving aside the strict notion of indemnification it states: 'by liability insurance, the insurer agrees to cover the risk that the insured incurs of having to indemnify third parties for the damages and losses caused by an event that was defined in the contract and for the consequences of which the insured incurs civil liability in accordance with the law'.

In order to grasp the notion of liability insurance, Article 73 must be completed with Articles 74 of the LCS (legal direction) and 76 of the LCS (direct action). For this reason, this insurance may be defined as the contract where the insurer agrees, within the legal and contractual limits, to pay the indemnification to which the insured is obliged as being liable for the damages caused to third parties on the basis of the specific liability that is mentioned in the contract – and, more generally, for events that occurred in the course of the duration of the contract – as well as assuming the juridical direction of the defence against the third parties' claims, the expenses caused by them and the deposit of the corresponding bail bonds.[262]

*235.* From the legal definition of Article 73 of the LCS as well as from the ones proposed by doctrine, it can be deduced that liability insurance covers the risk that a debt comes to burden the patrimony of the insured. The purpose is not to preserve a thing or specific right like other property insurance does (e.g., fire insurance) but the whole patrimony of the insured.

However, it should be clarified that liability insurance does not cover every debt arising in the patrimony of the insured because there is no insurance that covers all liability that a person may incur. Liability insurance covers damages that may be

262. M.A. Calzada Conde, *El seguro de responsabilidad civil* (Pamplona: Aranzadi, 2005).

suffered by third parties as consequence of the occurrence of damaging events defined in the policy. The insurer may assume in the policy contractual liability and torts. Everything will depend on the specific delimitation of the risk made by the contracting parties, which in this type of insurance contracts acquires major significance.

*236.* Furthermore, the debt must be a debt to indemnify. We are not dealing with liability as an element of the obligation – Article 1911 of the CC. It is a debt to indemnify by reference to damages and loss. In short, the purpose is to repair damages, the consequences of which have been transferred to the liable party, and which will now be assumed by the insurer, within the limits fixed by the policy. In addition, such debt must be imputable to the insured based on objective criteria (risk) and subjective criteria (fault). It is not relevant whether the material author of the damaging event is the insured or a person for whom the insured is vicariously liable. On the contrary, the absence of the insured's liability implies that the insurance undertaking is equally not carrying liability (e.g., force majeure or exclusive fault of the victim).

Finally, it should be pointed out that the person who will receive the indemnification is not the insured but a third party. This is exactly a characteristic that distinguishes this contract from the rest of property insurance. The third party, person unconnected to the insurance contract, is entitled to the right for compensation as a damaged party.

## §3. Purpose

*237.* The purpose of liability insurance is to keep intact the patrimony of the insured from economic consequences related to possible liability. This has been obscured sometimes by the phenomenon of compulsory liability insurance, especially, automobile insurance because in these cases insurance is used as mechanism to protect third parties. Sometimes, even when coverage of compulsory insurance appeared to be insufficient, such postulates have been applied to non-compulsory insurance in order to adequately protect the victims.

In non-compulsory insurance, third parties are protected by the solvency of the insurer; nevertheless, this payment by the insurer is not the purpose of the insurance but the means through which the patrimony of the liable person is kept intact.

Because of these reasons, liability insurance occasionally tends to be confused with accident insurance. Our case law had the opportunity to indicate the differences between them, and found the most important one was the difference in the risk covered. In liability insurance the purpose is to cover risks that threaten the possible a liable party and not the risk that threatens a third party. Thus, the insurer will be obliged to pay the third party within the limits of the insured sum only if the respective liability of the insured is determined. On the contrary, accident insurance tries to cover the risk that a person suffers (corporal injuries) regardless of the existence of liability.

## §4. The Insured Interest

*238.* In liability insurance, the object that is threatened by risk of liability is the current and future of the patrimony of the possible liable person. Hence, the insured interest is undetermined.

Establishing an unlimited guarantee in the contract constitutes the most convenient coverage, but usually an insured sum is fixed with different limits: per victim, insured event, time periods, personal or material damages.

Because there is no determined value of the insured interest, it is not necessary to discuss cases of underinsurance and overinsurance. Nevertheless, those rules are perfectly applicable in insurance contracts where the maximum amount of the liability is established by reference to the value of the specific good (e.g., liability of depositary).

In contrast, multiple insurance may occur. Proportional distribution among different insurers in function of the insured sum will not pose problems if insurance contracts in question foresee certain insured sums or if the guarantee is unlimited in all of them. If, however, there is concurrence of insurances with limited and with unlimited guarantees, several solutions are possible, among them, that the distribution may be done in function of the respective premium.

## §5. The Insured Event

*239.* One of the most controversial matters in liability insurance relates to the definition of an insured event. In that respect, the doctrine has elaborated different theories:

(a) The insured event is the event from which the liability debt is born.[263]
(b) The insured event does not occur until the moment where the third party judicially or extra-judicially brings a claim against the insured that caused the damage.
(c) The insured event is a complex event that lasts from the damaging event until judicial or private recognition of liability.
(d) It has also been argued that, in this type of insurance contracts, there is no insured event from the technical-legal perspective.
(e) The parties may freely establish which events constitute insured events.

The reasons for such different opinions lie on the one hand in the lack of simultaneity of the different events that are part of the risk process, and on the other hand on the fact that there are many events that are connected to the insured event, basically the damage-causing event, the occurrence of damage to the third party and the third party's claim.[264]

---

263. SSTS 20-3-1991 (Civil). RAJ 1991/2267, 23-12-1992 (Civil). RAJ 1992/3323, 10-11-1995 (Civil). RAJ 1995/8254.
264. M.A. Calzada Conde, *El seguro de responsabilidad civil* (Pamplona: Aranzadi, 2005).

*240.* However, there are substantial disagreements to determine which event is relevant to different effects. For example, regarding the duties with general character that arise from the occurrence of the insured event, the relevant fact is the event that causes damage to the third party. In order to determine the exclusion of certain causes, the relevant fact is the action or lack of action of the insured. Finally, the event that causes the arising of the obligation of the insurer is the claim of the third party. The highest court decided in favour of the first theory (insured event is the event that causes damage). This interpretation, of impeccable legal technique, is used to generate, in practice, serious difficulties to the insurers. Indeed, deciding that the insured event is the event that causes damages results in a burden when the verification of the damaging event and the claim by an injured third party passes a prolonged period of time. In such case, there is uncertainty for the insurer who does not know whether claims will be filed after the duration period of the contract. However, the insurer must consider as an insured event the damaging event that happens during the validity of the policy. The mere expiration of the corresponding liability period should release in a definitive way to the insurer who, in the meantime, must keep respective provisions in the contingency event of a potential claim.

*241.* The described situation motivates the reform of Article 73 of the LCS, by which the existing practices in the insurance market and the clauses that limit the period during which the insurer covers potential claims (the so-called claim made clauses) are legalized. Specifically, the rule mentions two types of clauses:

(a) Clauses for posteriority coverage limit the insurer's coverage to cases in which claims for damage have been filed within a time period not shorter than one year upon the ending of the last extension of the contract, otherwise the ending of its duration period.
(b) Retroactive coverage clauses limit the insurer's coverage to the injurer's claims filed during the validity period of the policy, provided that such coverage is extended to the situations in which the arising of the indemnification obligation on the insured's account could have taken place before, at least a year before the beginning of the contract, even when such contract has been extended.

### §6. The Insurer's Obligation

*242.* The insurer's obligation consists in confronting the insured's liability debt, assuming the juridical direction against the claim of third parties and covering the respective expenses, or in both cases. This obligation will arise when the claim of a third party occurs.

## I. Insurer's Obligation Regarding the Liability Debt of the Insured

*243.* If the insured's liability is determined judicially or extra-judicially, and the case is covered by the contract, the insurer must take care of the liability debt of the insured by paying third parties. But sometimes, the third parties do not use this option and simply claim against the insured and the insurer denies coverage. In such a situation, if the insured has been obliged to pay a third party, she or he will have the right to demand the corresponding reimbursement from the insurer according to the contract.

A different matter involves whether the insured is entitled to demand the corresponding sum that is owed to him or her. The highest court supports the insured's title to demand the indemnification – although with the purpose of paying third parties. If the insured does not pay third parties, the insurer always has the option of suing the insured for unjust enrichment or opposing the payment exception against the claim of the third parties.

*244.* Other decisions of the highest court have stated that once a third party claims, the insured has the right to require that, in compliance of the contract, the insurer pays the third party and subsidiarily the reimbursement of the amount paid to the third party if such payment has already occurred.

Stating that the insured may claim against the insurer without referring to the third party's claim lacks legal grounds because otherwise the insurer would be exposed to direct action of the injured. It is not possible that the insured who did not pay a third party and the third party itself are both simultaneously entitled to demand the respective sum from the insurer unless the payment made to any of them releases obligations and, therefore, may be opposed against the other.

Lastly, the present Article 20 of the LCS has clarified that compensation for delay in complying with the insurer's obligation can be demanded by third parties directly. However, such charge is not owed when direct action is exercised by the insurer of the third party on the basis of subrogation.

## II. Juridical Direction in Civil Liability Insurance

*245.* Article 74 of the LCS prescribes that in the absence of an agreement to the contrary it is up to the insurance undertaking to take care of the insured's juridical direction against the claim of the injured, which includes assuming incurred expenses. It is clear that this provision is intended for cases in which the injured claim is filed against the insured, not for those claims against the insurer. When this last case happens, the insurer will manage his or her defence.

With regard to legal defence, Article 38 of the LCS is not applicable because it is designed for expert's opinions of damages, basically goods.

The evolution of liability insurance has lead hereto: this activity and the expenses incurred have been formally included in the insurer's obligation. The insurance interest requires the insurer to have the power of decision.

The direction of the insurer's juridical defence must be limited to cases in which the claim is filed against the insured (extra-judicial or judicial in civil court), but it is excluded when it is filed against the insured in criminal procedure. In such case, the insured is free to assign the defence to the insurer because the right to individual defence prevails over the existence of insurance. Nevertheless, it arises in liability claims filed before a criminal jurisdiction.

*246.* On the contrary, the insurer's obligation of managing the legal defence does not arise when the claim is referred to a liability that is different from the one protected by the policy, or when dealing with an excluded risk.

In the broad sense, direction of juridical defence must be understood as the power to manage and use the liability debt that burdens the insured. It is a right and an obligation of the insurer derived from liability insurance. Thus, it cannot be stated that juridical direction is by itself an autonomous coverage. However, there are policies in the market that cover liability and also include legal defence coverage against payment of a corresponding premium to cover the new coverage. Hence, we are before a policy with two different insurance contracts, one of liability and another of legal defence.

All expenses from juridical direction, as it has been explained, are on the insurer's account, and that is logical if it is assumed that he or she defends his or her own interests.

The insurer's juridical direction is flanked by the insured's duty to provide the necessary collaboration to enable the operation of the defence.

*247.* In cases where the person who caused damages is also insured with the same insurer (it does not matter the insurance modality that the third party has contracted) or where any other conflict of interests exists among the insurer and the insured (connection between the person who caused damages and the insurer), the insured has the option to entrust his or her juridical defence to another person.

In conclusion, as is logical, the insurer is subject to the general regime of liability. Thus, the insurer will be contractually liable to the insured if, due to his or her negligent behaviour in the managing of the defence, he or she causes damages of the insured.

## III. Statute of Limitations on the Insured's Action

*248.* The insured's action against an insurer derives from the insurance contract and, therefore, is subject to the two-year statute of limitations. The LCS does not have any specific rule about the statute of limitations for liability insurance. At first, the *dies a quo* will be determined by the claim of third parties because this is what causes the insurer's obligation.

Nevertheless, in the case of judicial claim, the judicial declaration will decide on the insured's liability. In this line, the highest court has considered that while the insured's liability is not recognized or declared, the statute of limitations will not start running and thus the statute cannot be applied when the insured and insurer are sued in the same procedure. If the insured is acquitted and she or he claims for legal expenses, the solution will be the same.

If the insurer rejects coverage and the insured does not institute the proceedings against the third party but decides to recognize her or his liability or make a settlement, the term will begin running upon the date of the third party's extra-judicial claim.

§7. Duties of Policyholder/Insured

*249.* As in every insurance contract, a number of duties arise for the policyholder/insured in liability insurance, and they are governed by Article 10 and following Articles of the LCS.

With respect to the duties of declaration of risk, communication of its aggravation, existence of other insurance contracts and transfer of insured interest, we refer to the chapter about obligations of policyholder/insured.

In liability insurance, the duty to communicate the occurrence of the insured event, its circumstances and consequences must mention the moment when the damage is caused against third parties – that is to say, the moment in which the damage may lead to the insured's liability has occurred.[265]

*250.* The insured must strive to mitigate the damage suffered by third parties. The person who caused the immediate damage is the one who can better develop salvage activities even when that person is not the policyholder or the insured. If that person does not perform any salvage activities, we cannot state that we are before a mere breach of duty but an extension of the insured's liability. The so-called failure to come to the aid (criminal classification) incurred by the insured constitutes a first breach of this duty; however, policies usually foresee this case as an exclusion of risk. This practice is considered debatable.

There are some specific duties to be complied with by the insured, such as the duty to cooperate with the juridical direction assumed by the insurer and to give notice to third parties about the existence and contents of the contract.

*251.* According to the duty to cooperate with juridical direction, the insured must behave so as to make it possible, to facilitate and not to block the defence against third parties. The law does not establish any sanction for breach of such duty. When policies only mention the damages caused by breach, there is no problem. If other types of sanctions are prescribed, we would face limitative or even abusive clauses.

Furthermore, when the insurer refuses to assume juridical direction against third parties, she or he will be rejecting the coverage and the duty to cooperate declines.

*252.* The general duty to cooperate is materialized through specific duties. In the first place, the insured has the duty not to recognize his or her liability unless with the insurer's consent. Nevertheless, recognition of the occurrence of facts, liability for persons for whom the insured is legally accountable or recognition by the insured due to stress that surrounds insured events that caused serious prejudice to persons do not involve breach of this duty. In second place, the insured must inform the insurer about all reclamation by the third parties. Such reclamation is any serious declaration of third parties, even when they are informally made but are intended to require the insured to pay damages. In the third place, the insured must communicate all facts that occurred in relation to the liability and transmit the documents received. Finally, the insured should transfer the defence to the insurer, which

---

265. See Part II, Ch.4.

implies transferring all necessary powers to the attorneys and bailiffs that are assigned by the insurer, offering all the cooperation that is needed and refraining from hindering the insurer's work.

### §8. Direct Right of Action or 'Cut Through'

### I. Notion, Nature and Function

*253.* Article 76 of the LCS involves the definitive implementation in our legal framework of the direct right of action, generally applicable to all cases of liability insurance, including insurance contracts of compulsory and non-compulsory compliance. The rule tends to provide protection to the injured who has suffered damages caused by an insured person. Indeed, together with direct right of action against the person who caused damages derived from the liability and as a consequence of the mentioned provision arises the right of injured third parties against the insurer. Consequently, the injured has the right to require compensation for damages not only against the first debtor but also against the insurer. The injured may also directly demand compensation so that the indemnification does not form part of the insured's patrimony.

There are different theses that have been supported with respect to the foundation of the right to direct action. Some authors and case law of the highest court consider that its origin comes from the same insurance contract. Others understand that even though it requires the existence of the contract, the right to direct action finds its direct foundation in the intention of the same law. There is even a thesis that finds its foundation in the injuring event.

*254.* Given the importance of Article 76 of the LCS, let's analyse its literal text:

> The injured or his heirs will have right to direct action against the insurer to require compliance with the obligation to indemnify, without prejudice to the insurer's right to recover against the insured in cases where damages suffered by third parties have been caused by the insured's wilful mischief. Direct action is not affected by exceptions that the insurer has against the insured. However, the insurer may oppose exclusive fault of the injured and also personal exceptions. Due to the effects of direct action, the insured is obliged to inform injured third parties or their heirs about the existence of the insurance contract and its contents.

According to the mentioned Article 76 of the LCS, the injured or his or her heirs are entitled to direct action. Thus, the notion of injured is not limited to the direct 'victim' of the event, but it also comprises persons that suffered damages imputable to the insured according to the respective liability rule. Therefore, in case of decease, heirs are the injured. On the contrary, and although this result is obvious, the insured cannot be considered as an injured. In conclusion, there is a right to direct action against an insurer when, in accordance with liability law, there is a right to act against insured-liable in order to require indemnification for respective damages, and such liability is protected by the insurance contract.

*255.* Nevertheless, insurance contract legislation may exclude certain persons from being considered as injured third parties. This way, it is usual to exclude from coverage certain persons connected to the insured. They will be entitled to act against the insured regarding her or his possible liability but not if this clause is considered to be opposed against the injured.[266] The reasons that motivate such exclusion are diverse; sometimes the purpose is to avoid possible cases of collusion; other times it is understood that such persons are not third parties from the economic point of view; in short, it is believed that, in the absence of insurance, such liabilities are presumed not to be compulsory.

## II. Exercise of Rights by Third Parties Against Insured and Insurer

*256.* Third parties have two actions one against the insured to claim repair of the damage (liability) and another against the insurer to require compliance of that obligation of the insured to indemnify (direct action of liability insurance).

Currently, it is solid case law doctrine that the insurer and insured are solidarily obliged against third parties. However, scientific doctrine is critical to this position because, besides the different origins of insured and insurer, the purpose of the insurance is that once the insured's obligation is established, which implies the obligation of the insurer, the insurer comes into position of the insured for the payment, thereby avoiding actual payment; such a situation does not occur, as is known, in solidarity obligations.

## III. Exceptions Opposite Against Injured Third Parties

*257.* Article 76 of the LCS has tried to guarantee the autonomy of the right of third parties vis-à-vis the contractual relationship that connects the insurer with the insured. Hence, the mentioned provision recognizes that direct action is immune to exceptions that the insurer may have against the insured. The right of third parties is autonomous vis-à-vis the insured's right against the insurer, although it certainly assumes the existence of an insurance contract that offers a determined coverage. There is also an unquestionable connection between the insured and the insurer with regard to injured third parties.

*258.* Consequently, the problem is centred on determining the exceptions that the insurer may impose on the injured, considering exceptions in a broad sense, which includes any possible defence that the insurer may use against third parties. Schematically, we can consider exceptions those that may be opposed against injured parties:

---

266. See the SSTS 21-3-2000 (Civil). RAJ 2000/2426; 9-3-2000 (Civil). RAJ 2000/1517; 16-5-2000 (Civil). RAJ 2000/3579.

(1) Exceptions derived from damaging events:
   (a) Absence of damaging event or absence of insured's liability, as occurs when there is exclusive fault from the side of the victim.
   (b) Reduction of the indemnifiable quantum because the insurer is liable in the same terms as the person who caused damages, and thus in the possibility to reduce the indemnification given the concurrence of faults.
(2) Exceptions derived from difficulties of the compulsory relationship arising among insured and third parties: circumstances that affect the life of the obligation, such as expiration of rights due to statute of limitations, *plus petitio*, payment, compensation and so on.
(3) Exceptions derived from the insurance contract:
   (a) Absence of a valid insurance contract that covers the kind of liability imputed to the insured.
   (b) Exceptions that find their origin in policy clauses: fixation of maximum economic limits of coverage and exclusion clauses (objective, territorial or temporary) of the risk. Sometimes, such clauses have been classified by case law as limitative (subject to Article 3 of the LCS), and a causal connection between the excluding fact and the damaging event has been required in respect to this type of clauses.
(4) Personal exceptions of the insurer against the injured. They are derived from the fact that the injured persons are minors or legally incapable, and these exceptions may stem from personal relationships, such as the possibility of compensating the payment with a claim that the insurer may have against the injured person due to an existing different relationship with the insurer, or they can stem from a transaction and prescription of the direct action.

*259.* On the contrary, the insurer cannot allege against the injured, the personal exceptions that he or she may have against the insured. Hence, the insured's breach to comply with his contractual duties cannot be opposed against third parties.[267]

Another problem to be discussed is the insurability of damages caused by wilful mischief. The same Article 76 of the LCS establishes 'the insurer's right to recover from the insured in cases where due to wilful mischief of the insured's behaviour, damages have been caused to third parties'. Such statement seems to admit that the insurer must indemnify these insured events, given the possibility of later recovery. However, this interpretation clashes head on with Article 19 of the LCS, which establishes the insurer's release when the insured event has been caused by wilful mischief of the insured.

*260.* With the intention of reconciling both rules, some authors and the highest court have supported the thesis that even though damages caused by wilful mischief of the insured are not covered, the insurer must indemnify on the basis of a direct

267. See the SSTS 16-5-1991 (Penal). RAJ 1991/3677 y 11-7-1991 (Penal). RAJ 1991/5779 about lack of payment of premium.

action because it is not possible to oppose an exception based on fraudulent behaviour of the insured. Article 76 of the LCS grants the insurer the option to recover against the insured afterwards.[268]

However, other authors have understood that the insurer should only indemnify the insured when the policy does not exclude fraudulent insured events.

Finally, the thesis has also been supported that insurers cannot cover damages derived from fraudulent behaviour of the insured. The explanation to the cited mention of Article 76 of the LCS lies in the fact that the legislator was thinking of those assumptions in which the insurer indemnify before certifying the fraudulent character of the insured event.

## IV. The Insurer's Right of Recovery Against the Insured

*261.* Article 76 of the LCS only considers the right to recovery in cases where the insured has wilfully caused damages to third parties. Nevertheless, it is the general opinion that the insurer enjoys such right as long as, due to lack of opposition to exceptions of Article 76 of the LCS, the insurer has had to pay third parties without being obliged to do so according to law or contract.

There are two situations where the right of recovery arose. First, the actual payment made by the insurer to third parties. Second, such payment has been made in situations where, in spite of the right to oppose an exception against the insured, the insurer was obliged to pay because of the non-opposability of the exception against a direct action.

*262.* In return, the right to recovery will not arise when the indemnified event is not covered by the contract. Nor will the right of recovery exist when the insurer is entitled to an opposable exception but left it unused; nor in those cases where certain circumstances are opposed by the insurer and they are rejected by the tribunal not because they are unopposable but because of other causes (e.g., nullity of contractual clause).

The right to recovery is subject to the statute of limitations and jurisdiction established by the LCS.

The passive subject of this right is the insured-liable, that is, the person whose liability has been protected by the insurance and, therefore, whose patrimony has been improperly protected by the insurance. Such right of recovery does not make sense against the policyholder. It is not applicable either against co-liable third parties.

268. See STS 29-5-1997 (Penal). RAJ 1997/3637. More recently SSTS 7-2-2001 (Penal). RAJ 2004/358; 20-7-2004 (Penal). RAJ 2004/5465; 8-3-2006 (Penal). RAJ 2006/5706; 27-9-2006 (Penal). RAJ 2006/8360; and 21-3-2007 (Penal). RAJ 2007/2125. However, SSTS 27-4-2007 (Penal). RAJ 2207/3858; 8-5-2007 (Penal). RAJ 2007/2873; 10-5-2007 (Penal). RAJ 2007/4732; 24-4-2008 (Penal). RAJ 2008/2909.

# Chapter 6. Legal Expenses Insurance

*263.* Legal expenses insurance is regulated by Articles 76(a)–76(g) of the LCS.[269] This regulation is the result of the implementation of Directive 87/344/CEE of 22 June 1987 into Spanish national law. Besides providing minimum contents to this branch of insurance, the directive tries to solve potential conflicts of interests between insured and insurer, and it also governs relationships between legal protection insurers and associations of attorneys.

Legal expenses insurance is defined by the Spanish legislator as the contract by which the insurer agrees to pay the expenses that the insured incurs as a consequence of her or his participation in an administrative, judicial and extra-judicial or arbitration proceedings; and to provide legal, judicial and extra-judicial assistance linked to the insurance within the limits established by the law and the contract (Article 76(a) of the LCS). However, payment of fines and indemnification of any expense from sanctions imposed on the insured by administrative or judicial authorities are excluded (Article 76(b) of the LCS).

Legal expense insurance will be subject to a separate contract, which will be materialized in a separate policy or as a separate chapter in a single policy together with other guarantees, in which case the nature of the legal expenses and the amount of the relevant premium are specified (Article 76(c) of the LCS).[270] The organic legislation also recognizes this autonomy in Article 6 of the TRLOSSP while considering legal defence insurance as an independent type of insurance contract. Likewise, this is the reason for the delimitation of this insurance as opposed to other legal activities that are provided within the coverage of liability insurance, travel assistance and use of vessels of maritime ships (Article 76(g) of the LCS).

*264.* However, in Spain, there is no compelling specialization system of insurance undertakings. Article 5(h) of the TRLOSSP authorizes choosing among the following modalities of management:

(1) Entrust the management of claims with respect to legal expense insurance for a different entity.
(2) Ensure the specialization and independence of the personnel who provide services in legal defence insurance.
(3) Afford in the insurance contract the insured person the right to entrust the defence of his or her interests, from the time that he or she has the right to claim from the insurer under the policy, to a lawyer of choice and without waiting until the conflict of interests arises.

---

269. About legal defence insurance, the following may be consulted: A. Olmos Pildaín, *El seguro de defensa jurídica* (Pamplona: Aranzadi, 1997); A.J. Tapia Hermida, 'Arts. 76 a)–76 g) LCS. Seguro de defensa jurídica', in *Ley de contrato de seguro. Comentarios a la Ley 50/1980, de 8 de octubre y sus modificaciones*, AA.VV. Dir. F. Sánchez Calero, 3th edn (Pamplona: Aranzadi, 2005), 1449ff; J. Viciano Pastor, 'Arts. 76 a)–76 g) LCS. Seguro de defensa jurídica', in *Comentarios a la Ley de contrato de seguro*, AA.VV. (Coords J. Boquera, J. Bataller & J. Olavarría) (Valencia: Tirant lo Blanch, 2001), 867ff.

270. The STS 20-4-2000 (Civil). RAJ 2000/2981 insisted on these requirements to distinguish it from the legal direction of liability insurance.

*265.* To protect the insured when he or she is facing potential conflicts with the insurer diverse rights, the following are established:

(1) The insured has the right to freely choose a bailiff and lawyer who will represent and defend him or her in any type of proceeding.
(2) Lawyer and bailiff who are designated by the insured are not subject, in any case, to the instructions of the insurer.
(3) The insured will have the right to submit to arbitration any difference that may arise between him or her and the insurer about the insurance contract.
(4) These rights should be included in the policy and the insurer must inform the insured about them when a conflict of interests arises.

## Chapter 7. Aviation Insurance

*266.* Aviation insurance covers risks inherent to air navigation. Therefore, according to this concept, neither the type of insured interest (passengers, aircraft, etc., but also luggage) nor the nature of the insured events (e.g., liability) prevails but only the fact of providing coverage to risks exposed to air navigation.[271]

A body of national and international rules is currently applicable to aviation insurance. In the international arena, we have to point out the 1929 Varsovia Convention for the unification of certain rules related to international air transport, and its 1955 Hague Protocol, the 1961 Guadalajara Convention and the four additional Protocols of Montreal; and the 1952 Rome Convention regarding the unification of certain rules related to damages caused by the aircraft to third parties on the surface. The European Union has also enacted laws of great significance for aviation insurance.[272]

*267.* Internally, the law for air navigation of 21 July 1960 applies and its scope is concise. Article 126 of the law simply states that aviation insurance has the purpose of guaranteeing risks that are proper to navigation and that affect the aircraft, merchandise, passengers and freights, as well as liability derived from damages caused by the aircraft to third parties on the ground, water or while flying. Later on, Articles 127 and 128 established the compulsory character of passenger insurance, aircraft and damages on the surface. This law tells us a little more. Consequently, we have to use the LCS for all issues that are not governed by its provisions, without forgetting the important role policies play in the absence of legal regulation nor the fact that these insurance contracts are necessary to protect large risks.

271. About aviation insurance, consult M. J. Morillas Jarillo, 'Seguros y responsabilidad civil en la navegación aérea', in *Estudios en homenaje al Prof. J. Duque*, AA.VV., vol. II (Valladolid: Universidad de Valladolid, 1998); J.L. Rodríguez Carrión, *Los seguros marítimos y aéreos*, in *Tratado de Derecho mercantil, Derecho de la Navegación*, AA.VV. (Dirs M. Olivencia, C. Fernández-Novoa & R. Jiménez de Parga), vol. 5 (Madrid: Marcial Pons, 2003).

272. Regulation on the liability of airlines in case of accidents; Regulation on the concession of licenses to airlines, because according to this regulation a subscription of insurance is required to obtain the license; Regulation as well as regulation about insurance requirements for airlines and air operators.

# Chapter 8. Theft Insurance

## §1. Legal Framework and Concept

*268.* The legislator treats theft insurance in Articles 50–53 of the LCS, and this legal classification confers its essence.[273] Article 50 establishes the concept of theft but in a broader way than criminal law, stating that it covers damages from unlawful removal of insured things by third parties.[274] In other words, the concept offered by Article 53 includes different criminal types: theft (Article 237 Criminal Code (CP)), stealing (Article 234 CP) and misappropriation of vehicles (Article 244 CP). Nevertheless, policies use terminology that tries to approach criminal concepts. For example, theft is compared with the criminal concept of theft with violence, spoliation (also known as robbery) in which one recognizes the criminal concept of theft with violence on persons, and stealing without violence. Furthermore, policies specify that theft and spoliation – in its contractual acceptation – are covered while excluding losses, stealing and cases of employee disloyalty, although they can be covered through payment of the corresponding premium.

*269.* There is doubt about the cited exclusions as to whether they are clauses that delimit the risk or clauses that limit the insured's rights. Case law has decided to classify such exclusions as limitative clauses and, therefore, subject to the protective regime described in Article 3 of the LCS.[275] However, it seems better justified to declare such limitations void since it is contrary to a compulsory rule because the definition of risk is established by the legislator and Article 2 of the LCS declares all provisions contained in the insurance contract law compulsory.[276]

Finally, Article 50 of the LCS prescribes that the insured risk comprises not only the loss of stolen objects but also the damage caused by the committance of any form of crime.

## §2. Duty to Report the Theft

*270.* It is not rare that the insurer requires the insured to submit the denunciation of the occurrence of the crime. The legislator has not foreseen anything in this respect in the provisions that govern theft insurance; therefore, the general regime

273. For deeper information on theft insurance, the following may be consulted: J. Duque Domínguez, 'Seguros de incendio, contra el robo, de transportes terrestres y lucro cesante', in *Comentarios a la Ley de contrato de seguro*, AA.VV. (Ed. E. Verdera) (Madrid: CUNEF, 1982), 762 ss; L. Ferrando Villalba, 'Arts. 50 a 53 LCS. Seguro de robo', in *Comentarios a la Ley de contrato de seguro*, AA.VV. J. (Coords Boquera, J. Bataller & J. Olavarría) (Valencia: Tirant lo Blanch, 2001), 605 y ss; F. Sánchez Calero, *'Arts. 50 and ff. Seguro contra el robo'*, in *Ley de contrato de seguro. Comentarios a la Ley 50/1980, de 8 de octubre y sus modificaciones*, AA.VV. (Dir F. Sánchez Calero), 3th edn (Pamplona: Aranzadi, 2005), 905ff.

274. About the theft concept, see J. Gómez Calero, 'El concepto de robo en la Ley de contrato de seguro', *RES*, 1981, n° 28, 425ff.

275. SSTS 10-5-1989 (Civil). RAJ 1989/3751 and 8-3-2002 (Civil). RAJ 2002/1915.

276. See the SSTS 10-5-1989 (Civil). RAJ 1989/3751 and 8-3-2002 (Civil). RAJ 2002/1915.

of duty to salvage may be applied (Article 17 of the LCS). Effectively, this duty has to be included because the purpose of the denunciation is to facilitate the recovery of the insured object that has been stolen. If this is the applicable regime, it seems doubtful that the insurer might subordinate her or his obligation to indemnify to the insured's compliance with the duty to denunciate, even when the policy stipulated so. Article 17 of the LCS establishes that the breach of duty to salvage grants the insurer the right to reduce the indemnification. In our opinion, as the text is compulsory, it prevents the insurer from being released from her or his obligation to indemnify despite the contractual clause.

## §3. Obligation to Indemnify

*271.* The insurer's indemnification – established in Article 51 of the LCS – necessarily comprises the value of the insured's interest when the insured object is stolen and is not found within the delay that is contractually agreed on, and the damage caused by any form of crime on the insured object.

On the contrary, the insurer is released from any obligation to indemnify when the insured event is due to gross negligence of the insured, policyholder or any person who depends on them or lives with them (Article 52.1 of the LCS).[277] In the same manner, the insurer is not obliged to carry out indemnification when the insured object is stolen outside the place described in the policy or due to its transport, unless any of those circumstances has been consented to by the insurer (Article 52.2 of the LCS). The precept expressly admits the possibility of contrary agreement and it is usually done so in the policy.

However, we cannot deduce that the insurer always covers insured objects located in any place. On the one hand, it is frequent that the insurer demands the adoption of certain safety measures to assume coverage of insured objects (e.g., installation of reinforced doors). On the other hand, the indemnity is limited when the objects are found in places where the risk of theft is higher (e.g., objects in garages, storerooms and other places of exclusive use that do not communicate with the living quarters of the house). In conclusion, we face specific assumptions where high risks lead the insurer to contractual precautions, which do, however, not exonerate her or him from the duty to comply with the regime established by Articles 3 – limitative and harmful clauses – and 10–12 of the LCS – declaration of risk.

*272.* Money, jewellery and objects with special value usually receive a different treatment in policies because they are subject to high risks and because of their high value. Thus, the policy will rule.

Finally, Article 53 of the LCS regulates the right of the insured to abandon, distinguishing between two situations when the object reappears before the deadline established in the policy has passed, in which case the insured must accept to take

277. The STS 10-5-1989 (Civil). RAJ 1989/3751 declared that the exception should be approved by the insurer.

back the object unless otherwise agreed. If the object reappears after indemnification has been received, the insured may choose between keeping the indemnification and acquiring the object again while returning the money.

# Chapter 9. Agricultural Insurance, Hail Insurance, Livestock Insurance

*273.* Agricultural insurance[278] has the purpose of covering the risks that threaten agricultural, forestry and livestock activities. Agricultural risks normally refer to products of exploitation along the whole productive cycle and before their commercialization or transformation.

The regulation of agricultural insurance contracts in Spain enjoys certain practices that were criticized in certain systems that had been tested by the State with more or less success. Currently, the law with the most significant practice is Law 87/1978 of 28 September, combined crop insurance (LSAC), that, is putting an end to the tortuous path of agricultural insurance in Spain.[279]

*274.* One of the keys to success of agricultural insurance in Spain lies in the joint intervention of public and private agencies and in the procedures that are set up to facilitate the coordination of its actions:

(1) Creation of the agricultural insurance state agency (*Entidad Estatal de Seguros Agrarios* (ENESA)) as a coordinating body and connection with the administration for activities related to agricultural insurance (Articles 17 and 18 LSAC).
(2) Coverage of combined agricultural insurance is done in a co-insurance regime by insurance undertakings. Article 41 of Royal Decree 2329/1979, 14 September, which approves the Regulation for the Application of Combined Crop Insurance Law (RSAC) obliges insurance undertakings to form groups and participate in covering all risks, an order that has been carried out by the Spanish association of combined agricultural insurance undertakings (*Agrupación Española de Entidades Aseguradoras de los Seguros Agrarios Combinados*, S.A. (AGROSEGURO)).
(3) The Insurance Compensation Consortium acts as reinsurer and may even directly give coverage if private insurance undertakings do not arrive at covering the total amount (Article 10 of the ELCCS).

The purpose of the LSAC is to supervise multiple risks of agricultural, livestock and forestry productions (Articles 1 and 2 of the LSAC). Insurable risks are damages caused by abnormal variations of natural agents, in cases where technical means for preventive measures could not be used by the affected persons due to causes attributable to them or where the measures were inefficient (Article 3 of the LSAC). Annually, upon a proposal of the agricultural insurance state agency, the combined insurance plan is established by the government in which the progressive application of the law is specified (Article 5 of the LSAC).

278. For deeper study of this type of insurance, the following may be consulted: *El sistema español de seguros agrarios combinados: 25 años de protección a las rentas agrarias*, AA.VV. (Madrid: Ministerio de Agricultura, Pesca y Alimentación, 2003).
279. The LSAC is developed by Royal Decree 2329/1979, of 14 September by which the regulation for its application is approved.

Insurance contracts may be subscribed individually or collectively (Article 7 of the LSAC). The contracting is voluntary unless the government stipulates its compulsory application in accordance with Article 8 of Law 87/1978, 28 September, combined crop insurance (LASC).[280]

Insurance contracts are in accordance with general conditions that are complemented with special conditions for each agrarian line. Insurance undertakings establish fees for each type of crop and production zone on the basis of actuarial information obtained from the application of the insurance.

280. The government may state its compulsory application when, in a zone of production, more than 50% of persons that directly manage or work agricultural crops agree to subscribe to it, expressed through the organizations and associations of farmers without prejudice that the government may state so in serious cases. The agreement will fix types and minimum risks of compulsory subscription, and those who can be voluntarily and independently insured.

# Chapter 10. Catastrophe Insurance

## §1. Insurance Compensation Consortium

*275.* The high level of loss as a result of the Spanish Civil War created the need for the compensation consortium for catastrophic risks for goods, individual accidents and life insurance and to liquidate through them the insured events that had occurred during the war conflict. Nevertheless, the convenience to use these bodies in the liquidation of insured events of catastrophic nature was soon noticed. The system was consolidated with the law of 16 December 1954 and later it assumed new functions as needed.[281]

The evolution of the CCS legal framework is laid down in the Royal Legislative Decree (RDLeg) 7/2004 of 29 October, by which the adapted text of the Legal Statute of the Insurance Compensation Consortium was approved (ELCCS). The intense reform that the legal framework of the CCS has undergone in the past decade has thus been laid down in one single text.

*276.* At present, the CCS is a public enterprise[282] with a separate legal personality and with full capacity to act for the compliance of its purposes, and with a patrimony of its own that is separate from that of the state (Article 1 of the ELCCS).[283] In the absence of specific rules, in its legal status, the CCS is, in the exercise of its insurance activity, subject to the LCS and the TRLOSSP (Article 2 of the ELCCS).[284] In sections I and II of Chapter I, the ELCCS distinguishes between private and public functions. It would appear that public functions will be subject to public law.

## §2. Nuclear Risk

*277.* Law 12/2011 governs liability insurance in nuclear industry in harmony with international regulation (Treaties of Paris and Brussels). Objective liability is imposed and damages are limited until a maximum sum.

Insurance of liability of nuclear damages is compulsory (Article 12 of Law 12/2011); however, it is possible another financial solution like a credit surety.). In addition, Law 12/2011 introduces another compulsory insurance in order to cover radioactivity no nuclear liability.

281. About the consortium, the following may be consulted: Barrero E. Rodríguez, *El Consorcio de Compensación de Seguros* (Valencia: Tirant lo Blanch, 2000); R. Soto Vázquez 'El Consorcio de Compensación de Seguros', in *Derecho de seguros II*, AA.VV. (Dir. J.N. Martí Sanchez) (Madrid: CGPJ, 1996), 379 y ss; L.M. Almajano Pablos, 'El nuevo estatuto legal del Consorcio de Compensación de Seguros', *RES*, n° 67, 1991, 75ff.
282. About the significance of this category, see Law 6/1997 on organization and functioning of the state general administration.
283. SSTS 16-3-1995 (Civil). RAJ 1995/7786 y 27-10-1999 (Civil). RAJ 1999/7402.
284. SSTS 15-3-1991 (Civil). RAJ 1991/2260, 5-7-1994 (Civil). RAJ 1994/6432, 14-3-1998 (Civil). RAJ 1998/1566, 5-12-1996 (Civil). RAJ 1996/8808 y 24-11-1992 (Civil). RAJ 1992/9369; nevertheless, the STS 16-3-1995 (Civil). RAJ 1995/7786.

The Spanish atomic pool (Pool Atomico Español) has been constituted for the contracting of this insurance. At the same time, if the group of private insurance undertakings does not reach the minimum limit foreseen by Law 12/2011, the CCS will assume the difference until it reaches the indicated limit (Article 9 of the ELCCS).[285] On the other side of the insurance contract, the insured is the exploiter of nuclear facilities.

*278.* According to Article 3 of Law 12/2011, the coverage extends to personal and material damage, *lucrum cessans*, precautionary measures and decontamination. The period of liability is thirty years since accident in personal damages and ten years in material damages. However, the victim has to claim in three years since he has notice of the damages (Article 15 Law 12/2011).

## §3. Natural Catastrophe

*279.* The CCS has lost the monopoly that it used to have traditionally with respect to extraordinary risks. Currently, they can be covered with a separate insurance that may also be underwritten by private insurers. Nevertheless, a compulsory charge in favour of the CCS is kept in place that is not of the kind to motivate the contracting of private insurance because this would involve paying twice for the same coverage. In practice, the CCS is a de facto insurer for extraordinary risks and private insurers extend their coverage to other extraordinary risks that are not covered by the CCS. The exoneration of the charge in favour of the CCS would imply in practice an anti-selection of risks.

Regarding extraordinary risks, the CCS is subject to Articles 6–8 of the ELCCS but also to Royal Decree 300/2004 of 20 February by which the regulation of extraordinary risk insurance is approved and the resolution of 27 November 2006 about the clause of compulsory inclusion in extraordinary risk policies.[286]

*280.* In extraordinary risks, insurance contracting on behalf of the CCS is not directly performed with this body itself but through private insurers who will have to pay the corresponding obligatory charge so the CCS may pay the insured the corresponding indemnifications due to the occurrence of extraordinary insured events. The CCS may act as direct insurer when an extraordinary covered risk is not protected by private insurer (Article 8.1(a) of the ELCCS), or as a subsidiary insurer when an insured is still protected by an insurance policy and the insurer's obligations cannot be complied since they were judicially declared bankrupt, or when in

285. In force until Estates signs together protocols for 12.2.2004 of Treaty of Paris and Treaty of Brussels.

286. On extraordinary risks, consult I. Martínez Rodríguez & J. Bataller Grau, 'Il nuevo regime spagnolo dei rischi straordinari da parte del consorcio di compensazione delle assicurazioni', Dir.Ec.Ass., n° 3, 2004, 725 y ss; T.J. Correa, R. A. De Castro, 'Riesgos catastróficos y su conceptuación jurídica', *V Congreso Iberolatinoamericano*, t. II (Madrid, 1997), 387ff; A. García Barona, 'El sistema español de cobertura de las catástrofes naturales', in *Las consecuencias económicas de las catástrofes naturales. Prevención y seguro*, AA.VV. (Madrid, 2000), 107ff. and in *V Congreso Iberolatinoamericano*, t. II (Madrid: Editorial Española de Seguros, 1997), 401 and ff.

a state of insolvency the insured would be subject to intervention procedure to liquidation or this would have been assumed by the CCS (Article 8.1(b) of the ELCCS).

*281.* According to current legal framework, extraordinary risks[287] are those listed within branches enumerated by Article 6 of the ELCCS[288] that cover the following events:

(1) Pursuant to Article 6.1(a) of the ELCCS and Article 1(a) of the Royal Decree 300/2004, 20 February, which approves the regulation of extraordinary risks (RRE), certain phenomena of nature with extraordinary character: earthquakes and tsunamis, extraordinary floods, volcanic eruptions, atypical cyclone storms and fall of sidereal bodies and aerolites.
(2) By Article 6.1(b) of the ELCCS and Article 1(b) of the RRE, insured events violently caused as consequence of terrorism, rebellion, sedition, riot and popular tumult.
(3) Article 6.1(c) of the ELCSS and Article 1(c) of the RRE include extraordinary risks events or behaviours of the armed forces or forces of security in times of peace.

The coverage of the CCS will necessarily and exclusively protect the same persons or assets as are mentioned in the insurance policy (Article 8.2 of the ELCCS) and for the same amounts, although this obligation will be limited to indemnifications paid according to the LCS (párr. 2° Article 8.2 ELCCS), applying the proportional rule in case of underinsurance (Article 5.3 of the RRE).

*282.* The CCS' obligation to indemnify shows two important peculiarities:

(1) Article 8 of the RRE establishes a 'shortage' deadline (exclusion period) by virtue of which insured events are excluded when they occur within seven days after the date of issuance or effect of the subscribed policy.[289] Such deadline will not apply when there is a transfer of the policy to another undertaking with same coverage and without interruption; nor will it apply in the case of capital revaluation or when it was impossible to previously contract the insurance. The shortage deadline will not be applied to personal insurance either.
(2) Article 9 of the RRE concerns the deduction that will have to be assumed by the insured. It is limited to property insurance, not personal insurance, and assumes 7% of the indemnification that is due to insured events.

*283.* Additionally, because of its practical importance on this type of insured event, we must mention Article 7 of the RRE, which limits the coverage of complementary expenses (mud clearing and extraction of mud, rubble removal, deposit

287. See the STS 18-3-1996 (Civil). RAJ 1996/2241 on interpretation of included risks.
288. On the contrary, those insured events contained in Art. 6.2 of the ELCCS and 7 RRE are excluded.
289. See the SSTS 9-2-1990 (Civil). RAJ 1990/671 and 28-2-1998 (Civil). RAJ 1998/1163.

storage of goods, etc.) to 4% of the insured sum. This calculation will be subject to the underinsurance regime of Article 5 of the RRE.

Article 21 of the ELCCS gives jurisdiction to the curl court of civil jurisdiction and the absence of the requirement of a previous claim.[290] However, the same law, in its Article 20 contains certain peculiarities with respect to the liquidation of the insured event, for which Article 10 of the RRE clarifies now that the consortium is not bound by valuations performed by the insurer.

290. About its influence on the statute of limitations (prescripción), see the SSTS 2-2-1995 (Civil). RAJ 1995/729 y 24-11-1994 (Civil). RAJ 1994/8944.

# Chapter 11. Credit and Suretyship Insurance

*284.* The LCS has decided to regulate credit insurance separately from suretyship insurance. This decision is based on the existing difference between the risks covered in both insurance contracts. In credit insurance (Articles 69–72 of the LCS), the intention is to cover the creditor (insured) whose credit is not satisfied due to insolvency of the debtor.[291] On the contrary, suretyship insurance (Article 68 of the LCS) aims at covering the mere breach of obligation attributable to the debtor (policyholder) in relation to the creditor (insured).

## §1. Credit Insurance

*285.* Article 70 of the LCS concerns those cases where insolvency causes the insured event,[292] and that enumeration pretends to be exhaustive not merely enunciative. The interpretative problems posed by this provision have increased because Law 22/2003 of 9 July on bankruptcy has not expressly foreseen new categories applicable to the debtor's insolvency. In our opinion, the four assumptions of Article 70 of the LCS are:

(1) Reference to bankruptcy declaration by a final judicial decision must be understood as a reference to bankruptcy in which the phase of liquidation has been opened (Disp. Adic. 1ª of the bankruptcy law).[293]
(2) Reference to the judicial approval of a convention on the waiver of debt used to be interpreted by doctrine as a synonym of *concordal judiciaire* obtained within the procedures of '*suspension de pagos*' and of '*quita y espera'*. Consequently, it would appear that the reference refers both to the convention that arose from an anticipated convention and to that 'ordinary' convention that may be approved in the course of the bankruptcy procedures when they have an amount due to creditors.
(3) The third assumption concerns the case of an unsuccessful forced execution of the debtor's assets. Its draft is inspired by the old Article 876 of the Ccom, which considered it as a necessary cause of bankruptcy. The current Article 2.4 of the bankruptcy law considers as a sufficient reason to start bankruptcy proceedings the fact that execution or cautionary measures have been filed but the

291. More may be consulted about credit insurance in M.I. Candelario Macías, *Seguro de crédito y práctica concursal* (Madrid: Dykinson, 1999); R. Morral Soldevilla, *El seguro de crédito* (Madrid: Civitas, 2002); R. Marimón Durá, 'Arts. 69–72 LCS. Seguro de crédito', in *Comentarios a la Ley de contrato de seguro*, AA.VV. (Coords J. Boquera, J. Bataller & J. Olavarría) (Valencia: Tirant lo Blanch, 2001), 779ff; F.J. Tirado Suarez, *'Arts. 69 and ff. Seguro de crédito'*, in *Ley de contrato de seguro. Comentarios a la Ley 50/1980, de 8 de octubre y sus modificaciones*, AA.VV. (Dir F. Sánchez Calero), 3th edn (Pamplona: Aranzadi, 2005), 1215ff.

292. See STS 13-2-1990 (Civil). RAJ 1990/682.

293. The Disp. Adic. 1a. of the bankruptcy law foresees that, in those legal texts where nothing has been expressly said, references to bankruptcy must be understood as made to the tender in which the liquidation phase has been opened.

embargo did not provide sufficient free assets to pay. Doctrine demands that execution has been claimed by the insured and not by any other creditor.[294]

(4) Finally, there is the agreement between insured and insurer tending to recognize a claim as non-collectible.

On the expiration of the six-month deadline, lack of payment of the claim obliges the insurer to deliver 50% of the agreed coverage in advance.[295] Insurance undertakings follow the practice of paying in advance a percentage of the final amount of the indemnification when the insolvency is evident without having been verified so far. The total amount is only paid once the definite character of the debtor's insolvency has been conveniently proved.

*286.* In credit insurance contracts, the insurer agrees to only partially indemnify the total loss suffered by the insured. Consequently, the indemnification is a percentage of the final loss of the insured. Hence, the insured should take care of the portion that was not covered by the insurance ('*descubierto obligatorio*').[296]

However, the LCS allows inclusion of the nominal value of the claim and expenses of the debt recovery proceedings, the legal costs and any other expenses that were expressly agreed on.

Article 71 of the LCS establishes that the company must assume 50% of the final loss, but the percentage legally established that must be paid by the insurer is a maximum, not a minimum; therefore, nothing prevents the limit to be 100%. In practice, it usually fluctuates between 15% and 25%.

*287.* Lastly, Article 72 of the LCS establishes the following duties that must be complied with by the insured:

(1) On the insurer's request, the insured must exhibit books and any other document that may have relation with the credit or insured claims.
(2) He or she must provide the necessary collaboration during judicial proceedings to obtain payment of the debt, and the direction of the proceedings will be assumed by the insurer.
(3) Once the indemnification has been satisfied,[297] the insured must, on the insurer's demand, assign to him or her the claim against the debtor.

294. The STS 25-10-1995 (Civil). RAJ 1995/7738 subsumes in the assumption of fact of Art. 70.3 of the LCS a case of mortgage constitution by the debtor in favour of another creditor who is not the insured.
295. The STS 28-7-1990 (Civil). RAJ 1990/6185 considered included in Art. 70.2 of the LCS the subscription of a wait and see agreement. See also the STS 4-7-2000 (Civil). RAJ 2000/5726, which estimated a simple lack of payment as cause for the 50% payment in advance.
296. SSTS 20-2-1984 (Civil). RAJ 1984/698 y 25-10-1995 (Civil). RAJ 1995/7738.
297. See the SSTS 2-2-2001 (Civil). RAJ 2001/1685; 10-10-2000 (Civil). RAJ 2000/9186; and 7-3-2001 (Civil). RAJ 2001/2729.

§2. EXPORT CREDIT INSURANCE

*288.* Its regulation is found in Law 10/1970 of 4 July[298] by which a public limited company is created with a majority participation of the State, called the Spanish Company for Export Credit Insurance (CESCE). This law was further carried out by Decree 3138/1971 of 22 December and defines the different modalities of insurance (private buyers, public buyers, global policy and special global policy, banking risks, protecting of markets, attendance to fairs and increase of costs) leaving the possibility open to create others).

*289.* Finally, it is important to point out two laws:

(1) Order ECO/180/2003 of 22 January on the coverage on account of the State, of risks derived from foreign trade of foreign investment and foreign economic transactions modified by Order ITC/962/2006 of 13 March.
(2) The Royal Decree 1327/1999 of 31 July by which certain aspects of medium and long-term export credit insurance on account of the State implementing the Council Directive 98/29/CE of 7 May 1998 regarding harmonization of the main provisions concerning export credit insurance for transactions with medium and long-term cover. According to the introduction of the royal decree, this directive has the purpose of 'assuring that coverage for export operations is based on uniform principles to not distort competition among undertakings in the European Union'.[299]

*290.* The purpose of export credit insurance is to cover its risks and it constitutes a tool for the export activity.[300] Through these insurance contracts, losses of export undertakings and financial corporations due to claims arising out of export operations of commercial and political or extraordinary insured events are covered. It also covers losses produced by other operations and risks that affect export activity and have been expressly established (Article 1 of Decree 3138/1971).

There are different modalities: risks of contract resolution, risks arising out of expedition or from seller's credits, claims arising out of export operations or of buyer credit insurance, those from pre-financing credit of exports with firm orders, complementary guarantees to financial entities and institutions, market research, attendance to fairs, cost increases, exchange differences, international investment and documentary credit.

---

298. Previously to this regulation, but of great interest are the works of F. Del Caño Escudero, *Seguro de crédito a la exportación* (Madrid, 1965); and R. Jiménez de Parga Cabrera, *El seguro de crédito a la exportación* (Madrid: Tecnos, 1965). More recently, J. Hernández Martí, 'Seguro de crédito a la exportación', in *Contratación internacional*, AA.VV. (Coord. C. Espulgues Mota), 2th edn (Valencia: Tirant lo Blanch, 1999), 770ff.

299. About these last legal advances, see C. Vargas Vasserot, 'El seguro de crédito a la exportación y su desarrollo normativo en la Unión Europea', *RES*, 2001, n° 107, 421ff.

300. See the SSTS 3-2-1981 (Civil). RAJ 1981/347; 22-12-1981 (Civil). RAJ 1981/5348; and 20-2-1984 (Civil). RAJ 1984/698.

In export credit insurance, a compulsory deductible is also applied so as to make the insured assume a portion of the risk. Furthermore, the classification of the buyers-importers made by the insurer is an important element to delimit the risk.

## §3. Suretyship Insurance

*291.* Pursuant to Article 68 of the LCS, suretyship insurance is the contract by which the insurer agrees that in case of breach of the legal or contractual obligation of the policyholder's insurance, she or he will indemnify by way of payment or sanction the insured for the damages suffered within the limits established by law or contract.[301] Nevertheless, under the freedom of contract, insurers offer other guarantee insurance (with caution) with a different structure.[302]

In suretyship insurance, the insured is the person who receives indemnification (by way of payment or sanction) for patrimonial damage due to the policyholder's breach of her or his legal or contractual obligations. The insured cannot coincide with the policy. Hence, we are in front of an insurance on behalf of others. At the same time, pursuant to Article 68 of the LCS, the policyholder will be the debtor of certain legal or contractual obligations.[303]

*292.* The atypical characteristics of suretyship insurance lead to relative confusion when it comes to determining the applicable rules. Suretyship insurance that does not fit into the type described in Article 68 of the LCS leads the judge to apply general provisions of the insurance contract law, reasoning by analogy, or, when proceeding, with rules applicable to guarantee contracts – that in Spanish law are found in the bond deposit list in Articles 1822 and following of the CC. Although this atypical feature leads to legal insecurity, the insurance is perfectly valid.

It is not necessary that the interest in suretyship policies is determined but it is necessary that such interest exists.[304] According to Article 68 of the LCS, the insured interest in suretyship insurance is materialized in the obligation, either legal

301. There is large bibliography about caution insurance among which we cite J.M. Embid Irujo, 'El seguro de caución: Régimen jurídico convencional y naturaleza jurídica', *The law,* 1986-2, 1064ff; J.M. Embid Irujo, 'El seguro de caución como garantía', in *Nuevas entidades, figuras contractuales y garantías en el mercado financiero*, AA.VV. (Madrid: CGCOCC, 1990); J. Camacho de los Ríos, *El seguro de caución. Estudio crítico* (Madrid: Mapfre, 1994); M.P. Barres Benlloch, *Régimen jurídico del seguro de caución* (Pamplona: Aranzadi, 1996).

302. In practice, problems are posed when trying to differentiate caution insurance from other similar concepts. The SSTS 19-5-1990 (Civil). RAJ 1990/3741; 30-7-1991 (Civil). RAJ 1991/5425; 7-4-1992 (Civil). RAJ 1992/3031; 5-6-1992 (Civil). RAJ 1992/5002; and 26-1-1995 (Civil). RAJ 1995/172 have shown how complicated it is to distinguish between bail bond and caution insurance. The difference between them is the accessory character of the bail bond, the compensatory character of the caution insurance contract as well as the different statutes of limitations that rule them. About the differences among caution insurance and a demanded guarantee see the SSTS 30-3-2000 (Civil). RAJ 2000/2314; 5-7-2000 (Civil). RAJ 2000/6010; and 13-12-2000 (Civil). RAJ 2000/10438.

303. The SSTS 19-5-1990 (Civil). RAJ 1990/3741 and 14-3-1993 (Civil). RAJ 1993/2879 considered that the non-payment of premium by the taker releases the insurer from her or his obligation. However, the STS 30-6-1990 (Civil). RAJ 1990/4949.

304. See the STS 20-2-1989 (Civil). RAJ 1989/1212.

or contractual, that must be complied by the policyholder and has been described in the contracted policy. The obligation may be to do or not to do.

*293.* In Article 68 of the LCS, the risk that the legislator has intended to cover is concretized at the time of the breach. The concept of breach is not specified in Article 68 of the LCS and, therefore, it is necessary to use the policies that exist in the insurance market. Hence, the determination of the insured risk must be done in the policy.[305]

Article 68 of the LCS considers a property insurance contract in which the indemnification is characterized by the legislator as 'compensation' for the insured or 'sanction' for the policyholder who breached his or her obligation. According to the legislator, suretyship insurance must cover the 'incurred patrimonial damage'.

*294.* In conclusion, the right of recovery as recognized by Article 68 of the LCS lets appear the following differences with subrogatory action of Article 43 of the LCS:

(1) They cause different obligation levels and, therefore, it would appear that the right of recovery cannot be contractually excluded.
(2) The actions in which the insurer is subrogated (e.g., Article 43 of the LCS) are those that the insured has against the liable third party, whereas in suretyship insurance the actions are against the policyholder.
(3) The right of reimbursement gives an action that is proper to the insurer and that surpasses Article 43 of the LCS.

305. The SSTS 18-2-1993 (Civil). RAJ 1993/1243 and 14-4-1993 (Civil). RAJ 1993/2879 considered that the discrepancy about valuation of works is not an assumption of breach.

# Chapter 12. Construction Insurance

*295.* The importance of the construction sector in the economy is beyond any doubt. It is, therefore, not strange that the insurers have designed products that are specific for this sector. Furthermore, the legislator has tried to protect buyers of housing through insurance.

## §1. Advance Payment Insurance for Construction and Sale of Housing

*296.* In Spain it is frequent to pay in advance during the construction or even before construction has started in order to acquire housing. The number of abuses in housing construction that occurred in the decade of the 1960s leads the legislator to promulgate Law 57/1968 of 27 July on advance payments for construction and sale of housing, with a goal of avoiding irreparable prejudices in domestic households with loss of important sums of money and lack of delivering of the house.

The current regime obliges housing promoters who are not officially[306] protected and claim to receive money before finishing the works to open independent checking accounts to deposit the received amount and subscribe a caution insurance or bank guarantee. Hence, caution insurance is compulsory. The policyholder is the promoter, whereas the insured is the acquirer of the future home. The insured risk materializes when the deadline to begin or deliver the home has expired without these events having taken place. The insured sum is the amount paid as advance payments so that each time the acquirer pays in advance, the policyholder must pay the respective premium and the insurer will increase the value of the covered amount. The indemnification will comprise the sums delivered plus legal interest.[307] Finally, the point is to expedite the payment by declaring that the insurance contract together with the document that certifies that works were not started or the executive title was not delivered.

## §2. Construction All Risks Insurance

*297.* The policy of contractor's all risk insurance covers the risks all the way from the inception of works till the definitive delivery of the building, at which moment coverage of another insurance starts, that is, the insurance that is governed by the *Ley de Ordenación de la Edificación*. We come back to this later on. This policy is frequently subscribed to in practice although it is of voluntary subscription. As far as the legal rules of it are concerned, this contract does not enjoy explicit regulation; therefore, the general provisions of property insurance will have to be

306. Officially protected housing has characteristics that are established by current law and are addressed to persons with the lowest income. Its price is controlled by the administration, and also the persons who have access to this housing may receive subsidies and strong tax incentives.

307. This way has been established by the additional provision of Law 38/1999 of 5 December on building management.

applied in conjunction with policy conditions. Hence, every discussion of this type of contract must involve the study of the different policies that exist in the market, so as to make it difficult to make general statements that are not contradicted by contractual praxis. However, there are some common characteristics:

(1) The insured in this type of insurance is the constructor.
(2) Two risks are covered. First, material damages resulting from construction work and premises. This insurance is subject to the principle of universality of the risk – that is to say, all risk insurance – because it covers any material damage except what is expressly excluded. Second, it also covers constructor's liability considering it for construction works, employer's liability and 'cross' liability.
(3) Obviously, the insured event must fall on the insured interest, and it is here that this type of policy offers most flexibility: damage to construction works and premises are compulsory, whereas the coverage of construction machinery, the construction team and pre-existing goods are optional.

## §3. Insurance Contract Types in Construction Management Law

*298.* Law 38/1999 of 5 December on construction management law (law for zoning and development (LOE)) and other matters[308] governs liability of the agents who intervene in the construction process, which is a liability regime of great importance in the insurance sector because the LOE itself establishes a system of guarantees that are based on their insurance.[309] Specifically, the legislator mentions the possibility of using an insurance covering material damages or caution insurance.[310] The first option is more widely used in the market.

*299.* First, annual liability for material damage that is due to vices or defects in the execution and that affects the completion or termination of the work is covered by insurance in which the policyholder is the constructor and where the acquirer is the insured. The minimum amount to be insured is 5% of the final cost of works' execution, including professional fees. Deductibles are forbidden.

---

308. Article 1 of the LOE establishes that the law has the purpose of regulating essential aspects of the building process, establishing obligations and liabilities of the agents who intervene in such process, as well as necessary guarantees for its development, assurance of quality through the compliance of basic requirements for buildings and adequate protection of users' rights.
309. About insurance contracts introduced by the LOE, see C. Boldó Roda, 'Régimen de garantías por daños materiales ocasionados por vicios o defectos de la construcción', *RES*, 2000, n° 103, 531ff; M.J. Peñas Moyano, 'Edificación y seguro: modalidades contractuales exigidas como garantía en la LOE', *RES*, 2002, n° 110, 145ff; J. Brenes Cortés, *Garantías por defectos en la construcción en la Ley de ordenación de la edificación: especial referencia al seguro de daños decenal* (Valencia: Tirant lo Blanch, 2005); A. Cabanillas Sánchez, 'La responsabilidad civil por vicios en la construcción en la reciente Ley de Ordenación de la Edificación', *ADC*, 2000, 405ff; Carrasco Parera, Cordero Lobato & González Carrasco, *Comentarios a la Ley de Ordenación de la Edificación*, 3th edn (Pamplona: Aranzadi, 2005); J. Estruch Estruch, *La responsabilidad en la construcción: Regímenes jurídicos y jurisprudencia* (Madrid: Civitas, 2003).
310. See Art. 19.9 of the LOE, which contains risks excluded by the regulator.

Second, triennial liability to cover material damages caused in the building due to vices or defects of constructive elements or premises that affect the habitability is covered by insurance subscribed by the promoter in which the insured capital will be, at least, 30% of the final cost of works including fees, and where deductibles are only allowed if they do not exceed 1% of the insured sum.

Finally, decennial liability for material damage caused by the manifestation of vices or defects in the building structure is covered by insurance of the promoter that covers 100% of the final cost of the execution, including fees, and where deductibles are allowed if they do not exceed 1% of the insured capital.

*300.* Currently, decennial liability insurance is compulsory when housing is the final purpose of the building.[311] In the future, the other two insurance types may be declared compulsory by royal decree.

The legislator has prescribed certain measures that should preserve the efficacy of the rights of the building acquirer. Thus, the premium must be paid before the reception of the work;[312] also once the cover comes into force the insurance cannot be resolved or rescinded before the end of the agreed duration term. In addition, the registration of public deeds of declaration of new building works in the registry office of property is subject to accreditation of the insurance contracts that are compulsory.

---

311. Article 105 of the law for tax and administrative measures as well as tax matters published by the BOE 313 of 31 Dec. 2000, exonerates its contracting to auto-promoters of uni-familiar houses and rehabilitations.

312. Nevertheless, if installment payments are agreed for later periods, lack of payment will not give right to resolve the contract or release the insured from his or her obligation to indemnify.

# Chapter 13. Other Property Insurance

## §1. Its Atypical Character

*301.* Besides the types of property insurance already mentioned, one usually finds in the insurance market a heterogeneous group of insurance contracts that present a common denominator: they are property insurances on goods that are not classified in the LCS, that cover the insured interest of a specific risk that has not been expressly covered by the legislator. It is customary that, next to fire and theft insurance, other risks, called 'additional' or 'extensive' risks, are included in the policy, especially in multi-risk policies.

There are multiple potential risks that surround an object and the legislator has only classified some of them. The LCS chose to regulate those that enjoy more tradition (e.g., fire insurance) or that are widely practised in the current insurance market (e.g., liability insurance). It was never the legislator's intention to exclude the other possible objects of coverage. Consequently, such atypical insurances are perfectly valid because the LCS does not contain *numerus clausus* of contractual modalities. The mere reading of Article 6 of the TRLOSSP, which governs insurance industries, demonstrates the existence of insurance contracts that are not included in the LCS. Nor must we forget the prevalence of the autonomy of the will that continues to be the central crux of our legal framework and thus of insurance law. It is stated that Article 2 of the LCS has restricted its scope of application, but this does not imply its disappearance. All these considerations allow us to conclude that any risk that has not been considered by the legislator is insurable at the sole condition that such risk exists and that it is not illicit.

## §2. Legal Framework

*302.* Lack of classification does not involve lack of rules because such risks are subject to Title I of the LCS (Articles 1–24 of the LCS), which contains general provisions that are applicable to ground insurance, and section 1 Title II (Articles 24–44 of the LCS), holding general provisions applicable to property insurance (especially designed for property insurance of goods). What is left remains within the scope of party autonomy and that explains why the parties to these insurance contracts enjoy a higher freedom of contract. Thus, in order to delimit these risks, we will exclusively depend on the draft of the policy. The parties, or rather, the insurer, will have full freedom to delimit the risk according to her or his convenience. The absence of counterweight of legal regulation of the risks insured gives the policies' clauses the exclusive role to govern the contractual relationship. Apart from the general legal provisions, the party autonomy will be the only source of obligations for the parties.

§3. MODALITIES

*303*. The most contracted for risks are the following: explosion, lightning hit, electric damages, smoke, collision or clash of ground vehicles, aircraft fall, sonic waves, vandalism or bad faith acts, humanitarian actions and strikes, spillage or leak from extinction facilities, rain,

# Part IV. Motor Vehicle Insurance

## Chapter 1. Motor Vehicle Insurance: Compulsory and Voluntary

### §1. Introduction and Terminological Clarifications

*304.* The most widespread compulsory liability insurance (SRC) is, without a doubt, the one that covers civil liability in respect of the use of motor vehicles.

Occasionally, reference is made to compulsory motor vehicle liability insurance with the expression 'motor vehicle insurance'. Nevertheless, the technical sense of this expression is the denomination of administrative authorization simultaneously granted to insurance companies for accidents suffered by passengers in motor vehicles, non-rail ground vehicles (including all damages suffered by these ground vehicles, motor vehicle or not), transported merchandise (including luggage and other transported goods) and ground motor vehicle liability (including carrier liability). Such administrative authorization will also cover the risks that are accessory to the mentioned types of insurance, such as theft, fire and so on of motor vehicles.[313]

Thus, before discussing the compulsory motor vehicle liability insurance, it is convenient to mention, at least briefly, the various coverages that may also be contracted for to prevent other risks that are related to motor vehicles. The reason lies in the fact that insurance undertakings offer, jointly with the compulsory insurance, diverse other insurance contracts that are usually included in the same policy but without losing their autonomy.[314]

*305.* First, it is customary to subscribe, jointly with the compulsory insurance, to a voluntary SRC that covers scenarios and amounts above those covered by compulsory insurance. Their regulation, which is contained in the LCS, differs from the compulsory insurance regulated by the Royal Legislative Decree 8/2004 of 29 October which approves the consolidated law on liability and insurance in circulation of motor vehicles (TRRC SCVM) because the established singularities are not applicable to voluntary motor vehicle liability insurance.

Another insurance of which the subscription enjoys a long tradition is passenger insurance. This can be qualified as accident insurance,[315] and it has the purpose of attributing some amounts to the passenger vehicle designated in the policy. On the

313. See Art. 6.1 of the TRLOSSP.
314. Article 2.5 TRRC SCVM.
315. STS 8-3-1996 (Civil) RAJ 1996/1937.

basis of this coverage the driver will receive the amount stipulated in the policy because he or she will never be covered by liability insurance when causing the insured event.[316]

*306.* At the same time, it is possible to cover fire and theft of the motor vehicle as well as the breaking of glass. These property insurances only particularity lies in the insured object: the motor vehicle. Finally, insurers used to include also services for emergencies in highways insurance and legal defence.

These types of coverages are usually placed under 'full comprehensive insurance'.

*307.* Compulsory liability insurance must be the subject of attention not only because of the ongoing expansion of the motor vehicle traffic phenomenon and of the social alarm created by the number of deaths produced by accidents in this sector but also because of its influence in the legal framework of other compulsory SRC and the voluntary SRC.

Nevertheless, it is adequate to mention the doctrinal debate about the capability of the current motor vehicle SRC system to take care of its social function. Considering its evolution (obligatory, direct action, opposition of insurer exceptions in relation to the injured party, calculation of the indemnities on the basis of a scaled system, etc.) and with the purpose of better protecting victims of these accidents, a part of the doctrinal writers promotes the replacement of compulsory and voluntary SRC by a compulsory accident insurance and a guarantee fund in favour of potential victims.[317] However, doctrinal writings also recognize that the legislative option of facing this problem through an SRC system of compulsory subscription is strongly consolidated in the world. Therefore, it appears to be 'unpredictable to establish as to when such transformation may happen'.[318]

## §2. Legal Framework for Motor Vehicle Liability Insurance

*308.* The regulation of compulsory motor vehicle SRC insurance is found in Law 122/1962 of 24 December, named the 'law about use and traffic of motor vehicle' the consolidated text of which (currently repealed) was approved by Decree 632/1968 of 21 March.

Throughout the time, this consolidated text has been subject to various and profound modifications, albeit not solely based on the requirements of the ECC (today, the European Union (EU)). Among these, the modification made by Disp. Ad. 8ª of Law 30/1995 of 8 November for organization and supervision of private insurance (1995 de LOSSP)[319] must be pointed out. Apart from thoroughly amending the

316. SSTS 24-5-2001 (Civil) RAJ 2001/3377 y 22-12-2001 (Civil) RAJ 2001/10131.

317. See M.A. Calzada Conde, *El seguro voluntario de responsabilidad civil* (Madrid: Montecorvo, 1983), 417–418; M.A. Calzada Conde, *El seguro de responsabilidad civil* (Pamplona: Thomsom-Aranzadi, 2005), 22 and 137–138.

318. See, among others, F. Sánchez Calero, *Ley de Contrato de Seguro* (Pamplona: Thonsom-Aranzadi, 1999), 1126.

319. Law 30/1995 of 8 Nov. about organization and supervision of private insurance.

whole Title I of the mentioned consolidated text, the new law changed the name of the law to the 'law on civil liability and insurance of motor vehicle traffic' and introduced the annexe with the famous 'scale' – a system for the calculating damages caused to persons in traffic accidents. Such scale includes a legal system of quantitative delimitation of indemnity amounts for personal damages that can be claimed as a consequence of motor vehicle traffic.

*309.* Finally, and after other modifications, Law 34/2003 of 4 September that implements European Community rules in insurance, authorized in its final provision the government to prepare and approve a new consolidated text of the law on liability and insurance for motor vehicle traffic insurance, including the power to 'regularize, clarify and harmonize the legal texts that will be consolidated'. Pursuant to this law, Royal Decree 8/2004 of 29 October was enacted. It approves the consolidated text of the law on liability and insurance for motor vehicle traffic (TRRC SCVM), text that must be complemented with Royal Decree 1507/2008, 12 September by which the regulation on liability and insurance for motor vehicle traffic is approved (RRC SCVM). Since then, both the TRRC SCVM and the RRC SCVM have been modified on several occasions. The first was modified by Law 21/2007, of 11 July Law 18/2009, of 23 November, and by Law 21/2011, of 26 July. The RRC SCVM was modified by Law 18/2009, of 23 November.

The basic legal system on this subject ends with the functions that are related to this insurance of the Insurance Compensation Consortium (CCS), which are governed by Article 11 of Royal Legislative Decree 7/2004 of 29 October on the consolidated text of the Legal Statute for the Insurance Compensation Consortium (ELCCS), and also by Article 11 of the TRRC SCVM.

*310.* The mentioned legal framework contains a specific regulation relating to civil liability arising from motor vehicle traffic (Chapter I of Title I and annexe of the TRRC SCVM), the establishment of a compulsory SRC and the specific rules for this insurance regime (the rest of the consolidated text).[320]

That is to say that with respect to those subjects that are not governed by TRRC SCVM and regulatory rules for their implementation, one must use the help (supplemental law) of the Civil Code for liability matters and the LCS for liability insurance.[321]

*311.* When the compulsory SRC appears in the same policy together with other coverage types (e.g., in a fully comprehensive policy) or when there is an extension of compulsory SRC scope, all the different branches covered will be governed by the LCS.

---

320. See above

321. Article 2.6 of the TRRC SCVM which is harmonious with Art. 2 of the LCS.

One should also consider the criminal scope of Article 636 of the 1995 Criminal Code, which qualifies 'performing activities without complying with compulsory liability insurance legally required for the practice of those activities', as an infringement against public order. Also its Article 117 admits the possibility of the injured to exercise direct action against the insurer, within a criminal procedure, without prejudice to the right of recourse against whoever it may concern.

## Chapter 2. Liability System in Motor Vehicle Traffic

*312.* The TRRC SCVM establish (Chapter I of Title I and annexe of the TRRC SCVM) a legal framework that is specific for liability in motor vehicle traffic and that partially modifies the general system of liability contained in Article 1902 and following Articles of the Civil Code. According to this special liability regime:

(a) Given the risk created by driving motor vehicles, their drivers are liable for damages suffered by persons or goods caused during traffic.
The driver will only be exonerated of liability from damages suffered by persons (corporal damage) when it can be proven that damages were solely caused by behaviour or negligence of the injured (the so-called exclusive guilt of the victim)[322] or by force majeure unrelated to driving or vehicle operation. For these purposes, vehicle defects or breaks of their defective parts or mechanisms do not constitute 'force majeure'.[323]
With regard to damages suffered by goods (material damages), the driver will be liable to third parties when her or his liability is established according to Article 1902 and following articles of the Civil Code, Article 109 of the Criminal Code and provisions of the TRRC SCVM.
Therefore, with regard to personal damages, a quasi-objective liability system is established, whereas with regard to material damages, the general liability system of guilt stipulated in the Civil Code remains almost intact.
In both cases, personal damage and damage to goods, if negligence of the driver and of the injured concur, it will lead to an equitable distribution of liability and indemnity amounts, on the basis of the respective importance of the corresponding guilt.[324]
(b) The owner who is not the driver of the insured motor vehicle will be liable for damages that are caused to persons and goods by the driver, if the owner is linked to the driver by any kind of relationship as stipulated by Articles 1903 of the Civil Code and 22 of the Criminal Code (parents, businesspersons, etc. in respect to minor children, assistants, employees). This liability will cease when the owner in question proves that she or he observed the due diligence of a '*bonus pater familias*' to prevent the damages.[325]
The owner, no driver of a vehicle without compulsory insurance, will be liable with the driver for damages caused to persons and goods except when he proves that the vehicle had been stolen.[326]
(c) In order to delimit the objective scope of this liability regime, the concepts of 'motor vehicle' and 'traffic events' are fundamental. In case of damages in which the vehicle cannot fit within the motor vehicle concept or in other cases

322. Entre otras, SSTS 2-2-1994 (Civil). RAJ 1994/860, 1-2-1995 (Civil). RAJ 1995/728; 31-1-1997 (Civil). RAJ 1997/253, 1-4-1998 (Civil). RAJ 1998/1868.
323. STS 14-6-1995 (Civil). RAJ 1997/2888.
324. Article 1.1. del TRRC SCVM.
325. STS 23-9-2002 (Criminal). RAJ 2002/9026.
326. Article 1.1 of TRRC SCVM.

when existing motor vehicles, actions or omissions cannot be qualified as traffic events, the general liability system of the Civil Code will be applied.

*313.* To establish what a motor vehicle is, positive and negative criteria are used. On the one hand, considered as a motor vehicle is any vehicle, special or not, that is suited for running on the ground surface and motor-driven, including motorcycles, trailers and tractor-trailers, whose entry into service requires administrative authorization in line with what is set out in legislation on transport, the use of motor vehicles and road safety. On the other hand, expressly excluded are: 'railways, trams and other motor vehicles that run through proper traces'; electric motor vehicles that are considered as toys in defined terms of the current legislation and wheelchairs.[327]

To establish what traffic events are,[328] positive and negative criteria are considered. Traffic events that result from risks created by driving of motor vehicles in garages and parking lots, as well as on interurban routes and grounds both public and private, and on routes and places that even though having not been properly furnished for traffic use, are actually used with the same purposes.[329]

*314.* Events expressly excluded from traffic events are:[330]

(a) Events that result from performing sports events with motor vehicles in circuits specially built for that purpose or set up for those events.
(b) Events that result from industrial or agricultural tasks performed by motor vehicles that are especially built for these purposes except when such vehicles run on routes or places mentioned previously.[331]
(c) The movement of motor vehicles on roads or land on which legislation on transport, the use of motor vehicles, and road safety is not applicable, such as port or airport facilities.
(d) Events that use motor vehicles for committing intentional crimes against persons and goods.[332] Nevertheless, it will be considered as a traffic event[333] the use of motor vehicles in any of the forms described by the Penal Code that constitutes a violation of traffic safety.[334]

*315.* In a 2001 legislation, a new explicit exclusion of driving motor vehicles as an instrument to commit intentional delicts was introduced again.[335] With such exclusion it was intended to solve the strong controversy that exists in doctrine and case law arising from diverse decisions of the supreme tribunal that in the second

327. Article 1 of the RRC SCVM.
328. See SSTS 10-2-2000 (Civil). RAJ 2000/9192 and 4-7-2002 (Civil). RAJ 2002/5900.
329. Article 2 RRC SCVM.
330. Article 1 of the TRRC SCVM and Art. 2.2 of the RRC SCVM.
331. Among others, the SSTS 10-10-1996 (Civil). RAJ 1996/7554, 3-3-1998 (Civil). RAJ 1998/1044, 10-2-1998 (Civil). RAJ 1998/752, 7-5-1998 (Civil). RAJ 1998/3238, and 25-10-2000 (Civil.) RAJ 2000/9588.
332. Article 1.4 of the TRRC SCVM y Art. 2.3 of the RRC SCVM.
333. Article 2.3 of the RRC SCVN.
334. Including the assumption of Art. 382 of the Criminal Code.
335. It was in Art. 21 (b) of the 1964 regulation for motor vehicle insurance.

half of the 1990s condemned insurers to indemnify victims of intentional crimes, on the basis of the consideration that the intentional character of the damage cannot be opposed by the insurer against the injured without prejudice for the possibility of the insurer to recover damages from the 'intentionally' liable.[336] Nevertheless, in view of the supreme tribunal decisions on this matter made after 2001, it does not appear that the controversy has been solved.[337]

*316.* The establishment of uniform and compulsory criteria and limits for the evaluation of personal injury damages in traffic accidents have special importance and meaning.

On the one hand, it stipulates that damages suffered by persons include the '*lucrum cessans*' (value of the loss suffered and of the profit that was expected or susceptible to be expected, or that is known to have originated from the causal event) and moral damages.[338]

On the other hand, the calculation of damage to persons must observe the criteria and limits that are established by the annexe of the law (known as sliding fee scale),[339] the importance and meaning of which is not limited to motor vehicle liability matters but extends to the calculation of the indemnity in other sectors.

The fee scale consists of charts that determine amounts for indemnity purposes corresponding to the damage suffered by persons, victims of traffic accidents (death or corporal injuries that cause permanent or temporary disability). The amounts mentioned are updated annually by resolution of the General Direction for Insurance and Pension Funds.

Its introduction mainly responds to technical needs of the insurance and reinsurance sectors, but it is also a reaction to strong differences among the levels of indemnity that are laid down by the courts in similar cases.

*317.* The enacting of the fee scale gave rise to a vivid controversy in case law and in doctrinal writings on diverse topics related to its application, such as its constitutionality.

The issue of the unconstitutionality of the fee scale was based first and mainly on the fact that it fixes and limits indemnities for bodily injury, and, on the basis of questionable arguments, does not apply to material damages (that in principle can be calculated objectively); second, on the fact that it limits indemnities for these type of accidents and not for others, discrimination that violates the principle of equality before the law, which is guaranteed by Article 14 of the CE.

*318.* The historical decision of the constitutional Court No. 181/2000 of 29 June gave response to ten questions on constitutionality and declared that such fee scale,

336. Among others, see the SSTS 29-5-1997 (Criminal). RAJ 1997/3637, 10-7-1995 (Criminal). RAJ 1995/5438, 4-11-1998 (Criminal). RAJ 1998/7777, 8-4-2002 (Criminal). RAJ 2002/5093, 7-2-2001 (Criminal). RAJ 2001/358.

337. See about the matter F. Arnau Moya, 'El Contrato de seguro y los daños causados dolosamente', *RES*, 2005, n. 122–123, 571ff.

338. Article 1.2 of the TRRC SCVM.

339. Article 1.2 of the TRRC SCVM.

in general, observes the Constitution because it is required by the collective and universalized traffic risks that need to be insured, that it does not violate rights to life and safety because the patrimonial indemnity is not a demonstration of them (Article 15 of the CE), that it does not violate the principle of equality before the law (Article 14 of the CE) nor the principle of the right of defence (Article 24.1 of the CE).

The Constitutional Tribunal only admits that the fee scale violates the right to legal defence insofar as Table V (indemnity for temporary disability), letter B, strictly evaluates correction factors for the indemnity, and so prevents the victim from proving larger prejudice. It also decided that this rule must be applied only in case of absence of fault and not if there is relevant fault by the person who caused the accident. However, four judges expressed a dissenting vote, stating that, in this assumption, global consideration of risks must prevail and that the (majority) decision will incite litigation around proving the fault of the liable person, with all the consequences of it that are detrimental for the system.

# Chapter 3. Compulsory Liability in Motor Vehicle Insurance

## §1. WHO IS OBLIGED TO BUY THIS INSURANCE?

*319.* Once the special regime of liability that we analysed in the previous chapter is established, our legal framework obliges all owners of vehicles that are habitually stationed in Spain to contract for each vehicle an SRC that covers up the quantitative limits established by regulation, that liability.

There is a presumption that the owner of a vehicle is the natural person or legal entity whose name appears the vehicle in the respective public registry.

The owner will only be released of his or her obligation to subscribe to the SRC when this is contracted by any person with interest in the insurance who shall express the concept that contracts.[340]

*320.* It is considered that a motor vehicle has habitual stationing in Spain:[341]

(a) When it has a Spanish registration. It is expressly indicated that a temporary or definite condition of the vehicle's registration is not relevant to determine the place of habitual stationing.
(b) When, in the absence of registration due to the type of vehicle, it has an insurance plaque or distinctive sign similar to the registration that was issued in Spain.
(c) When, in the absence of registration, insurance plaque or distinctive sign, due to the type of vehicle its user has domicile in Spain.
(d) Vehicles that caused accidents in Spain that lack registration or have registration that does not belong to them or do not belong to them anymore.
(e) Vehicles imported from other Member States of the European Union, during a maximum of thirty days counted from the date the buyer accepted delivery of the vehicle, even when it was not registered in Spain. To this end such vehicles may be temporarily secured by a secure border.

## §2. EXTENSION AND EXCLUSIONS OF THE COMPULSORY COVERAGE

*321.* Compulsory motor vehicle liability insurance should cover against the payment of one premium up to the regulatory fixed amount of the civil liability as stipulated by Article 1 of the TRRC SCVM, that is, the civil liability arising from damage caused to persons and goods as a result of the participation in traffic of the insured motor vehicle in the whole territory of the Economic European Area and of the other States that are affiliated to the multilateral agreement of guarantee. Such coverage shall include any stay of the insured vehicle in the territory of another Member State of the European Economic Area for the duration of the contract.[342]

340. Article 2.1 of the TRRC SCMV.
341. Article 2.1 of the TRRC SCMV.
342. Article 4 TRRC SCVM.

The maximum amount of coverage of compulsory subscription insurance (which shall be updated according to European price indices) mounts up:[343]

(a) For personal damages: up to EUR 70 million per insured event, whatever the number of victims.
(b) For damages to goods: up to EUR 15 million per insured event.

The personal damages caused shall be quantified in any event according to the criteria and within the compensation limits established in the scale set out in the annexe to the TRRC SCVM.

The medical assistance, pharmaceutical and hospital expenses shall be paid to the amount required for the sequelae to heal or begin to heal, as long as the expenses are duly justified based on the type of assistance provided. Compensation in case of death shall include burial and funeral expenses according to the local customs where the service is provided, to the amount that shall be justified.[344] However, medical assistance, pharmaceutical and hospital expenses and burial and funeral expenses in case of death be considered as falling within the amount set by personal damages.[345]

When personal damage and damage to goods coincide and the compensation for the latter exceeds the maximum amount of the compulsory insurance, the difference shall be charged to the remainder that may be left over from the personal damage compensation up to the maximum limit.[346]

If the amount of the compensation were higher than the amount of the coverage afforded by the compulsory insurance, this maximum amount shall be paid and charged to this compulsory insurance and the rest, up to the total amount of the compensation, shall be paid by the voluntary insurance or the person responsible for the accident, as appropriate,

*322.* When the insured event occurs within a State that is not Spain but it is affiliated with the multilateral agreement of guarantees and the event was caused by a vehicle that has habitual station in Spain, the limits of the compulsory coverage to be applied are the ones fixed by the Member State in which the insured event occurs. If the insured event occurs within a Member State of the Economic European Area, the limits of the compulsory insurance fixed by Spain will be applied only when they are superior to the ones established in the State where the insured event has occurred.

*323.* In addition, the following exclusions from compulsory insurance can be opposed by the insurer against the injured:[347]

343. Article 4.2 TRRC SCVM.
344. Number 6, section One of the TRRC SCVM Annex.
345. Article 10.2 of the RRC SCVM.
346. Article 10.1 of the RRC SCVM.
347. Article 5 of the TRRC SCVM.

(a) All the damage and prejudices caused by injuries or death of the driver of the vehicle who caused the insured event.
(b) Damage caused by the insured event to vehicle insured, to goods that were being transported and to goods that are property of the policyholder, insured, owner, driver, and their spouses and relatives until third degree of consanguinity or affinity.
(c) Damage to persons and goods caused by stolen vehicles, considering as such, exclusively, behaviours typified as theft and vehicle handling in Articles 237, 244 and 623.3 respectively, of the Criminal Code.[348] In such situations Article 11.1.c) of TRRC SCVM will be applicable, which means that coverage will be provided by the Insurance Compensation Consortium.

Also excluded from coverage is the damage that is caused by driving under the influence of alcohol or toxic drugs, narcotics or psychotropic drugs. However, this exception will not be opposed against the victim without prejudice to the insurer's right of recovery. The victim will collect from the insurer and this one will recover against liable persons who drove in such conditions.[349]

## §3. Conclusion, Perfection, Documentation and Insurance Accreditation

*324.* The regime of conclusion and performance of the contract offers some special characteristics as compared with rules contained in LCS.[350]

A distinction must be made between the case where the negotiation process starts with the application for insurance or with an insurance proposal made by the insurer.

In the first case the insurance application has the effect of covering the risk during a period of fifteen days from the time where the demand was stamped by the insurer or by his or her agent.[351] The insurer may reject the application within a period of no more than ten days upon its presentation. The rejection, which must be in writing and must specify the reasons, shall be addressed to the policyholder in any form as long as it offers proof of the receipt. The insurer acquires the right to receive the premium that corresponds with the mentioned fifteen-day coverage. If the insurer does not reject the contract after ten days, it will be considered that the contract was admitted. If the ten-day period has passed and the insurer has not rejected it, the insurer will have to remit the insurance policy within a ten-day term.[352]

---

348. Article 8 RRC SCVM.
349. Article 10.a) of the TRRC SCVM.
350. STS 7-4-1994 (Civil). RAJ 1994/2730.
351. See the SSTS 15-2-2002 (Civil). RAJ 2002/1620 and 8-10-1999 (Civil). RAJ 1999/7317.
352. Article 12.1 RRC SCVM. The DGSFP has established that the communication has to be directly addressed to the taker and it is not valid communication performed to the intermediary; and that registered mail with acknowledgment receipt is an efficient method to perform such communication.

*325.* When negotiation starts with an insurance proposal for compulsory insurance made by an insurance undertaking or its agent, the proposal will be binding on the insurer for fifteen days. The insurance contract will be completed on acceptance of the proposal by the policyholder. However, in case the policyholder does not pay the first premium and the policyholder is at fault, the insurer will have the right to resolve the contract by written notice to the policyholder, sent by registered mail with acknowledgement of receipt or through any other means admitted by law, unless she or he requests the payment of the premium according to the terms of Article 15 of the LCS. Once the policyholder accepts the proposal, the insurer will deliver the insurance policy in ten days.

Among other functions, the CCS will have to cover the liability that arises from motor vehicle traffic when the risk has not been accepted for coverage by any insurance undertaking, or when two proposals of compulsory insurance were rejected by two insurers and outside the hypothesis that the risk has been accepted by another insurer upon the CCS' request. The insurer that rejects or does not accept the subscription of compulsory insurance must issue a certificate that proves such fact upon written request by the interested party.

*326.* The insurer must deliver the insurance policy to the policyholder. The policy must contain clear and specific reference to the applicable rules for this type of insurance and other provisions that govern insurance contracts, its organization and the supervision of private insurance. Furthermore, once the premium is collected, the insurer will deliver the transfer slip of the payment to the policyholder.[353]

Every motor vehicle should at all times have documents on board that prove the subscription to a current compulsory SRC (certificate of insurance policy). The transfer slip of the payment of the premium is considered as such a document for the current insurance period.[354]

Whereas an agent of the public authority on duty requests the presentation of supporting documents that prove the existence of the insurance and such proof cannot be showed (which will be penalized with a fine), she or he will report this to the proper authority who will order the immediate seal and deposit of the vehicle if at the term of five days the existence of the insurance is not proved.

*327.* Failure to comply with the obligation to contract compulsory liability insurance will give rise to administrative sanctions, such as prohibition to circulate within the national territory, deposit of the vehicle at the cost of the owner if it is not insured and a fine according to the criteria determined by law.[355]

---

353. Article 13 RRC SCVM. STS 29-10-1997 (Civil). RAJ 1997/7342.
354. Article 14 RRC SCVM.
355. Fine from EUR 601 up to EUR 3,005. The 50 per 100 of the amount collected for this cause will be delivered to Insurance Compensation Consortium, to compensate in part indemnifications that he must pay to the injured in compliance of the obligations legally established in relation to compulsory auto insurance. The STS (Court 3.a.) of 23 Nov. 2005 declares the nullity by operation of the law of determined aspects of Art. 29 of the RRC and SCVM related to administrative sanctions for breach of obligation to get insured 'they do not contain the proceeding of compulsory file of administrative-penalty actions, once a criminal decision is produced for the same facts'.

It is important to notice that Article 636 of the 1995 Criminal Code classifies as a misdemeanour against public order, the behaviour of performing 'activities without compulsory liability insurance when such insurance is required by law', by punishing authors with a fine of one or two months.

## §4. Insurer's Obligation to Pay the Indemnity to the Injured: Direct Action and Exceptions Regime

*328.* In order to hasten compensation of material damages that may arise from the use and traffic of vehicle motors, the insurer will provide copies of the so-called European accident statement to be used by the driver for notifying of the occurrence of an insured event to his or her insurer.[356]

Whoever has subscribed to an insurance contract should prove its validity so as to allow the persons involved in a traffic accident to obtain as soon as possible information about the insurance contract and about the insurer.

The informative card index of insured vehicles (FIVA) has also been established to provide persons involved in a traffic accident with the necessary information allowing them to obtain as soon as possible information about the circumstances related to the insurer that covers the liability of each of the vehicles involved in the accident.[357]

According to the SRC for automobiles, the insurer must, within the scope of compulsory insurance and at the expense of this compulsory insurance, compensate the injured with an amount for personal and property damages. The injured or her or his heirs will have a direct action against the insurer to claim such benefit, the action expiring after one year.

Special mention goes to the obligation of insurance undertakings to present a grounded offer of indemnification within three months upon the receipt of the injured claim in case liability had been determined and the damaged calculated; otherwise, a grounded response to the claim must be presented. The requirements that must be complied with by the grounded offer and response are established. The grounded offer will be 'satisfied' or 'consigned' to avoid interest on arrears. Its failure will constitute administrative infringement and will imply accrual of the mentioned interest.

In any case the insurer should guarantee liability up to the amount of the compulsory insurance and pay the amount required by judicial authorities to the insured allegedly liable according to Articles 764 and 765 of the Civil Procedure Law.

*329.* The regime for direct action[358] prescribed that the insurer will only be able to oppose a legally limited number of exceptions against the injured's direct action in the following cases:

356. Article 8 TRRC SCVM. Agreements between insurers to speed up the liquidation of the insured event cannot denature the legal framework, which is why such agreements are not possible to be opposed against the insured and injured.
357. Article 23ff. RRC SCVM and query done before the DGSFP.
358. Articles 7, 6 and 5 of the TRRC SCVM and supplementary Art. 76 of the LCS.

(a) Damage and prejudice from physical injury, or death of the driver who caused the insured event.
(b) Damage to the insured vehicle, to transported goods and goods that are property of the policyholder, insured, owner, driver and their spouses or relatives up until the third degree of consanguinity or affinity.
(c) Damage to persons and goods caused by a stolen vehicle (in such case the coverage is given by the CCS).

*330.* However, despite the categorical terms of Article 6 of the TRRC SCVM, which limits the available exceptions (Article 5 of the TRRC SCVM), the insured's pretension is not totally immune from defences. As pointed out in Article 7 of the TRRC SCVM the insurer will be exonerated of her or his obligation to pay the injured if she or he proves that the event does not lead to liability according to the special liability system for damages caused by circulation of motor vehicles. Furthermore, she or he can call on the defence that the circumstances go beyond the scope of the policy coverage and would imply an extension of the risk covered by this policy to an event that is not produced by traffic, the non-existence of the application for insurance, the end of coverage and the occurrence of the accident outside the territorial scope of the compulsory insurance.

In addition, in automobile insurance, the insurer may oppose the exceptions of Article 76 of the LCS. Also, the insurer may allege the non-existence or absolute nullity of the insurance contract and the resolution of the contract properly notified to the policyholder.

*331.* The rules about compulsory auto insurance expressly state that the insurer cannot oppose the injured's direct action:[359]

(a) The lack of coverage in cases of damage due to driving under the influence of alcohol or toxic drugs, narcotics or psychotropic substances.
(b) Contractual exclusions of coverage that exclude the use or driving of the vehicle by persons without driver license, the lack of compliance with legal obligations on technical aspects of the vehicle's safety, or unlawful use (other than theft) of motor vehicles that belong to others or without the owner's express or tacit authorization.
(c) Non-use of the European accident statement.

If the calculation of the indemnity on the basis of the Baremo results in higher amounts than the maximum amount of the compulsory insurance coverage, it will be paid at the expense of the mentioned compulsory insurance and the voluntary insurance or by the person who is liable for the insured event as the case may be.

*332.* If the insurer is late in paying the insurance money in the context of compulsory auto insurance, the indemnification will be governed by Article 20 of the LCS and by some other regulations. Article 9 of the TRRC SCVM observes a

359. Article 5 TRRC SCMV.

regime of consignment of the indemnity that is used by the insurer to avoid the possible adverse effects of the delay resulting from penal correction.

Finally, one shall also take into account that a direct action against the insurer can be performed by the victim or his/her heirs in the form prescribed by Article 12 and following articles of the TRRC SCMV.[360]

## §5. The So-Called Recourse Action of the Insurer

*333.* The purpose that underlies the legal framework of the compulsory SRC is to protect the victim and, as was mentioned, this leads to a strict regime of opposability of non-exceptions by the insurer as opposed to the direct action of the injured. This is why once the indemnity is paid to the injured, the insurer is given the right to perform a recourse action – which will end after one year upon the date of payment to the injured – against the following persons:[361]

(a) The driver, the owner of the vehicle that caused the accident and against the insured if the caused damage was due to intentional behaviour of any of them or if the driving was performed under the influence of alcohol or toxic drugs, narcotics or psychotropic substances.[362]
(b) The third party that is liable for the damages.
(c) The policyholder or the insured for reasons stipulated by LCS and in the own insurance contract.
(d) Anyone who could be entitled to the recourse action in accordance with the law.

*334.* The law expressly mentions ‘recourse action’. In fact, although the matter is arguable, there is action in the hypothesis described by (a) and (b), whereas hypothesis (b) refers to the insurer’s subrogation into rights of the insured against the liable third party and/or before his or her insurer.[363]

The technical qualification of these cases such as a recourse action or subrogatory action will influence deeply the legal framework that an insurer may begin. Thus, if hypothesis (b) is qualified as subrogation, the same exceptions can be raised as those that could be opposed against the insured.

360. This is the testimony of the judge order referred by Art. 13 of the TRRC SCMV, which will be sufficient executive title to proceed against the insurer and the injured cannot act without it.
361. Articles 10 of the TRRC SCMV. STS 29-10-1997 (Civil). RAJ 1997/7342.
362. STS 8-7-2003 (Civil). RAJ 2003/4338.
363. See in the sense indicated in the text, the SAP of Madrid of 19 Jun. 1999 and authors such as A. Tato Plaza, *La subrogación del asegurador en la Ley de contrato de seguro* (Valencia: Tirant lo blanch, 2002), 78ff; M.A. Calzada Conde, *El seguro de responsabilidad Civil* (Pamplona: Thomsom-Aranzadi, 2005), 152; against, understanding that in the assumption of (b) we are also before a recovery action, M. J. Morillas Jarillo, *El seguro de automóvil. El aseguramiento obligatorio de la responsabilidad civil automovilística* (Barcelona: Bosch, 1992), 633; on his side, R. Alonso Soto, *El Seguro de la culpa* (Madrid: Montecorvo, 1977), 456–457, considers all assumptions of subrogation and Duque Domínguez, ‘Subrogación en el seguro de automóviles a todo riesgo y derecho de repetición del asegurador frente al asegurado’, *Rev. Der. Cir.* (1967), 405ff., takes the concept of solidary surety.

For the rest, one shall remember that the presumptions of a recourse action are that the insurer had effectively paid the injured or has been obliged to pay due to the fact that the exceptions stemming from the internal relationship of the insurer-insured could not be invoked. Obviously, the recourse action will not be successful when the alleged circumstances are rejected by the court, not because of their non-opposability against the injured but, for example, because they did not occur or because the contractual clause that supports them is not valid.

## §6. Functions of the Insurance Compensation Consortium in Relation to Auto Liability Insurance

*335.* The CCS has important functions in relation to auto liability insurance. Generally, the CCS is responsible for the defence and promotion of compulsory subscription of motor vehicle insurance and it is also responsible for the information system that leads to the FIVA.

As was mentioned before, the CCS must assume liability arising from motor vehicle traffic in those cases where the risks are not accepted by insurers. Also, the CCS must cover the liability that arises from the participation in traffic of vehicles that belong to the State, autonomous communities, local corporations and public agencies that depend on them, when they have applied this insurance with the consortium.

*336.* But apart from these two last functions, in which the consortium becomes an insurer of the compulsory auto insurance, it has also the following functions:[364]

(a) To indemnify those who suffer personal injury caused by insured events in Spain when the vehicle is unknown.
(b) To indemnify personal injury and damage to goods caused by a vehicle habitually stationed in Spain when such vehicle is not insured.
(c) To indemnify personal injury and damage to goods caused by an insured vehicle habitually stationed in Spain, that was stolen (Articles 237 and 244 of the Criminal Code).[365]

Personal injury and damage to goods suffered by those who freely agreed to be passengers of the vehicle that caused the insured event, knowing that the vehicle was not insured or that it had been stolen, will be excluded from indemnification by the CCS, but only if this agency proves that such passengers were aware of such circumstances. With respect to damage suffered by goods, in both cases the CCS will apply the deductions that are provided for by regulations:

– To indemnify personal injury and damage to goods when, in cases of compulsory insurance or in cases described in previous paragraphs, controversy arises

364. Article 11 TRRC SCVM.
365. SSTS 4-12-1997 (Penal). RAJ 1997/8719, 18-10-1999 (Penal). RAJ 1999/8128, 28-5-2001 (Penal). RAJ 2001/7173, which includes theft use within the coverage of the CCS.

between the CCS and the insurance undertaking about the question of who must indemnify the injured. If it is resolved or agreed that the insurance company should pay, this will reimburse the CCS for the indemnified amount, augmented with interest at a rate of 25% as from the date that the amount was paid.

- To indemnify personal injury and damage to goods when the Spanish insurer of the vehicle habitually stationed in Spain has been declared bankrupt or been dissolved, or is in a state of insolvency, and subject to liquidation with intervention or if this intervention has been assumed by the CCS.

*337.* In these circumstances, the injured will have a direct action against the CCS, which will be able to exercise recourse under the same conditions as those under which insurers can do so. The recourse is directed against the owner and the person who is responsible for the accident when the vehicle is not insured, or against the perpetrators, accomplices or concealers of the theft of the vehicle that causes the insured event, as well as against the person liable for the accident who knows about the theft.

The CCS will not be able to submit the payment of the indemnity to the condition that the injured proves that the liable person cannot pay or refuses to pay.

However, one should notice that the case law of the criminal chamber of the highest court has developed toward the civil court's doctrine on the limits of coverage of the CCS, according to which the CCS covers only amounts insured by compulsory insurance.[366]

*338.* Finally the CCS has to reimburse indemnifications paid to injured residents of other states of the European Economic Area by compensation agencies in the following cases:

(1) When the vehicle that caused the accident has its habitual stationing in Spain or when it cannot be identified by the insurance undertaking.
(2) When the accident occurred in Spain and the vehicle that caused the accident cannot be identified.
(3) When the accident occurred in Spain and the vehicle is habitually stationed in third countries affiliated with the green card system and cannot be identified by the insurance undertaking.

366. Among many decisions of the civil court of the supreme tribunal: SSTS 28-9-1994 (Civil). RAJ 1994/7309; 19-10-1994 (Civil). RAJ 1994/7489; 9-5-1995 (Civil). RAJ 1995/3628; 25-1-1995 (Civil). RAJ 1995/169; 13-6-1995 (Civil). RAJ 1995/4851; 19-12-1995 (Civil). RAJ 1995/9152; 13-2-1998 (Civil). RAJ 1998/983; 31-3-1998 (Civil). RAJ 1998/2042; and 27-5-1999 (Civil). RAJ 1999/3934. The doctrine of the civil court has been also followed by the criminal court, among others in the STS 8-2-2001 (Penal). RAJ 2001/2492; 29-5-2001 (Penal). RAJ 2001/4576; and 16-10-2003 (Penal). RAJ 2003/7617.

§7. Insured Events Occurring in a State Other than the State of Residence of the Injured

*339.* The adaptation of the internal legal framework to the demands of community regulation has necessitated the introduction of a set of rules tending to facilitate victims' claims for insured events that are caused by vehicles that have habitual stationing and are insured in a Member State of the European Economic Area but only if:

(a) The place of the insured event is in Spain and the injured has residence in another Member State.
(b) The place of the insured event is in a Member State other than Spain and the insured has residence in Spain.
(c) The insured events occurred in third countries affiliated to the green card system when the injured has its habitual residence in Spain or when the vehicle that caused the accident is habitually stationed and is insured in Spain (Article 20 TRRC SCVM).

*340.* Title III of the TRRC SCVM regulates the problem. Briefly, the established system is the following:

(1) Insurance undertakings domiciled in Spain and branches of third-country insurers with an establishment in Spanish territory must designate in the other EEA Member States a representative for the handling and liquidation of the insured event in the state of residence of the injured (Article 21 of the TRRC SCVM).
(2) The injured who is not a resident of Spain will be able to submit her or his claim to the insurance undertaking established in Spain or to the representative designated by that undertaking in her or his own state of residence. The insurance undertaking or its representative must react to the claim within a period of three months and present a motivated offer if the liability has been determined and also if the damage has been assessed. Otherwise, if the insurance undertaking repels the claim, it must explain legal grounds for the claim. Once the deadline has expired without a motivated offer, delay interests will be calculated according to the applicable legislation in each case and taking into account the place of occurrence of the insured event (Article 22 of the TRRC SCVM).
(3) The injured who has residence in Spain can directly address the insurance undertaking of the vehicle that caused the accident when the insurance undertaking is not authorized in another Member State or address its representative in Spain for the handling and liquidation of the insured event (Article 23 of the TRRC SCVM).
(4) The CCS will act as an information body providing necessary information enabling the injured to claim the insurance undertaking or its representative for the handling and liquidation of the insured event (Articles 24 and 25 of the TRRC SCVM).

(5) OFESAUTO has the qualification of a claim settlement institution before which the injured with residence in Spain can bring claim for indemnification if in three months after the date of presentation of the claim neither the insurance undertaking of the vehicle that caused the accident or its representative designated in Spain for the handling and liquidation of the insured events, neither of them have formulated a motivated answer to the claim; or if the insurance undertaking did not designate a representative for the handling and liquidation in Spain except if the injured presented the indemnification claim directly to the insurance undertaking of the vehicle that caused the accident and received a motivated response from the undertaking within the three months upon the submission of the claim. Nevertheless, the injured cannot present a claim before the OFESAUTO, in its capacity claim settlement institution if the injured has exercised the right to direct action against the insurer (Articles 26 and 27 of the TRRC SCVM).

Furthermore, if it is not possible to identify the vehicle or if two months after the accident it is not possible to identify the insurance undertaking, the injured resident in Spain can request indemnification before OFESAUTO, on its condition as indemnification agency for insured limits of compulsory subscription valid in the country where the insured event occurred (Article 29 of the TRRC SCVM).

(6) The OFESAUTO will also act as a bureau to process insured events that occurred in other countries by vehicles habitually stationed in Spain or insured in Spain on the basis of international insurance certificate, called green card or border insurance. In the same manner, it will assume this function on the name of the national bureau of the relevant state for accidents that occurred in Spanish territory with intervention of a foreign vehicle habitually stationed in a Member State of the multilateral agreement of guarantee or insured though green card issued by another national office or borders insurance (Article 21 of the RRC SCVM).

# Part V. Personal Insurance

## Chapter 1. General Provisions on Personal Insurance

### §1. Concept and Legal Framework of Personal Insurance

*341.* Personal insurance constitutes the second-largest category of all insurance contracts. As opposed to property insurance, personal insurance is characterized by the fact that it is the physical person her- or himself who is exposed to risk.

Regardless of the position chosen about the nature of an insurance contract (compensatory or dualistic), there are important differences between property insurance and personal insurance. In property insurance, the insurer's obligation is measured by the effectively suffered loss, whereas in personal insurance, the insurer must pay the agreed insurance money even when the insured event does not cause any damage. Also, in contrast to what occurs in property insurance, the amount of the insurer's obligation in personal insurance is fixed *a priori* by the parties, which explains why this branch is sometimes called the insurance of sums. Definitely, in personal insurance, the existence of an effective damage and its value is irrelevant.

*342.* Strictly speaking, the mentioned characteristics only attach to life insurance, whereas insurance covering accident, sickness and health care, for example, mainly share the principles governing property insurance because in many cases the insurer has the tendency to repair an actual damage (e.g., health care expenses). However, nuances are important here because personal insurance has had a clear influence here, giving rise to the introduction of specific rules, such as the rule prohibiting the insurer's subrogation of the insured's rights.

Article 80 of the LCS uses the element of risk as delimiting criteria for personal insurance contracts, which 'comprise all risks that may affect the existence, corporal integrity or health of the insured'. Although this rule implies a reference to life, sickness and health care insurance, which is submitted to its own rules (Articles 83–106), the provision cited does not specify the risks that may be covered by the insurer and refers to any atypical contract in which the insured is the object of risk or an object of the insurable interest exposed to the risk. Hence the importance of the rule because general provisions of personal insurance will be applied to those atypical contracts that fit within the concept proposed by the regulator.

*343.* Title III of the LCS concerning personal insurance is divided into four sections, one with general provisions (Articles 80–82) and the next three dealing with life insurance (Articles 83–99), accident insurance (Articles 100–104) and sickness and health care insurance (Articles 105 and 106), respectively.

The section about general provisions, with only three provisions, contrasts with its equivalent in property insurance that contains, as is well-known, twenty-one chapters. Originally, it was intended to increase the number of common rules about personal insurance but such effort was replaced by the system indicating the applicability of rules of one kind to another. In this way, rules on life insurance are declared to be applicable to accident insurance if they are compatible with its nature (Article 100 of the LCS), and the rules on accident insurance are applicable to sickness and health care insurance when the said rules are compatible with the cited insurance contracts (Article 106 of the LCS).

*344.* In addition to this defective legislative technique, there is also the fact that Title I of the LCS (Articles 1–24), which is entirely applicable to personal insurance, appears to be exclusively drafted for property insurance, which causes a number of interpretation problems. And the reason is that general provisions of Title I of the LCS can only be transferred with difficultly to personal insurance because, except in cases as described in Articles 7, *in fine*, and 20.1° that refer to the beneficiary or special rights of the life insurance policyholder, general provisions of the LCS seem to have been conceived only with a view to property insurance.[367]

Finally, there are certain provisions that are located among the general provisions concerning property insurance that may extend personal insurance (e.g., Article 33 of the LCS on co-insurance). Nevertheless, general provisions for property insurance have little efficiency in personal insurance because property insurance is ruled by different principles and many of them – compensatory principle, transfer of insurable interest, mortgage, secure loan or privileged creditors – are not applicable to personal insurance, whereas other principles, such as expert liquidation[368] and subrogatory action (Article 82 of the LCS) are only partially applicable.

## §2. Collective or Group Insurance

*345.* According to the number of insured, personal insurance can be either individual insurance or group insurance, as prescribed by Article 81 of the LCS. This provision states that contracts may be subscribed with reference to risks related to one person or to a group of them.[369]

367. Paradigmatic results in this case Art. 8 which, when regulating the minimum content of the policy, obliges ‘designation of insured objects and their location’ without any reference to personal insurance.
368. Article 104 of the LCS, referrers to Art. 38 of the LCS and STS 4-6-1994 (Civil). RAJ 1994/4584.
369. The first regulation in Spain about group insurance is Order of 16 Dec. 1943, that tried to be complemented with Order of 3 Feb. 1949, about general conditions for collective retirement insurance or indemnity in case of death; Order of 2 Dec. 1957 about cumulative policy of individual accidents; of 5 Oct. 1959 about the prohibition to individually extend group insurance and of 3 Jun. 1968, that rules collective insurance of life and accident risk of entitled to passive accounts in credit

Indeed, Article 81 of the LCS expressly allows the contract to be subscribed for the benefit of a group of persons and imposes the only requirement that the group be identified by a common characteristic different from the insurance's purpose.

*346.* According to the provision, group insurance constitutes a single contract by virtue of which every person in the group is insured. Out of one single contract, a number of insurance relationships between the insurer and each member of the group are born. The group has to be identified by a common characteristic that cannot be the intention or wish to be insured. Nevertheless, the LCS does not demand a minimum number of persons to make a group. It is a contract subscribed on behalf of another person due to the fact that the policyholder is not covering his or her own interest but acts on behalf of the persons of the group.

The splitting up of the contracts on the basis of different relationships bears important consequences. On the one hand, it may produce separate effects of the insurance contract and the separation of each of these relationships. On the other hand, breach of certain obligations or duties – that is, of the pre-contractual declaration of the risk, declaration of the insured event and so on – will have an influence, at first, on the relevant legal relationships but not on the contract[370] as a whole.

*347.* The policyholder is the person who stipulates the contract,[371] assumes contractual obligations[372] and should previously accept in writing limitative clauses in accordance with Article 3 of the LCS.[373]

In practice, it is usually a legal entity – for example, a financial service provider – that takes the policyholder's position, but it is the insured who really assumes the obligations, especially the premium. Thus, the DGSFP correctly considers that the insured is the person who can dispose of the contract.

The insured is the person that suffers the risk. Pursuant to Article 81 of the LCS, the insured must comply with the required characteristics in order to belong to the insured group. It is problematic to specify when the relationship between the insurer and insured arises. On this matter many theses have been supported, although case law insists on the existence of the relationship upon the notification given by the policyholder to the insurer.[374]

*348.* The legal position of the beneficiary does not present special traits while compared with individual insurance. Nevertheless, the particular configuration of

---

establishments. This set of rules was replaced by Order of 24 Jan. 1977 that pretended to prove general and uniformed conditions for group life insurance. From our standpoint, that Order is currently repealed.

370. F. Sánchez Calero, 'Art. 81. Seguros de grupo', *Ley de Contrato de Seguro*, 3th edn (Pamplona: Aranzadi, 2005), 1675–1676.
371. STS 14-12-1983 (Social). RAJ 1983/6205.
372. STS 26-2-1985 (Social). RAJ 1985/702.
373. SSTS 14-6-1994 (Civil). RAJ 1994/4818 y 21-6-1994 (Civil). RAJ 1994/4967.
374. SSTS 25-6-1986 (Social). RAJ 1986/3736, 22-7-1996 (Social). RAJ 1996/6377, 2-2-1998 (Social). RAJ 1998/3250, 12-2-1998 (Social). RAJ 1998/1803 and, mainly, 15-10-1985 (Social). RAJ 1985/4726.

this contract implies that the beneficiary normally will be designated by the insured, who will also have the right to revoke such designation.[375]

The policyholder must pay the premium, which is why the compliance with the obligation to pay has to be made in one invoice.[376] Its amount is determined as a function of the number of insured persons, which must not be a fixed number but can vary along the insured relationship.

The formal elements of the policy are the membership form and the insurance certificate. The policy that is a signed document between the policyholder and the insured does not give rise to special problems. From our standpoint, an extensive interpretation of Articles 5 of the LCS and 76.2 of the ROSSP leads us to consider that the insured has the right to demand from the insurer the delivery of the policy. The membership form is the document declaring that the insured complies with the characteristics that are required to be incorporated into the insured group. It should be delivered to the insurer, via the policyholder. Subsequently, the insurer will declare through the insurance certificate that the referred person has the insurance condition.

*349.* The disparity between policy and insurance certificate gives rise to the difficult problem of establishing which document must prevail. With regard to this matter, two theses have been supported, the prevalence of the insurance policy over the insurance certificate[377] as well as the opposite. The matter should have been solved from the beginning on the basis of the '*in dubio pro asegurado*'[378] rule, which means that the most favourable interpretation for the insured should prevail. Because the drafting of both documents is the insurer's responsibility, their obscurity should equally come down on the insurer's shoulders. On the subject, it is important to bear in mind that the insured would suffer a situation of defencelessness because normally she or he will not have access to the policy until the occurrence of the insured event.

*350.* Nowadays, businesspeople often contract private insurance in favour of their workers as a better alternative to the obligatory regime of social security. The traditional set of rules that apply to voluntary improvements of the social security regime in accordance with Articles 39 and 191 and following to the General Social Security Law (LGSS) has been supplemented with the regulation on plans and pension funds (currently Royal Decree 1/2002 of 29 November of the RPFP). Since then compulsory application for complementing or improving pensions has become a rule. Article 193 of the LGSS was clearly affected by the rule because it limits the allowed improvements to those that are directly negotiated by undertakings with respect to improvements on temporary obligations or subsidies of temporary disability, maternity or risk during pregnancy. Improvements with respect to retirement pensions, permanent disability or disability derived from death and survival

375. R. Illescas Ortiz, *El seguro colectivo o de grupo* (Sevilla: Cámara Oficial de Comercio, Industria y Navegación de Sevilla, 1975).
376. STS 12-6-1996 (Civil). RAJ 1996/4760.
377. STS 15-3-1985 (Social). RAJ 1985/1345.
378. STS 27-6-1985 (Civil). RAJ 1985/3485.

are absolutely forbidden. Setting up these internal funds for improvements' management is prohibited except in cases included in the fourteenth transitory provision of the 1995 LOSSP.[379] In the same manner the obligation is introduced to constitute pension plans in the employment system or agreement of specific insurance contracts for these purposes.[380]

Two jurisdictional orders, the social one for insurance contracted as a complement to social security and the civil courts for matters that are clearly private law, give rise to a duality of interpretation. This must be taken into account since case law from the civil court does not bind the social court.

## §3. Prohibition Against Insurer's Subrogation

*351.* Considering personal insurance as an insurance of sums, there is no subrogation of the insurer in the claims that the insured may have against the third party that is liable for the insured event covered by the policy. These claims remain in the sphere of the insured who may combine the insurance money from the insurer and the indemnity derived from civil liability. The fact that personal insurance is by nature an insurance of sum authorizes the beneficiary to receive these two amounts without infringing any imperative principle inherent to these insurance contracts.

A different regime is proposed with respect to the insurance of health care expenses where the subrogation of the insurer is admitted. Health care expenses include amounts that the insurer is committed to in health care and the costs of the provision of medical services when it is assumed by the insurer. As a result, because sickness and health care insurance have the referred expenses as main obligations, they fall within the scope of the application of the rule. Also included are those insurance contracts in which health care expenses meet other obligations as it occurs in accident insurance.

The regulator admits subrogation in Article 82 of the LCS but does not say anything about its regulation. Consequently, we must seek it in the content of Article 43 of the LCS for property insurance.

379. Credit undertakings, insurance undertakings and brokers corporations and agencies are allowed to keep internal funds for management of commitments for pensions contracted previously to 10 May 1996; see Art. 38 and ff for regulations on implementation for pensions commitments.

380. On that matter, see R. La Casa García, *Contrato de seguro y previsión social complementaria en el ámbito laboral: (régimen jurídico de los contratos de seguro que pueden instrumentar compromisos por pensiones)*, (Madrid: Mapfre, 2000).

## Chapter 2. Accident Insurance

### §1. Concept and Regime Applicable to Accident Insurance

*352.* This insurance can be defined as the contract by which the insurer has to indemnify the damage caused by bodily injury that arises from violent, sudden and external cause, that was not intentionally generated by the insured, and that caused temporary or permanent disability or death.[381]

Articles 100–104 of the LCS regulate accident insurance. Consequently, as accident insurance ranks among personal insurance contracts, the general provisions for all types of insurance and also the specific provisions must be taken into account (Articles 1–24 of the LCS) along with the provisions that are applicable for personal insurance (Articles 80–82 of the LCS).

Accident insurance has a hybrid nature and shows a mixture of characteristics of sum insurance and property insurance. This duality is demonstrated by the insurer's obligation, which is divided into two parts: on the one hand, the sum to be paid in case of death, temporary or permanent disability, and on the other hand, the expenses for health care. However, this mixed nature should not make us forget that this is one insurance contract.

*353.* Choice for the systematic inclusion of accident insurance was made by the legislator. Indeed, the debate about its nature was focused on the question of whether the rules on property should be applied to accident insurance (Articles 25–44 of the LCS). The LCS chose to exclude this possibility because accident insurance is to be classified among personal insurance contracts. Nevertheless, it is convenient to point out in advance that some 'property insurance' rules apply: for example, the insurer's subrogation is admitted in the case of health care expenses (Article 82 of the LCS); the existence of multiple or cumulative insurance must be notified (Article 101 of the LCS); and there is the possibility for expert proceedings to resolve disputes during the liquidation of the insured event (Article 104 of the LCS).

According to the referral made by Article 100 of the LCS, Articles 83–86 and 87.1 of the LCS also apply to the beneficiary in life insurance. Its qualification as personal insurance is reinforced, and doubts about the perception of the insurer's benefit by a third party are solved because the accident covered by the policy may cause the insured's death.

*354.* Private doctrinal legal qualifications do not impede that from the perspective of the organic set of rules for the insurance sector; accident insurance has been included within the section that deals with direct insurance, other than life insurance (Article 6 TRLOSSP), even though the same rule enables life insurers, when certain requirements are complied, to cover accidents as a complementary risk.

---

381. F. Sánchez Calero, 'Art. 100. El riesgo de accidente. Normas aplicables del seguro de vida', *Ley de Contrato de Seguro*, 3th edn (Pamplona: Aranzadi, 2005), 2088ff.

Finally, it is important to note that although obligatory insurance for travellers is subject to a special regulation (Royal Decree 1575/1989, 22 December) it is qualified as accident insurance. The same qualification has to be granted to passengers insurance, which is stipulated together with motor vehicle civil liability.

## §2. Insured Risk

*355.* The legislator prescribes that an accident is a 'corporal injury' that is generated by a violent, sudden, external and non-intentional cause by the insured that causes temporary or permanent disability or death' (Article 100 of the LCS).[382] As a result, the accident must cause an injury to the insured's body, which, in order to be considered an accident in accordance with LCS, must meet a series of requirements:[383]

(1) The cause of the injury must be external to the body of the insured.
(2) The event that caused the accident was not caused by the insured.
(3) The corporal injury suffered by the insured must have a sudden non-predictable and inevitable origin. In other words, it should be a corporal injury, the cause of which is sudden, and of immediate affectation and not a more or less extended pathology that presumes a progressive deterioration.[384]
(4) The sudden, violent, external and non-voluntary event must cause a corporal injury to the insured, that is to say, a decrease in the corporal integrity physically and psychologically.

Without prejudice to the legal limitation of accident contained in Article 100 of the LCS, the parties may also use a flexible approach of the cause, time and territorial scope of the insured risk. The limitation must be within the legal limits.[385]

---

382. A number of decisions have considered including myocardium attack within the concept of accident. Analysis of this case law can be read in A. Lois Caballé, 'La consideración del infarto de miocardio como accidente en la jurisprudencia del Tribunal Supremo', in *El contrato de seguro en la jurisprudencia del Tribunal Supremo*, AA.VV. (Coords J. Bataller, J. Boquera & J. Olavarría) (Valencia: Tirant lo Blanch, 1999), 822ff. Among the last decisions in regard to the civil court it may be read the decision of 31-7-2000 (Civil). RAJ 2000/8675 y la STS 27-12-2001 (Civil). RAJ 2002/3087 where consolidated doctrine in this jurisdictional order is shown.
383. A. Lois Caballé, 'Art. 100. Concepto de accidente', in *Comentarios a la Ley de contrato de seguro*, AA.VV. (Coords J. Boquera, J. Bataller & J. Olavarría) (Valencia: Tirant lo Blanch, 2001), 1141–1147. See also the SSTS 20-6-2000 (Civil). RAJ 2000/5295 and 5-6-2001 (Civil). RAJ 2001/6669.
384. The expression 'violent' referred to in Art. 100 of the LCS does not necessarily refer to the causal event in itself, but to its injuring efficiency, in a way that consequently injuring cause is not only the traumatic cause but any other cause of fast injuring action, considering the expressions 'injuring ', 'fast', 'sudden' or 'unexpected' as synonymous.
385. For more information on this matter, consult I. García Martín, 'El seguro de accidentes', in *Contratos mercantiles*, AA.VV. (Dirs A. Bercovitz Rodríguez-Cano & M.A. Calzada Conde), 2th edn (Pamplona: Aranzadi, 2001), 859ff.

§3. Insurer Obligation

*356.* The insurer's obligation is carried out by paying out the insurance money in the form of capital or rent as previously agreed in the policy. In Spain, it is customary that the risks of death or permanent disability (total and partial) are given a lump-sum cost, whereas temporary disability leads to payment of a daily amount during its existence. Furthermore, if it is expressly provided in the policy, health care will also be paid by the insurer according to the conditions laid down in the contract, which cannot exclude necessary and urgent care.

Insured risk here has already been mentioned and as we know the insured event is the materialization of the risk. Nevertheless, it is still a question when does it occur. On this issue, the social court of the supreme tribunal has decided that the relevant time is the date when the sequels are established. Recently, however, this case law trend has radically changed and joined the doctrinal view that the insured event occurs on the date of the accident, although the consequential damage (disability or death) appears afterwards.[386]

*357.* Once the insurer has notice of the event that causes injury or death, he or she will have to decide basically on two matters. First, whether the event is covered by the contract or, in other words, whether an insured event has occurred. Second, when the answer to the first question is affirmative, what is the amount of the obligation. In addition, if the insured event is caused by the insured with malicious intent, the insurer will be released of the obligation[387] and if it is caused with malicious intent by the beneficiary, the designation made in his or her favour will be void (Article 102 of the LCS).

After the occurrence of the insured event is accepted, the next step is to quantify the insurer's obligation. The least conflictive hypothesis will be the insured's death because there are few matters to discuss, the facts having already been ascertained after the insured's death. The proof of death is the responsibility of the beneficiary who will have to present to the insurer, according to the usual requirements imposed by policies, a death certificate from the civil registry, a medical death certificate and a letter of payment or declaration of exemption of successions tax properly issued by the Ministry of Economy (Treasury), although required documents differ from insurer to insurer.

*358.* Corporal bodily injuries pose more problems. Pursuant to Article 104 of the LCS, determination of the degree of disability caused by accident will be made by the insurer after the insured has submitted the medical certificate of disability, according to scales fixed in the policy. Disability must be demonstrated by the insured, who must provide evidence of the relationship among the injuries suffered and the disability. Furthermore, the insurer may ask as many complementary reports

386. This way was established by STS 1-2-2000 (Social). RAJ 2000/1069, ratified by the SSTS 14-3-2000 (Social). RAJ 2000/2857; 21-3-2000 (Social). RAJ 2000/2872; 18-4-2000 (Social). RAJ 2000/3698 and 2000/5154; 3-11-2000 (Social). RAJ 2000/9661; 6-11-2000 (Social). RAJ 2000/9632; and 21-11-2000 (Social). RAJ 2000/10295, among others.

387. SSTS 9-11-1990 (Civil). RAJ 1990/8535 and 20-11-1991 (Civil). RAJ 1991/8468.

about the consequences of the insured event as she or he deems necessary. In particular, in the absence of justification, policies usually force the insured to be examined by doctors designated by the company when the insurer considers it necessary in which case the insurer assumes the costs.

*359.* Once the insurer has received the required documents from the insured, she or he has to notify its indemnity proposal in writing. The LCS does not prescribe a term, so the insurer can take this decision but it has to be taken as soon as possible. However, the arrears regime of Article 20 of the LCS will be applied.

The last phrase of Article 104 of the LCS prescribes that if the insured does not accept the insurer's proposal, the parties will submit the decision to medical experts in accordance with Article 38 of the LCS. This provision regulates the extra-judicial proceeding for liquidation of an insured event in property insurance.[388]

## §4. Multiple Insurance in Accident Insurance

*360.* Article 101 of the LCS obliges the policyholder to notify the insurer about the subscription of any other accident insurance for the same insured. In our opinion, the reason lies in the defence of the indemnity principle. Also, because in accident insurance this principle only applies with regard to health care expenses, it was necessary to establish a special regime.[389]

The policyholder is the person who must notify. Nevertheless, the insured may also do so releasing the policyholder from this obligation. The notification may be carried out in any form. The insurer who will subscribe to the contract must be notified of previous and future insurance contracts. Finally, Article 101 of the LCS stipulates that a breach of this duty may only give rise to a claim for damages.

388. The STS 27-10-1998 (Civil). RAJ 1998/8513 considered that the imperative character of the expert proceeding of Art. 104 of the LCS cannot be claimed by one who did not use it before.
389. J. Bataller Grau, *El seguro múltiple* (Valencia: Tirant lo Blanch, 1998), 17ff.

## Chapter 3. Sickness and Health Care Insurance

*361.* Sickness and health care insurance enjoy a concise regulation in LCS. Article 105 of the LCS governs the insurer's obligations, and Article 106 of the LCS refers to accident insurance when the rules are compatible.

Both insurances cover the same risk: sickness that is a perturbation of the health condition, or an abnormal situation of the body.[390] However, it does not seem that sickness is by itself the risk to be assumed by the insurer but rather the sickness that implies the help of third parties, the cost of which has to be faced, besides the fact that, as a general rule, sickness will hinder the practice of professional activity or simple normal life. Nevertheless, any specification of the covered risk will always have a relative character because its delimitation must be made in the policy.

*362.* Thus, it is possible to deduce that there is one type of contract with two subtypes according to the insurer's obligation:

(1) In *sickness insurance* the insurance undertaking is obliged to pay a lump-sum amount, the payment of health care expenses or a combination of both. The lump-sum amounts usually comprise indemnity for surgery intervention, daily hospital indemnity for surgery intervention, daily indemnity for any cause and indemnity for temporary total disability. Likewise, the insurer may agree to pay the insured for health care and pharmacy expenses. These expenses are governed by the principles of property insurance because the insurer must reimburse the insured for the expenses that were effectively generated. As a result, Article 82 of the LCS admits that the insurer may subrogate the insured's rights in order to be compensated as much as possible.

(2) In *health care insurance* 'the insurer directly assumes the obligation to provide medical and surgery services', although it would be more adequate to state that the insurers directly manage and organize the provision of these services by professionals chosen by the insured and, being such managers, the insurers are committed to pay their direct cost.[391] [392] The insurer's obligation is normally performed by offering to the insured a team of doctors among whom the insured is entitled to choose.[393] The insurer also determines the procedure that must be followed in order to use its medical services.[394] In practice, problems occur when the insured uses the services of a professional or centre not included because the policy only authorizes this in case of vital urgency.

---

390. J. Garrigues, *Contrato de seguro terrestre*, 2th edn (Madrid, 1982), 565.
391. F. Sánchez Calero, 'Art. 105. Prestaciones del asegurador en estos seguros', *Ley de contrato de seguro*, AA.VV. (Dir F. Sánchez Calero), 3th edn (Pamplona: Aranzadi, 2005), 2151ff.
392. *Ibid.*, 2159ff.
393. The STS 2-11-1999 (Civil). RAJ 1999/7998 sentenced the insured directly for negligent surgical intervention of an authorized doctor that was recommended by the insurer.
394. The STS 17-7-2000 (Civil). RAJ 2000/6178 sentenced the insurer to pay hospital expenses because in the scope of that territory the insurer lacked the necessary means to provide the committed care.

In any case, it is the insurer who pays directly the doctors for the cost of services received by the insured, although in some cases the insured is required to pay a small percentage of the cost. Also, when the insurer directly assumes the provision of services, he or she also assumes the civil liability *in eligendo* or *in vigilando* for providing defective services.[395] Such liability will have to be shared with the professional and hospital that performed them.

The STS 30-5-2000 (Civil). RAJ 2000/5088 ratified the rejection of the coverage by the insurer because the hospital did not have an agreement with the insurer that had expressed its refusal to pay the treatment.

395. See STS 2-11-1999 (Civil). RAJ 1999/7998.

# Chapter 4. Life Insurance

## §1. Concept and Classes

*363.* Life insurance may be defined as the insurance contract by which the insurer agrees to pay a single or periodic amount of money to the insured or beneficiary when an insured event related to the duration of human life occurs. It is characterized as being an insurance of sum or in other words insurance of abstract coverage need, which means that the insurer's obligation is an amount of money fixed *a priori* in the contract.

There exists a wide variety of life insurances. Taking into account the insured risk, in a simple way, they can be classified as life insurance for death (term life insurance), survival insurance and mixed insurance.

*364.* In insurance for death, capital or an insured amount is paid in case of the insured's death. This type of insurance covers, in general, all causes of death, except those expressly excluded in the policy (Article 91 of the LCS). At the same time it is possible to distinguish between lifelong insurance that covers an unlimited period of time until the death occurs and temporary insurance, the coverage of which is for a limited time.

In survival life insurance, the insurer's obligation arises when the insured is alive on a certain date.

Mixed life insurance combines, to some degree, life and death risks.

*365.* Recently, new products have been designed to channel savings, overcoming monetary depreciation through different formulas: stipulating a percentage increase of the obligations, reassessing obligations according to benefit participation or linking insurance to money market investment funds, without prejudice that the life risk is contracted together with other complementary risks.

However, life insurance can also be classified on the basis of the insurer's obligation. According to this criterion, the insurance may be for a capital or a periodic rent.

## §2. Personal Elements

*366.* Especially when the covered risk is death, life insurance is characterized by the plurality of personal elements that overcome the usual elements of the insurance contract.

The insured may be any person who is older than 14 years and persons not lacking legal capacity. The insured and the policyholder do not need to be the same person. In insurance for the death of another person the insured's consent will be necessary except if his or her insured interest insurance may be proven through other means (Article 83.2 of the LCS).[396]

*367.* Together with the policyholder and the insured, there is a third contractual position: the beneficiary.[397] With respect to the beneficiary, Articles 84–88 of the LCS constitute the legal framework that is intended solely for death insurance. Nevertheless, also in other types of insurance the possibility of designating a beneficiary has been accepted unanimously by doctrine and case law, and it is a reality not only in survival life insurance but also in accident, sickness and health care insurance.

The designation of the beneficiary is a unilateral declaration of will that, according to Article 84 of the LCS, exclusively belongs to the policyholder.[398] It is not necessary to have the insurer's consent or knowledge of the beneficiary or insured when this is another person different from the policyholder in order to designate the beneficiary.

*368.* The beneficiary may be designated in the policy, later by written declaration notified to the insurer or by will, and in any other form that is more beneficial for the insured.[399] Regarding the types of designation, it may be nominative or generic, individual or collective, and for a definite or indefinite amount.

Nominative designation is about indicating the name and last names of the beneficiary in the case of a physical person, and the corporate name in the case of a legal entity. Generic or indefinite designation, as provided by Article 85 of the LCS, may be in favour of children, heirs and the spouse. The expository character of the provision allows new hypotheses for generic designation in favour of relatives, family and so on, being necessary to fix rules for limiting what is indefinite.

*369.* The designation may be for one or many beneficiaries, and in the second assumption they may be designated as a group and coinciding temporarily (co-beneficiaries), subsidiarily (the designated persons only acquire the beneficiary status if the person who precedes them never becomes a beneficiary) or alternatively

396. Case law has made a flexible interpretation to observe the concurrence of the insured's interest. SSTS 12-4-1993 (Civil). RAJ 1993/2993; 18-2-2002 (Civil). RAJ 2002/4142; y 25-2-2002 (Civil). RAJ 2002/4147.

397. For deep study about the beneficiary, consult C. Boldó Roda, *El beneficiario en el seguro de vida* (Barcelona: J.M. Bosch, 1998).

398. Insurance practice reveals that a conventional derogation of the article in group insurance in which the designation of the beneficiary is usually a right of the respective insured (STS 20-12-2000 (Civil). RAJ 2001/1509).

399. In group insurance the designation is usually made in membership form that the insured subscribe. In contracting practice there is some clause type in which different beneficiaries are established in successive order in case the taker does not choose. They are, from our perspective, null clauses contrary to the rules that grant the taker the exclusive right to designate a beneficiary. The taker is the only legitimized person to designate a beneficiary and in case he or she does not do it – due to mistake or intentional action – the benefit will be part of his or her patrimony as stipulated by Art. 84, in fine, of the LCS.

(assuming that there is no beneficiary specifically designated or rules for his or her designation, the policyholder and not the insurer must carry out the designation before the verification of the risk).

Finally, Article 86 of the LCS prescribes, although not expressly, that, in the case of co-beneficiaries, the policyholder can choose to determine or not which portion of the insured amount belong to each of them. In the absence of such a decision, the distribution will be proportional to the inheritance quota if the beneficiaries are heirs; if they are not heirs, the agreed obligation will be distributed equally. When the policyholder has defined which portion of the amount belongs to each beneficiary or if the legal solution applies, there exists a right to increase if another beneficiary does not acquire his or her share.

*370.* Revocation is an exclusive right of the policyholder. It does not require the consent of the insurer or insured when she or he is neither the policyholder nor the beneficiary. It may be carried out at any time, as long as the risk has not been realized and in any of the forms stipulated for the designation. Especially important from a practical point of view are the implicit acts such as modification of the designation and revocations that result from conclusive facts.[400] According to Article 87 of the LCS, the policyholder can revoke the designation of the beneficiary at any moment 'while the policyholder has not expressly renounced to such faculty in writing'. When the policyholder renounces to revoke, the position of the beneficiary becomes irrevocable and it changes from entitlement to a mere expectation to an entitlement to a real right of claim, the exercise of which will nevertheless only be possible when the risk is realized.[401]

*371.* Once the insured event occurs, the right of the beneficiary acquires full effect and enables her or him to directly demand from the insurer the fulfilment of the obligation. Such right is practised in the beneficiary's name and not the policyholder's name; it is autonomous, direct or immediate and this explains why the insured amount passes directly from the insurer's patrimony to the patrimony of the beneficiary without ever becoming part of the policyholder's patrimony.[402] However, Article 88 of the LCS enables heirs and creditors to demand the beneficiary for the reimbursement of the premium paid by the policyholder in fraud of her or his rights.

The beneficiary loses the right to the insurance's benefit for maliciously causing the insured's death (Article 92 of the LCS).

---

400. For example, new marriage of the taker in favour of her or his 'spouse', the insurance rescue or the assignment and pledge of the policy.
401. Until such condition is suspended, the beneficiary will be able to conditionally transfer her or his right, *inter vivos* or *mortis causa* – which presumes that in case of the previous decease of the spouse, the right will be transferred to the heirs – and exercise in its defence all actions that proceed to keep it being able to, for example, file reivindicatory action against the taker that infringing Art. 87 of the LCS, disposes of all or part of the insurance amount or also oppose an executive action by the taker's creditors against the insurance amount.
402. SSTS 22-12-1944 (Civil). RAJ 1944/1392; 8-5-1957 (Civil). RAJ 1957/1611; 2-1-1978 (Social). RAJ 1978/121 y 1-12-1987 (Social). RAJ 1987/8804. The typical and autonomous character of the right does not impede the insurer to oppose the beneficiary the exceptions that objectively derive from the contract, as those based on risk exclusions, limitative clauses and/or inexact declarations.

## §3. Withdrawal Right

*372.* As a consequence of European Community law, the faculty to resolve individual life insurance contracts with terms longer than six months has been introduced in the Spanish legal framework (Article 83(a) of the LCS).[403] This unilateral right of the policyholder does not require any motivation and the insurer cannot penalize it. The established deadline is thirty days upon the delivery of the policy or the document of provisional coverage. The communication will be addressed to the insurer by way of lasting, available and accessible support that proves notification. From the time the right to resolve is exercised, the coverage ceases and the premium will be returned to the policyholder except for the portion that is consumed corresponding to the time passed.

*373.* When the insurance contract is commercialized through distance contracts, the relevant legal provision is Article 10 of the law on distant commercialization of financial services to consumers (Law 22/2007, 11 July). This provision establishes that the thirty-day term to withdraw will be counted from the time that the consumer is notified that the contract was subscribed, or, if the consumer has not received the contractual conditions and the information of Article 7 of the mentioned law, the term to exercise the right of withdrawal will be counted from the reception of such information.

## §4. Declaration of the Insured Risk

*374.* The general regime of the duty of declaration of the risk is also applicable to life insurance. Nevertheless, Article 89 of the LCS forbids challenging the insurance as a consequence of an inexact or reticent declaration of the insured once the term of one year, or the shortest term established in the policy, has passed, unless there was an element of malice in the declaration.[404] There is also a special regime for declarations about the age of the insured (Article 90 of the LCS).

## §5. Premium and Guaranteed Values

*375.* Risk in life insurance presents singularities from a technical-actuarial viewpoint. The formation of the mathematical reserve in this type of insurance serves as

---

403. Insurance contracts in which the taker assumes the investment risk and insurance in which the guaranteed profitability is in function of investment assigned in the contracts do not enjoy resolution rights.

404. Insist in the need of malice does not occur SSTS 8-7-1996 (Social). RAJ.1996/5764 and 30-9-1996 (Civil). RAJ 1996/6822.

a technical foundation for investing the policyholder with certain rights described in Articles 94 and following Articles of the LCS:[405] rescue, reduction, cash advance, assignment and pledge of the policy.

Reduction is the special regime for default in payment of premium that tries to avoid the suspension or extinction of the contractual bound as a consequence of the default. The policyholder is entitled to reduction through express declaration or default in payment. The consequence is the reduction of the insurer's obligation.[406]

*376.* Right to rescue in the LCS may be understood as the policyholder's legal right to obtain part of the mathematic reserve through advanced resolution of the contract addressed to the insurer, without observing a pre-notice deadline or claiming just cause. Nevertheless, the doctrine mentions the possibility of partial rescue in which case there will be a partial resolution of the contract.[407]

The right to cash advance allows the policyholder to use a certain amount of money without waiting for the realization of the risk that is the object of the coverage. We are facing a right here that, as in the case of surrender, enables liquidity that must not be returned to the insurer.[408] From our standpoint, it is distinguished from surrender because whereas surrender presumes the total or partial resolution of the insurance, cash advance enables the policyholder to keep the insurance fully enforceable. The difference is not purely theoretical. If the surrender is partial, it is not possible to reimburse the money that the insurer delivered to reach the maximum benefit agreed in the policy and consequently the premium must be reduced because the benefit has also been reduced. On the contrary, cash advance simply presumes an advance on the provision and leaves the contract intact. The benefit will only be reduced if there is no restitution of the received amount but the premium will remain constant along the insurance relationship.

---

405. On mathematic provision and its legal incidents see N. LahoreLatorre Chiner, 'Art. 94. Los derechos de rescate y reducción como contenido obligatorio de la póliza', in *Comentarios a la Ley de contrato de seguro*, AA.VV. (Coords J. Boquera, J. Bataller & J. Olavarría) (Valencia: Tirant lo Blanch, 2001), 1089ff.
406. See N. Latorre Chiner, 'Art. 95. La reducción del seguro', in *Comentarios a la Ley de contrato de seguro*, AA.VV. (Coords J. Boquera, J. Bataller & J. Olavarría) (Valencia: Tirant lo Blanch, 2001), 1095ff; F.J. Tirado Suárez, 'Art. 95. Reducción del seguro de vida', in *Ley de contrato de seguro. Comentarios a la Ley 50/1980, de 8 de octubre y sus modificaciones*, AA.VV. (Dir F. Sánchez Calero), 3th edn (Pamplona: Aranzadi, 2005), 1870ff; J.L. Maestro Martínez, 'Los valores garantizados en el contrato de seguro sobre la vida (II)', *Rev. R.C.* (February 1996): 3ff.
407. See N. Latorre Chiner, 'Art. 96. El derecho de rescate', in *Comentarios a la Ley de contrato de seguro*, AA.VV. (Coords J. Boquera, J. Bataller & J.Y. Olavarría) (Valencia: Tirant lo Blanch, 2001), 1105 y ss; F.J. Tirado Suárez, 'Art. 96. El derecho de rescate', in *Ley de contrato de seguro. Comentarios a la Ley 50/1980, de 8 de octubre y sus modificaciones*, AA.VV. (Dir F. Sánchez Calero), 3th edn (Pamplona: Aranzadi, 2005), 1884ff; J.L. Maestro Martínez, 'Los valores garantizados en el contrato de seguro sobre la vida (II)', *Rev. R.C.* (February 1996): 3ff; M.S. Flores Doña, 'El derecho de revocación en el seguro de vida a favor de tercero', *CDC*, 1993, n° 12, 91ff.
408. See N. Latorre Chiner, 'Art. 97. El derecho de anticipo', in *Comentarios a la Ley de contrato de seguro*, AA.VV. (Coords J. Boquera, J. Bataller & J. Olavarría) (Valencia: Tirant lo Blanch, 2001), 1115ff; F.J. Tirado Suárez, 'Art. 96. Anticipos en la prestación', in *Ley de contrato de seguro. Comentarios a la Ley 50/1980, de 8 de octubre y sus modificaciones*, AA.VV. (Dir F. Sánchez Calero), 3th edn (Pamplona: Aranzadi, 2005), 1893ff; J.L. J.L. Maestro Martínez, 'Los valores garantizados en el contrato de seguro sobre la vida (II)', *Rev. R.C.* (February 1996): 3ff.

Assignment and pledge of the life insurance policy enable the insurance to circulate. Life insurance is an investment tool that may be transferred and even be used as a guarantee through pledge.[409]

409. C. Salinas Adelantado, 'Art. 99. La cesión y pignoración de la póliza del seguro de vida', in *Comentarios a la Ley de contrato de seguro*, AA.VV. (Coords J. Boquera, J., Bataller & J. Olavarría) (Valencia: Tirant lo Blanch, 2001), 1115ff; F.J. Tirado Suárez, 'Art. 99. Cesión y pignoración de la póliza del seguro de vida', in *Ley de contrato de seguro. Comentarios a la Ley 50/1980, de 8 de octubre y sus modificaciones*, AA.VV. (Dir F. Sánchez Calero), 3th edn (Pamplona: Aranzadi, 2005), 1921ff; A. Aurioles Martín, 'La pignoración de los derechos dimanantes del seguro de vida', in *Tratado de garantías de la contratación mercantil*, Madrid, t. II, *Garantías reales*, AA.VV., vol. 1, *Garantías mobiliarias*, 1996, 919ff; M.I. Martínez Jiménez, 'La cesión de la póliza de seguro', RDM, 1992, 93ff; J. Mejías Gómez, 'Cesión y pignoración de la póliza de seguro de vida', CDC, 1995, n° 17, 81ff.

## Chapter 5. Burial Services Insurance

*377.* Burial services insurance enjoys wide diffusion in Spain as is demonstrated by the annual reports of the DGSFP. In our opinion there are two reasons that explain the success of this type of insurance. On the one hand, burial services insurance has been conceived as a service that the insurer provides in difficult times for the family of the deceased. It is usually established in the policy that if the insurer could not provide the agreed-on services in their totality, reimbursement of the appropriate amount can be claimed. On the other hand, the premium is traditionally paid by instalments, monthly or quarterly, in the policyholder's domicile although this last practice has not been extended as in the past.

The economic importance of this type of insurance, its high level of turnover[410] and its tradition in our country, strongly contrast with the total absence of any prescriptions in the LCS about this type of insurance contracting. Consequently, the policy plays a central role together with the general provisions contained in the LCS. A complete legal framework has to begin from the qualification of burial services insurance as personal insurance, even when the particular obligation of the insurer is similar, in some matters, to property insurance.

*378.* In practice one of the most frequent problems is caused when the premium increases. In that regard, the DGSFP has chosen to admit the legality of this practice provided that the increase is parallel to the insured's ageing and the possible increase of service's costs. Nevertheless, it is provided that the premium increase must be announced two months before the end of the current period and that in case of non-acceptance of the contract modification, the insurance will continue to be valid, whereas the insured will have to bear the excess cost of the service at the time the insured event has occurred.

*379.* The typical and main object of this insurance is the burial service as specified in the policy. Usually, services include coffin, funeral car, cars for family and friends, funeral wreath, announcement of death in the press or in memoriam cards for the attendees placed in usual locations, necessary procedures for the burial, payment of certificates and fees, costs for religious assistance, funeral home, incineration, niche, gravestone and transfer of the deceased. Policies enable this coverage to be extended to include other services such as repatriation of remains, burial of a foetus or of children of less than thirty days of age, burial or incineration of amputated limbs and so on. That is why usually the insured amount does not constitute a limit for the indemnity but a reference for the calculation of the premium, the function of the insurer being to pay the funeral service. Nevertheless, if the insurer does not provide the services agreed, she or he will have to pay the heirs the proper amount.[411]

Notice of the death, and in this case, the deadline of forty days granted by Article 18 of the LCS, is not applied. Delays in the carrying out of the agreed services will give rise to liability for damages.

---

410. It has been estimated that 55% of the population has subscribed this type of insurance.

411. F.J. Tirado Suárez, *Los seguros de personas*, vol. 3 de *El seguro*, en *Tratado de Derecho mercantil* (Dirs Olivencia, Fernández-Novoa & Jiménez de Parga) (Madrid: Marcial Pons, 2006), 236.

# Part VI. Pension Plans and Pension Funds

## Chapter 1. Regulatory Framework

*380.* The basic elements of the regulatory framework for pension plans and pension funds are found in the Spanish Constitution. Article 41 of the Spanish Constitution expressly recognizes the freedom to establish assistance and complementary benefits. Indeed, Article 1.2 of the law for pension funds and pension plans stipulates with regard to pension funds that they are 'voluntarily incorporated and its benefits will never substitute social security benefits'.

The Spanish Constitution is also relevant for the social security framework from the perspective of the distribution of powers between the State and autonomous communities. Article 149, which governs the matter, has been the subject of interpretation by decisions of 27 November 1997 and of 18 March 1998 of the Constitutional Court. Doctrinal theory, based on the legal grounds of these decisions, vests the State with the exclusive power to regulate the contractual aspects but, as in the case of private insurance, the State may only dictate basic regulations for its organization of its institutional elements. The autonomous communities have the power to develop them.

This constitutional provision is currently implemented by Royal Decree 1/2002 of 29 November, which approves the Consolidated Text of the law for regulation of pension plans and pension funds (TRPFP) and by Royal Decree 304/2004 of 20 February, which approves the regulation for pension plans and pension funds.[412] It is also important to mention the Royal Decree 1588/1999 of 15 October, which implements the agreements made between employers and their employees with respect to pensions, and it intends to guarantee its effective compliance through the undertaking.

412. For deeper information on pension plans and pension funds, see F. Sánchez Calero, 'Delimitación y notas características de los Planes de Pensiones', in *Régimen jurídico de los Planes y Fondos de Pensiones*, F. Sánchez, L. Angulo, J. Duque, F.J. Tirado, M. Vérgez, J. Aguilar, L.F. Castresana & F. Mansilla, 2th edn (Madrid: Editorial Española de Seguros, 1989); R. La Casa García, *Los fondos de pensiones* (Madrid: Marcial Pons, 1989); A. Martínez Lafuente (dir.), *Estudios sobre Planes y Fondos de Pensiones* (Barcelona: Ariel, 1989).

# Chapter 2. Pension Plans

## §1. Definition

*381.* According to Article 1 of the TRPFP, pension plans have a contractual nature. The TRPFP also defines a persons' rights to receive capital or income in the event of specified contingencies (retirement, survival, widowhood, orphanhood or disability). Despite its contractual nature, pension plans cannot be qualified as insurance contracts.[413]

Pension plans must be included in a pension fund in order to comply with the payment of capitals or incomes derived from the plan's execution (Article 10 of the TRPFP).

## §2. Type of Pension Plans

*382.* From a taxpayer's viewpoint, pension plans may be split into three groups: those linked to employment (the promoter is any undertaking and its beneficiaries are its employees), those linked to a partnership (the promoter is an association or trade union and its beneficiaries are its partners, members or affiliates) and the individual system (the promoter is a financial undertaking and its participants are any physical person).

The other big classification established by the TRPFP chooses to focus on the type of obligation and, therefore, distinguishes between plans with defined benefits (plans with the purpose of paying certain amounts to the beneficiaries), plans with 'defined contributions' (the purpose is to pay the contribution amount, but it may not guarantee or define future obligations) and the mixed types.

## §3. Personal Elements

*383.* There are three categories of subjects in a pension plan:

(1) C*ontracting parties* are the subjects to the plan, that is to say, the promoters (undertakings, associations, trade unions that promote their creation or manage

413. F. Sánchez Calero, 'Delimitación y notas características de los Planes de Pensiones', in *Régimen jurídico de los Planes y Fondos de Pensiones*, ed. F. Sánchez, L. Angulo, J. Duque, F.J. Tirado, M. Vérgez, J. Aguilar, L.F. Castresana & F. Mansilla, 2th edn (Madrid: Editorial Española de Seguros, 1989), 19, stands out as having the distinguishing characteristic of the lack of a personal element essential to the definition contained in Art. 1 of the LCS such as the insurer. L. Angulo Rodríguez, 'Los planes y fondos de pensiones y la Ley de contrato de seguro', in *Régimen jurídico de los Planes y Fondos de Pensiones*, ed. F. Sánchez, L. Angulo, J. Duque, F.J. Tirado, M. Vérgez, J. Aguilar, L.F. Castresana & F. Mansilla, 2th edn (Madrid: Editorial Española de Seguros, 1989), 49, understands that plans do not guarantee by themselves the effectiveness of the defined obligation as the main distinguishing element.

them), the participants (the persons for whose interest the plan is created) and the beneficiaries (persons entitled to receive the benefits) (Article 3 of the TRPFP).

(2) Actuary inspectors whose intervention is compulsory. They are inspectors of the financial and actuarial contractual provisions.

(3) Guarantors who may be insurers or suretyship providers. Their participation is merely optional.

Pension plans are supervised by a supervisory commission except in pension plans for individuals when this function is assumed by the participant's ombudsman. The ombudsman also supervises the beneficiaries' rights.

## §4. Contents of Pension Plans

*384.* The contents of pension plans must comply with the basic principles set out in the TRPFP, essentially in Article 5:[414]

(1) Principles related to subjects: (a) principle of no discrimination that assures the entry of any subject that complies with the requirements defined by the plan (Article 5.1(a) of the TRPFP) and (b) principle of supervision by the supervisory commission except for individual plans (Article 7 of the TRPFP).

(2) Principles related to functioning: (a) principle of individual capitalization (Article 8.1 of the TRPFP), (b) principle of irrevocability of fees and their annual restrictions (Articles 5.1(c) and 5.3 of the TRPFP), (c) principle of attribution of the participants' rights (Article 5.1(d) of the TRPFP) and (d) principle of forced integration in pension funds (Articles 5.1(e) and 10 of the TRPFP).

*385.* Rights and obligations derived from a pension plan are articulated according to the correlation between the contributions of the participants and the benefits to be received by beneficiaries (Article 8 of the TRPFP). Fees and contributions are amounts paid by participants or promoters for the respective plan account of the fund.

The obligations to pay benefits are recognitions of economic rights (capital, income or a combination of both) in favour of beneficiaries of pension plans as a result of contingencies that are covered by the plan (retirement, total permanent work disability for habitual profession or absolute permanent work disability for any work, great disability and death of participant or beneficiary).

414. We follow the structure proposed by A.J. Tapia Hermida, *Manual de Derecho de seguros y fondos de pensiones* (Pamplona: Aranzadi, 2006), 301 and ff.

# Chapter 3. Pension Funds

## §1. Definition

*386.* Pension fund is a patrimony that does not have a legal personality subject to the compliance with one or more pension plans (Article 2 of the TRPFP).[415] Its legal title corresponds to participants and beneficiaries of integrated pension plans in accordance with the accounts in the fund (Article 8.4 of the TRPFP).

## §2. Personal Elements in Pension Funds

*387.* Pension plans have triangular structures. First, the legal title of the resources corresponds to the participants, or in their absence, to the beneficiaries. Their participation is implemented through the supervisory commission of the fund. The commission's main functions are to supervise the management and approve the merger with new plans. It may also represent the fund but this function can be delegated to the management undertaking (Article 14.2 of the TRPFP).

Second, its management may be handed over to a third party, which can be a public limited company that has pension fund management as its exclusive corporate goal and that complies with the requirements set out by Article 20 of the TRPFP, or an insurer who possesses the appropriate administrative authorization. The management undertaking is responsible for the internal and external administration of the fund. In any case, the management undertaking is obliged to submit reports about the accounting of the fund and about its own accounting as well. The management undertaking is responsible for the representation of the fund, as the case may be.

Finally, there is a third subject, the depositary who is in charge of the custody and the deposit of the securities and other financial assets that are integrated in the fund (Article 21 of the TRPFP) as well as of the surveillance of the management undertaking.

Also actuary experts are needed to verify the accounting of management undertakings and funds (Article 19.4 of the TRPFP).

## §3. Patrimony

*388.* Pension funds are characterized as four types of patrimonial masses:[416]

415. An analysis of the different theses about the nature of the fund can be found in J. Duque Domínguez, 'Notas delimitadoras y naturaleza jurídica de los fondos de pensiones', in *Régimen jurídico de los Planes y Fondos de Pensiones*, ed. F. Sánchez, L. Angulo, J. Duque, F.J. Tirado, M. Vérgez, J. Aguilar, L.F. Castresana & F. Mansilla, 2th edn (Madrid: Editorial Española de Seguros, 1989), 67–71.

416. See A.J. Tapia Hermida, *Manual de Derecho de seguros y fondos de pensiones* (Pamplona: Aranzadi, 2006), 335 and ff.

(1) They are *patrimonies that are* subject to the exclusive purpose of serving as a vehicle for investment of contributions according to the pension plan (Article 2 of the TRPFP).
(2) They are *separated patrimonies* because of the patrimonial independency established by the TRPFP, implying that debts of the manager are not transferred to the fund (Article 12 of the TRPFP). However, given the fact that participants are not the creditors of the contributions while being entitled to patrimonial assets of the plan, they suffer the consequences when the fund's assets increase or decrease, in accordance with the investment of the fund.
(3) They are *dynamic patrimonies* because they require an active management (Article 13 of the TRPFP) and the investment of the integrated financial resources (Article 16 of the TRPFP) due to the principle of transformation of contributions to plans and investment of pension funds.
(4) They are *collective patrimonies* because participants or beneficiaries are entitled to collective ownership.

# Part VII. Private Insurance-Social Security

*389.* Spain has an extensive social insurance system denominated 'social security'. It is defined as the group of public measures for the organization of a communal system for the prevention and remediation of personal risks through individualized pecuniary obligations. The Constitution itself, in its Article 41, gives a structure to the so-called constitutional model of the social security by establishing that 'public authorities will set up the public framework of the social security system for all citizens to assure sufficient social assistance and benefits in case of necessity, especially unemployment. Assistance and complementary benefits will be freely provided for'. The text of the law literally distinguishes among three levels: the contributive level, the welfare level or non-contributive level (for concrete contingencies: benefits for sanitary assistance, retirement, disability and child support) and the private complementary level (pension plans and pension funds).

The contributive level is organized into three regimes (a general regime and different special regimes) formed by differentiated social groups.[417] The general regime includes employed workers and self-employed workers (although they cannot strictly be considered workers, and also certain civil servants, full-time members of local corporations, managers of public limited societies who do not have effective control of such societies and others determined by the government). Special regimes are established for professional practices whose nature, peculiar time or localization, or whose type of productive process requires special treatment such as those related to forestall and cattle industries, coal mining, fisheries, self-employed work, civil and military public servants, housekeeping, student work and other groups determined by the Ministry of Labour.

*390.* One of the main purposes of the social security system is to economically support individuals who suffer damages as a result of an increase in expenses, decrease in income or both at the same time. In that sense, social security responds to the same objectives of social welfare and protection against specified risks as the insurance contract does. Social security is obviously different from insurance because it is not based on a contract and, consequently, not on the presence of free will, freedom and proportionality between premium and risk, which is characteristic of the insurance contract. The 'necessity' situations protected by the Spanish

417. The regulatory framework of the social security is basically described in the 1994 General Law of Social Security (consolidated text approved by Royal Legislative Decree 1/1994 of 20 June), in the Labour ProcedureJurisdiction Law (consolidated text approved by Royal Legislative Decree 2/1995Law 36/2011, of 7 April 10 October) and in the Infringements and Sanctions Law for Social Issues (refundida consolidated text approved by Royal Legislative Decree 5/2000 of 4 August).

social security systems include temporary disability, maternity, paternity, risks during pregnancy and natural breastfeeding, disability, retirement, unemployment, death and survival, accidents, and special situations further specified by Royal Decree taken on a proposal of the Ministry of Labour and Welfare affairs.[418] For historical reasons, health changes, disability and death have a different treatment according to whether the accident was professional (accidents occurred at work and professional sickness) or common (any accident and common sickness). The first one is the most beneficial one.

*391.* If the protected event occurs, the benefits of social security may be pecuniary, which usually happens, or 'in natura' basically in cases of sanitary assistance when technical service is provided. Economic benefits are sometimes indemnities, which are payments a *tanto alzado* made to the beneficiary (e.g., partial and permanent disability), but they usually imply periodic payment to be made on a lifelong basis (as in the case of pensions) or on a temporary basis (benefits for unemployment, maternity to temporary disability).

*392.* Public administration is responsible for the management of the social security system (collaboration of private initiative is also allowed) but only when it is not lucrative. The public management agencies of social security are three: the National Institute of Social Security, the Institute of Sanitary Management and the Institute of Major and Social Services. Other public agencies that may intervene in its management include the General Treasury of Social Security and the National Institute of Employment. Some private entities also support the social security management such as the mutual societies of social security for working place accidents and professional disease (they are options for insurance protection and, consequently, employers may choose among them in order to protect their employees contracting the correspondent public agency or any mutual society. In the second case, the mutual society will pay benefits derived from professional accidents caused by employees of the contracting employer or, if that is the case, benefits for temporary disability for common contingencies). Finally, private undertakings in general may provide a voluntary collaboration (they directly pay certain benefits to their employees in exchange for reduction of their contributions to be paid to social security) or a compulsory participation (the undertaking makes advanced payments for temporary disability to be compensated later with their contributions).

Social security is financed by two kinds of resources: State contributions consigned in the General Budget and quotas obligatorily paid by specified persons. In this way financing resources can be split up into contributive obligations financed by quotas and the non-contributive obligations financed by taxes or fiscal means.

418. Modification of Art. 38 of the General Law of Social Security introduced by the Organic Law 3/2007 of 22 March for effective equity of men and women.

# Part VIII. Insurance Intermediaries

## Chapter 1. Law of Establishment and Supervision

### §1. Legal Framework

*393.* LMSRP is the central regulation for intermediation of insurance in the Spanish insurance market.[419] However, it is necessary to point out that in the Spanish legal framework many applicable regimes for intermediation of private insurance coexist.

Indeed, the autonomous communities have almost unanimously acquired the power to organize and supervise intermediation of insurance contracts. There is thus distribution of powers. The LMSRP lays out the exclusive power of the State to supervise brokers of exclusive insurance and banking-insurance operators of exclusive insurance undertakings controlled by the DGSFP and for the rest of intermediaries who operate beyond the territory of one autonomous community. On the contrary, the power is given by the LMSRP to the autonomous community when brokers of exclusive insurance or exclusive banking-insurance operators of insurance undertakings are subject to control of the supervisory body of the community, or when intermediaries of other classes have domicile and operate in the territory of an autonomous community. Such powers are based on the development of organization and powers to implement them, which is why it is possible to notice the development of the communities' regulation on LMSRP.

However, LMSRP has reformed intermediation for private insurance in the Spanish legal framework on the basis of Directive 2002/92/CE of 9 December 2002, which is an important milestone in community law because it recognized freedom of establishment and free provision of services in insurance intermediation.

*394.* In this matter and in accordance with the LMSRP, intermediaries who are domiciled in Spain, will, once registered in the administrative registry for insurance intermediaries, be authorized to do their business in other Member States of the EU. In order to have access to these markets, it is sufficient for them to communicate to the DGSFP their intention and to provide the correspondent documentation. The DGSFP will later notify the authority of the host Member State within a one-month deadline. The activities can be started from one month after the mentioned communication (Article 40 of the LMSRP).

419. For more information, see *Comentarios a la Ley de Mediación de Seguros y Reaseguros Privados*, AA.VV. (Dirs V. Cuñat Edo & J. Bataller Grau) (Madrid: Civitas-Thomson, 2007).

In the same manner, intermediaries domiciled in other countries of the EU who intend to carry out insurance activity in Spain must follow the same notification procedure in their country of origin, and one month will be authorized to have access to the Spanish market (Article 65 of the LMSRP). These insurance intermediaries can be penalized by the supervisory authority of their home country and also by the DGSFP (Article 66 of the LMSRP), which is authorized to adopt intervention measures (Article 67 of the LMSRP).

## §2. Classes of Insurance Intermediaries

*395.* The LMSRP introduced the first major classification by making distinctions between insurance intermediaries to whom it dedicates Chapter I, Title II, and reinsurance brokers governed by Chapter II of the same title. Indeed, the legislator reserves a special chapter for reinsurance brokers in order to lighten the obligations and duties of its general regime in view of the singularity of the insurance contract distributed by these intermediaries.

The second classification made by the LMSRP distinguishes between insurance agents and brokers. Criteria used to differentiate are the degree of independency, professionalism and impartiality of the broker. The LMSRP tries to guarantee better compliance with this rule than the one that was required by the abrogated 1992 law of intermediaries.

*396.* Finally, regarding insurance agents, the LMSRP distinguishes between exclusive and non-exclusive or 'tied agents'. An exclusive agent is an agent who sells for one insurance undertaking and is non-exclusive or 'tied' if she or he serves as intermediary for more than one of them. When the insurance agent is a credit undertaking or a corporation controlled by a credit undertaking or with participation of a credit undertaking, the LMSRP calls it a banking-insurance operator, either exclusive or non-exclusive. Certain obligations are added with these names (Article 7 of the LMSRP).

## §3. General Duties of Intermediaries

*397.* In the reading of the LMSRP, the only article that governs the general obligations of insurance intermediaries (Article 6 of the LMSRP), to which other obligations that appear along with the legal text, should be added with better or worse legislative technique. Briefly, such duties are:

(1) Access to any type of intermediary insurance activity requires knowledge of financial subjects and private insurance, although the level of the required knowledge differs according to type. Royal Decree 764/2010, of 11 of June determines the knowledge requirements and also the basic principles to be applied in training programmes for intermediaries in private insurance, private reinsurance and for other persons that participate in the distribution in private insurance and reinsurance.

(2) Insurance intermediaries, whether they are physical persons or managers or directors of legal entities, must be of commercial and professional integrity.
(3) Intermediaries should register in the administrative registry for insurance intermediaries. This registry attempts to serve as a unique information source where the data of intermediaries can be found. It is under the supervision of the DGSFP and similar supervisory bodies in the autonomous communities. The intention is to guarantee, by doing so, the transparency of the insurance market, providing clients with a unique source of information about any intermediary. Moreover, the registry plays a central role in the supervision of intermediaries because registration is a requirement both to start and to cease intermediation activity in any category.
(4) Persons who intend to operate as private insurance intermediaries should choose one class of intermediation. Later, the activity will be circumscribed to the specific chosen category because the different classes of intermediaries are mutually exclusive except for the reinsurance broker activity, which can be performed simultaneously.
(5) Insurance intermediaries are subject to different duties of information and advice at the time of conclusion of the contract as well as during its performance. Before subscribing the contract, the intermediary must inform the policyholder about her or his identity, independency, claim proceedings against intermediary, and about the insurance contract itself. Furthermore, depending on the category of intermediaries she or he belongs to, the intermediary is obliged to inform whether she or he is obliged to perform exclusively with the insurer (the case is an exclusive agent) or whether she or he is not contractually compelled to perform intermediary activity exclusively with only one insurer, and does not advise on the basis of a duty of objectivity – if it is (the case of a non-exclusive intermediary). In addition, if the agent is a banking-insurance operator, she or he must communicate that the purpose of the advice is to facilitate the subscription of insurance and not another financial product. Advice on the basis of an objective analysis is obligatory – in the case of brokers (Article 42.2 of the LMSRP). Also claim proceedings against intermediaries must be informed about (Article 42.1 of the LMSRP).

With respect to the insurance contract, the intermediary is obliged to provide sufficient information for the promotion, offer and subscription of insurance contracts (Article 6.2 of the LMSRP). This obligation of advice, which was already figuring in the 1992 law on intermediation, has now been expanded by the LMSRP on the basis of European Community law. The legislator obliges the intermediary to provide the policyholder with a report specifying, according to the needs and demands of the client, the reasons that justify the provided advice. Such information must reply at least to the problems posed by the application of the client and will be adequate according to the complexity of the proposed insurance contract (Article 42.5 of the LMSRP). Therefore, the intermediary must explain her or his job, and this document will serve as evidence for the evaluation of the intermediary's diligence that until then had been impossible to challenge. Before the LMSRP, this contracting phase was completely oral and it was impossible to prove the diligence applied to the intermediary. The lack of coverage of the insurance contract has always been imputed to the insurer and until now there have not been decisions that recognize contractual civil responsibility of intermediaries because of negligent advising, demonstrating the existence of the mentioned problem.

The legislator tries to ensure the effectiveness of these provisions by requiring written evidence or the use of sustainable supports to record the information described in Article 42 of the LMSRP:

(1) All publicity and commercial documentation of intermediaries must mention the type of intermediation (Articles 17, 22, 25.3, 33.1 and 37.1 of the LMSRP). Also to ensure transparency, the rules prevent the use of such mention when the person does not have the specified category of intermediary (Article 7.2 of the LMSRP).
(2) Insurance intermediaries and insurance undertakings on behalf of their agents must reply to their clients' complaints (Article 44 of the LMSRP).

## §4. Insurance Agent

### I. General Regime for Insurance Agents

*398.* The classification as insurance agent is determined by the conclusion of one or many agent contracts with insurance undertakings and their subsequent inclusion in the administrative registry of intermediaries (Article 9 of the LMSRP). Therefore, the agency contract plays a central role in the legal regime of intermediaries.

With an obvious lack of proper legislative technique, Article 10 of the LMSRP prescribes that the insurance agency contract is governed by the agreement between the parties as supplemented by the prescription of Law 12/1992 of 27 May on the contract of agency. Obviously, the first source of obligations and duties of the agent is found in the LMSRP, although this is not expressly mentioned. The problem lies with deciding whether the law for agency contracts loses its mandatory character in the case of an insurance agent. A literal reading of the provision leads to this conclusion. It would have been more accurate and fair to understand that the law for agency contract continues to be obligatory because of the lack of justification for a differentiated treatment for insurance intermediation. Considering free will as the main source of obligations leaves the content of contractual clauses in the insurer's hands – except powerful companies as banks or retailers – while it is precisely this inequality between contracting parties that serves as justification for the protection of the agent and for the mandatory character of the law of agency.

### II. The Exclusive Insurance Agent

*399.* In accordance with Article 13 of the LMSRP, the exclusive insurance agent is the physical person or legal entity that, in performing an insurance agency contract with an insurance undertaking and in accordance with the administrative registration, agrees to perform intermediation activity of private insurance contracts.

However, besides legal capacity and commercial and professional honourability, the subscription of an insurance agency contract also requires the knowledge of financial subject matters and of private insurance.[420] Following the process laid down by the LMSRP, knowledge of financial subject matters and of private insurance is a preliminary requirement for subscribing an agency contract and finally recording the agency contract in the administrative registry of intermediaries. This process gives rise to difficulties, both with respect to the conclusion of the contract and with the registration, whenever the applicant does not have the required training.

*400.* The difference between exclusive and non-exclusive insurance agents lies in the fact that whereas the first operates for an insurance undertaking (with some reserves that will be explained later), the second performs for several of them. They both are linked to the insurer through an agency contract. Thus, the exclusive insurance agent is similar to the former agent under the abrogated 1985 law of production or to the agent of the presently derogated 1992 law of intermediation.

As has been noted, the exclusive insurance agent is tied to one insurance undertaking. Nevertheless, in accordance with the 1992 intermediation law, the exclusive agent may be authorized to subscribe a single agency contract with another insurer with respect to the intermediation of certain types of insurance where the authority body does not operate (Article 14 of the LMSRP). In the same manner, it is important to take into account that the frequent breach of this limitation is considered by the LMSRP as a serious infringement (Article 55 of the LMSRP), capable of leading to the cancellation of the administrative registration (Article 56 of the LMSRP).

*401.* Each insurer is compelled to keep a registry of exclusive agents whose registrations must be notified to the DGSFP to be included in the administrative registry of intermediaries (Article 15 of the LMSRP).

Finally, one should be aware that the logical consequence of the narrow link with the insurer is to consider the agent as a representative of the insurer in the communications with the policyholder (Article 12 of the LMSRP) and in payments and collections (Article 13.3 of the LMSRP).[421] Also, the insurer is invested with civil and administrative responsibility for his or her intermediaries and for the work performed by its dependents (Article 18 of the LMSRP), without prejudice of criminal or other types of responsibility that the agent him- or herself may incur.

---

420. Royal Decree764/2011 Resolution, establishes 200 hours of training and a minimum programme to develop.
421. SSTS 24-9-2002 (Penal). RAJ 2002/8590 y 26-11-2002 (Penal). RAJ 2003/170.

## III. Non-exclusive (*'Vinculado'*) Insurance Agent

*402.* Article 20 of the LMSRP defines a non-exclusive ('*vinculado*') insurance agent as a physical person or legal entity that, through the subscription of an insurance agency contract with several insurance undertakings recorded in the administrative registry of intermediaries, agrees to perform the intermediation activity of private insurance.

Finally, the demanded concept of multi-contract agent is included. Nevertheless, the rigorous requirements to have access to this type of intermediation, which we think are necessary, do not solve the problem that is caused by the absence of such requirements to become a broker (specifically the lack of qualification). This absence of requirements leads in practice to the violation of the prohibition to compete, which is characteristic of the exclusive agent concept. It also remains to be seen whether the administrative registry of intermediaries will operate efficiently to enable to detect and persecute the situations declared illegal by the regulator but tolerated by the market.

*403.* The entry access to the non-exclusive agent depends on the compliance with diverse requirements that are similar to the ones required to become an insurance broker (Article 21 of the LMSRP):

(a) First, the LMSRP concerns the authorization of the insurer with whom there is an exclusive agency contract, exonerating such consent in future subscription of agency contracts.
(b) Non-exclusive insurance agents who are physical persons must have legal capacity to practice commerce, and in the case of legal entities, they must be corporations or cooperatives registered in the commerce registry prior to their application for the administrative registration. Their by-laws must include performance of activities of insurance intermediation in the form of a non-exclusive insurance agency as a corporate goal. When the corporation has shares, they have to be nominative.
(c) Non-exclusive insurance agents that are physical persons must prove to have passed the training course or test on financial subjects and private insurance. Non-exclusive agency corporations must designate a board of directors that is responsible for insurance intermediation and at least half of its members or, in any event those members who are in charge of the technical direction or similar position, must prove to have passed the training course or the test on financial subjects and private insurance that comply with the requirements laid out by the Royal Decree 764/2011.
(d) Non-exclusive insurance agents, physical persons, members of the board of directors of legal entities and any member of the personnel that directly participates in insurance intermediation must be persons of commercial and professional honourability.
(e) They must present a memorandum about the types of insurance and about the insurance undertakings they deal with during their intermediation activity, about

the territorial scope of their activity and about mechanisms for solutions of conflicts related to client's complaints. It must also include an express reference to the training programme.

(f) Non-exclusive insurance agents will have at their disposal training programmes for employees and external assistants. Furthermore, insurance undertakings must take the necessary measures to train their non-exclusive insurance agents on the products that they deal with in their intermediation activity.

(g) They cannot act for reasons of incompatibility due to the fact that they cannot perform activities as another type of intermediary, or as an expert for policyholders, insured or beneficiaries in cases in which they had participated as insurance agents. This incompatibility also includes persons who are members of boards of directors of legal entities (Article 24 of the LMSRP).

(h) They should have a financial capacity that must always reach up to 4% of the total amount of the received annual premium. This financial capacity can be proved by the subscription of a bank guarantee or surety for no less than EUR 16,803 (Resolution DGSFP 23 September 2008) Nevertheless, a non-exclusive agent will be exonerated from satisfying this solvency requirement if there is an express agreement with insurance undertakings that the amounts paid by clients will be done by way of a direct deposit to open accounts in their names, or, if the case may be, when the non-exclusive agent offers immediate coverage to the policyholder on delivery of the receipt issued by the insurer, and in any case that the insurance money paid for indemnity is directly delivered by the insurers to policyholders, the insured or beneficiaries.

(i) There must be evidence that such agent possesses professional liability insurance or any other financial guarantee that covers in the whole territory of the European Economic Area the liability that may arise out of professional negligence (this insurance must cover EUR 1.5 million for all insured events (Disp. Transit. 3ª of the LMSRP)). This insurance can be omitted when the insurance undertaking that will subscribe the agency contract will also assume the professional liability insurance concerning the activity as non-exclusive insurance agent.

## IV. Banking-Insurance Operator

*404.* Being aware of the important growth of the insurance distribution through credit institutions, the legislator has provided a singular regime for this distribution channel. Thus originated the concept of banking-insurance operator, which is reserved for credit undertakings and corporations controlled by them or in which they have a participation, by concluding an insurance agency contract with one or several insurers and by registering in the administrative registry of intermediaries to perform the activities of intermediation in order to distribute insurance through their branches. (Article 25.1 of the LMSRP).

The regime for banking-insurance operators is regulated in Article 25 of the LMSRP, because the LMSRP defines the concept of banking-insurance by referring to the other two types of agents. In other words, the exclusive or non-exclusive banking-insurance operator is an exclusive or non-exclusive agent who, because of the characteristics of the distribution channel, must comply with certain additional requirements.

*405.* In order to have access to the administrative registry of intermediaries as exclusive or non-exclusive banking-insurance operators, the following requirements must be met:

(a) Be a credit institution or a corporation that is controlled by a credit institution or in which the credit institution has a participation; in this last case, their corporate goal must refer to the performance of activities that correspond with private insurance agents and exclusive and non-exclusive banking-insurance operators.
(b) There must be a designated board of directors that is responsible for insurance intermediation and at least half of its members or the persons who perform technical direction, or those with a similar position, must prove to have passed the training course or test on financial subjects and private insurance that meet the requirements established by resolution of the DGSFP. Moreover, any other person who participates directly in insurance intermediation should prove to have the necessary knowledge and competency for the performance of the job.
(c) Provide a training programme that credit institutions will give to persons who are part of the distribution network and directly participate in insurance intermediation.
(d) When acting as non-exclusive banking-insurance, the memorandum must indicate, besides the obligatory items for every non-exclusive agent, the network(s) of credit undertakings used by banking-insurance operators to practice their intermediation activity.

*406.* Finally, it is forbidden that distribution networks of credit undertakings may simultaneously act as auxiliaries of other intermediaries. In addition, if the banking-insurance operator acquires the legal form of corporation, there must be a contract for provision of services, organizing the assignment of distribution networks as well as the training by the credit undertaking of the persons participating in the distribution of insurance.

## §5. Insurance Broker

### I. Concept

*407.* An insurance broker is the physical person or legal entity that performs intermediation in private insurance without having contractual ties that point towards any predisposition in favour of insurance undertakings and that offers independent, professional and unbiased advice on insurance contracting (Article 26.1 of the LMSRP).

## II. Beginning of the Insurance Broker Activity

*408.* The insurance broker – physical person – or the insurance broker agency – legal entity – must comply with certain requirements in order to obtain and preserve registration in the administrative registry of intermediaries. Article 27 of the LMSRP is the responsible body for regulating the matter in accordance with the following rules:

(a) When insurance brokers are physical persons, they should possess the legal capacity to practice commerce. Legal entities must be corporations or cooperatives that are registered in the registry of commerce prior to the application for the administrative registration and whose by-laws must, in their section relating to the corporate purpose, mention the performance of insurance broker activity. If the corporation has shares, it must be nominative. Furthermore, they should facilitate information about the existence of close ties with other persons or undertakings.
(b) Insurance brokers who are physical persons must prove to have passed the training course or the test on financial subjects and private insurance that meets the requirements established by the DGSFP resolution. Broker's insurance corporations should designate one board of directors that is responsible for insurance intermediation; at least half of its members, and in any case the persons who perform technical direction or similar position, must prove to have passed the training course or test on financial subjects and private insurance that meets the requirements established by resolution of the DGSFP.
(c) In broker's insurance corporations, at least half of the managers must have adequate experience in performing managing functions. To this purpose, they will be considered to possess the required experience if they have, for at least two years, management, control and advisory functions in public or private entities, of a similar size to the envisaged business project or if they have carried out functions of comparable responsibility as individual businesspeople.
(d) Insurance brokers, physical persons, managers and persons who perform direction functions in insurance broker corporations and all the personnel that participate directly in insurance intermediation have to be persons of good commercial and professional repute.
(e) They are obliged to obtain professional liability insurance or to acquire any other financial guarantee covering in the whole territory of the European Economic Area the liability that may arise from professional negligence for an amount of EUR 1,120,200 per insured event and for an aggregate amount of EUR 1,680,300 for all insured events (Resolution DGSFP 23 September 2008).
(f) They must have financial capacity that should at all times reach 4% of the total amount of annual premiums received. This financial capacity may be proved through the subscription of a bank guarantee or a surety for an amount of no less than EUR 16,803 (Resolution DGSFP 23 September 2008). Nevertheless, these contracts will not be required when there is a contractual agreement with the insurance undertakings that money payments by clients must be directly done by way of direct deposit in open accounts on their name, or as the case

may be, the insurance broker must offer immediate coverage to the policyholder by delivering the receipt issued by the insurance undertaking. In any case, the insurance money that is due by the insurance undertakings by way of indemnities must be delivered by insurance undertakings to the policyholders, insured or beneficiaries directly.

(g) They must present a programme of activities that indicates at least the insurance groups and classes of risks that are intended to be intermediated; the principal guidelines and the territorial scope of the activity; the organizational structure including commercial systems, personal and material means available to comply with the programme; and the mechanisms for solving conflicts in case of claims of clients. Furthermore, for the three first corporate financial years, there must be a plan that indicates in detail the expected income and expenses, in particular, both generally and with respect to the insurance premiums subject to intermediation, together with a justification of the expectations and of their adequacy in view of the available means and resources. It must also include a training programme.

(h) They are not subject to an incompatibility as described by Articles 31 and 32 of the LMSRP, rules that try to guarantee the independency of the broker or of the broker agency.

*409.* Nevertheless, the LMSRP did not use the occasion to further regulate matters that are related to supervision of the activity and to the transition from exclusive or non-exclusive agent to insurance broker. The absence of a clear regime on this matter again leaves many and various practical problems without definitive solutions.[422] One of the unsolved problems concerns the role that the insurer(s)' consent plays in the setting up of a broker or broker corporation, or what happens with existing agency contracts that must be replaced by new ones in accordance with the new status of the intermediary.

## III. Independency, Professionalism and Impartiality of the Broker

*410.* In the legislative definition of broker (Article 26.1 of the LMSRP), the concepts of independency, professionalism and impartiality will be noticed. These characteristics of brokerage are materialized in the broker's obligation to inform any applicant of the question of whether, in the broker's judgment, the contract conditions are convenient and whether, according to professional judgment, the cover offered satisfies the needs of the client. At the same time, they will verify whether the policy complies with the requirements of efficiency and of full legal effect. Also brokers must provide information about any policy clause that is asked for by their clients and provide them with assistance and advice in case of occurrence of the insured event (Articles 26.2 and 3 of the LMSRP).

*411.* The broker's contractual independency from the insurer along with the strict requirements of access to and remainder in the market require that better

422. See STS 13-3-1999 (Civil). RAJ 1999/2146.

advice be given to the policyholder. The LMSRP sets the standard that advice must be given on the basis of 'objective analysis'. Such obligation, and this is one of the important and new features of the LMSRP, given its interpretation of the Community Directive, is satisfied when the advice is based on the analysis of a sufficient number of contracts covering such risks, and whereby in a way that it is possible to formulate a recommendation on the basis of professional criteria to find the adequate insurance contract that meets the client's needs. Thus, the standards will be met when the broker has compared at least three offers of insurance undertakings, or, in the case where the insurance contract is specifically designed by the broker, it has been negotiated with at least three insurers (Article 42.4 of the LMSRP).

Finally, Articles 31 and 32 of the LMSRP impose a strict regime of incompatibilities to try to guarantee the intermediary's independence.

## §6. Reinsurance Broker

*412.* The definition of reinsurance broker must start from the restrictive definition of the object of intermediation: reinsurance contracts. These brokers also have to be registered as such in the administrative registry of intermediaries. If the insurance brokerage activity is performed simultaneously, an additional registration for both classes of intermediation in the mentioned registry is required.

The registration in the administrative registry of intermediaries also demands the compliance of certain requirements contained in Article 35 of the LMSRP. This provision simply refers to the requirements compelled to its homonym insurance broker, while scaling down the demands. Lastly, reinsurance brokers must be physical persons with legal capacity, or corporation or cooperatives registered in the commercial registry with intermediation of reinsurances as their corporate goal; they must have passed the training course or aptitude test; if it is a legal entity, half of its managers should have experience, possess commercial and professional honourability and finally subscribe to professional liability insurance.

## §7. Supervision of Intermediaries

*413.* Insurance undertakings, insurance intermediaries and members of the management or board of directors are subject to supervision of the authority on intermediation of private insurance and reinsurance, and they will be sanctioned if they infringe any of the specified rules (Article 54 of the LMSRP). Article 55 of the LMSRP establishes a detailed list of infringements, dividing them into very serious, serious and minor infringements. This provision has its corollary in Article 56 of the LMSRP, linking the class of infringement with its correspondent sanction, which may amount up to the cancellation of the registration in the administrative registry for intermediaries.

## Chapter 2. Insurance Intermediaries and Insurance Contract

*414.* An insurance contract may be directly concluded between the insurer and the policyholder, but it is frequently made through an insurance intermediary. This situation makes it necessary to specify the contractual consequences generated from the participation of the intermediary in the subscription of the contract. However, intermediaries entertain different types of relationships with the parties to the insurance contract, which is why it is logical that their powers of representation and their incidence on the insurance contract also differ.

### §1. Insurance Agent

*415.* Insurance agents intervene in the conclusion of the contract on behalf of insurers and on their account, although normally such conclusion requires the express consent of the insurer. Communications that are addressed to the agent are considered to be addressed to the insurer (Article 12 of the LMSRP[423]).

Amounts paid by the client to the exclusive agent are considered to be paid to the insurance undertaking; payments made in the opposite direction do not produce the same effects (Article 13.3 of the LMSRP).

The LMSRP does not mention anything in relation to the amounts paid to non-exclusive agents. It seems that the policyholder is only released from her or his obligation when the non-exclusive agent delivers the premium receipt (Article 21.3 (g)) of the LMSRP). Such interpretation clashes with the characteristics of an agent. It would indeed be more in accordance with the nature of the agent to consider the policyholder to be released from any amount paid to an agent non-exclusive and to consider that the indemnity is not satisfied until it is received by the insured or beneficiary.

Here banking-insurance operators are also included because in this matter exclusive and non-exclusive agents do not differ.

### §2. Insurance and Reinsurance Brokers

*416.* Insurance brokers are intermediaries that perform their activity without keeping links that may presume any predisposition toward insurers. Consequently, communications between a broker and the insurer on behalf of the policyholder will have the same effect as if they had been made by the policyholder, except contrary indications are given by the policyholder. In any event, expressed consent of the policyholder must be specified in the case of subscription of a new contract or of modification or termination of a still valid contract (Article 21 of the LCS).

A consequence of the broker's independency from the insurer is that payments made by the policyholder to the broker are not considered as being made to the

423. STS 31-3-1998 (Civil). RAJ 1998/2039.

insurer.[424] There is an exception to this rule; if the broker delivers the premium receipt, the policyholder will be released (Article 26.4 of the LMSRP).[425] Indeed, in spite of the broker's independency, it may occur that the letter stating the relationship between the broker and the insurer invests the broker with certain rights. In such cases, the content of the agent's contract will prevail to determine its scope and to answer the question whether the insurer is directly bound.

Finally, reinsurance brokers have a simplified regime in the LMSRP, which does not mention the consequences of their participation in the condition of the reinsurance contract. From our viewpoint, their qualification as brokers leads us to establish an analogous extension of the regime designed for insurance brokers.

424. STS 25-6-2004 (Penal). RAJ 2004/4181.
425. STS 28-7-1997 (Civil). RAJ 1997/6309.

# Part IX. Co-insurance and Reinsurance

## Chapter 1. Co-insurance

### §1. Regulatory Framework

*417.* Article 33 of the LCS[426] has been included within the general prescriptions on property insurance, but co-insurance is actually a form of contracting that is applicable to any type of insurance. For this reason and making abstraction of its location, Article 33 of the LCS is applied by analogy to insurance contracts for persons and to maritime and aerospace insurance contracts in the absence of an agreement to the contrary.

Moreover, Article 33(a) of the LCS introduced in Spain the framework for communitarian co-insurance, originating in Directive 78/473 of 30 May on coordination of legal, regulatory and administrative provisions in co-insurance. This directive lacks practical interest due to the current development of communitarian freedoms.

However, contractual matters have great importance given the general provisions laid out by corporations that have insurers within their organizations.

### §2. Economic Function

*418.* The co-insurance technique is the most basic formula to face risks, the magnitude of which exceeds the insurer's capabilities, and it consists in distributing the risk among different insurers. It offers unquestionable advantages because it empowers the law game of big numbers to play between interested undertakings, because it facilitates the market entry of smaller undertakings and because it contributes to the standardization of conditions and the establishment of common fees.

### §3. Delimitation of Related Concepts

*419.* In co-insurance there is a preliminary agreement between insurers that generate two relationships, one 'internal' among insurers and another 'external' among insurers and the policyholder. One will notice that such previous agreement does not occur in multiple insurance. The differences between co-insurance and multiple insurance are even deeper because in co-insurance there is an absolute identity of

426. About co-insurance, see J.M. Muñoz Paredes, *El coaseguro* (Madrid: Civitas, 1996).

interest, risk and time that is decisive for the application of the framework for over-insurance instead of the double insurance framework.[427]

The distribution of the risk is horizontal in co-insurance and vertical in reinsurance. Indeed, whereas in co-insurance the different insurers do contract with the policyholder, in reinsurance the risk is borne by one insurer who contracts another undertaking that will cover damages in case the insurer's patrimony suffers damages when paying indemnities or benefits of the first insurance contract. Reinsurance is property insurance; co-insurance is a form for subscribing any type of insurance. A *pool* is an association of undertakings that provides insurance services with the purpose of distributing risks in the form of co-insurance or reinsurance.

### §4. Pre-agreement Between Insurers

*420.* One of the essential characteristics of co-insurance is the existence of an internal relationship between insurers that usually is stipulated as a general provision in all contracts subscribed under the co-insurance framework. This internal agreement determines the proportions of the insured risk to be covered by each insurer and consequently the payment of indemnities in the case where an event occurs, as well as the right of recovery that is set up in Article 33.2 of the LCS. Such right may be exercised by any insurer, usually the 'principal insurer', insofar as she or he paid more than the required amount stipulated in the co-insurer chart.

### §5. Relationship Between Co-insurers and the Policyholder

*421.* The so-called external co-insurance, which, in practice, is set up by one single policy, determines the distribution of quotas and the assumption of liability by the co-insurers. In this regard, Article 33.1 of the LCS sets up the general rule that insurers must face indemnity only in proportion to their respective quotas. Nevertheless, the law allows the agreement of different liability systems, such as solidary liability, although this possibility does not enjoy support in insurance practice.

In this matter it is necessary to mention the delegated insurer (the 'first insurer' or 'head') as governed by Article 33.1 of the LCS, which has eliminated from the market any other form of relationship with the policyholder. The use of a delegated insurer is preferred because it gives both parties the advantage of having a representative. About this power to represent, the LCS disposes that 'delegated insurers are legitimized to exercise all rights in order to receive all declarations and claims correspondent to the insured'.[428]

427. J. Bataller Grau, *El seguro múltiple* (Valencia: Tirant lo Blanch, 1998).

428. Power to represent of the delegated insured is analysed by the SSTS 23-10-1991 (Civil). RAJ 1991/7861; 31-3-1992 (Civil). RAJ 1992/2317; 29-6-1993 (Civil). RAJ 1993/5226 and 25-11-1999 (Civil). RAJ 1999/8282.

# Chapter 2. Reinsurance

## §1. Concept, Function and Notes

*422.* Article 77.1 of the LCS defines the reinsurance contract as the contract by which 'the reinsurer assumes the obligation to cover, within the limits established by law and by the contract, the debt arising in the patrimony of the reinsured as a consequence of its obligation assumed as an insurer in an insurance contract'.[429]

The economic purpose of reinsurance is to diminish and redistribute on a major scale the risks of the insured-reinsured through the division and dispersion of such risks.

*423.* In reinsurance we can distinguish the following:

(1) Reinsurance is *property insurance*, independent of the insurance that serves as its foundation.
(2) This contract is characterized by its *internationality*, which is not essential but customary in the reinsurance business.
(3) Treated as an insurance contract between professionals, the free will of the parties acquires a fundamental role. In consequence, Article 79 of the LCS expressly states that the LCS is not compulsory with respect to reinsurance.

## §2. Autonomy of the Relationships of Insurance and Reinsurance Contracts

*424.* A characteristic that defines the reinsurance contract is the lack of communication between the reinsurance contract and the insurance contract that serves as its foundation. The logical result is that the insured related to the reinsured lacks the right of bringing an action directly against the reinsurer (Article 78.1 of the LCS).[430] The insured may only act against its insurer after the insured event occurs. Nevertheless, in practice, policy clauses that dilute this absence of communication are included. Indeed, it is frequent to find clauses that allow a direct action against the reinsurer (*'cut through clausue'*), clauses of simultaneous payment that condition the payment of indemnity by the insurer to the previous payment of the reinsurer and clauses for control that enable the reinsurer to supervise the insurer.

Article 78.2 of the LCS aims at decreasing the autonomy of the reinsurance contract by giving the insured a privilege in case the insurer is subject to voluntary or

429. For deeper study of the reinsurance, see M. Broseta Pont, *El contrato de reaseguro* (Madrid: Aguilar, 1961); M.C. Hill Prados, *El reaseguro* (Barcelona: Bosch, 1995); L. Angulo Rodríguez, 'La desnaturalización del reaseguro tradicional', Anales de la Real Academia Sevillana de Legislación y Jurisprudencia, 1994–1996, vol. I, 215ff; AA.VV, *Estudios sobre el contrato de reaseguro* (Madrid: Editorial Española de Seguros, 1997); J. Sánchez Villabella, *El contrato de reaseguro* (Madrid: Editorial Española de Seguros, 2002); J.J. Vara Parra, *El contrato de reaseguro en el Derecho internacional privado* (Cáceres: Universidad de Extremadura, 2003).

430. J. Bataller Grau, 'La subrogación de los riesgos reasegurados: seguir la senda marcada por el legislador evita perderse en el bosque', RDM (2011), 125 ff.

forced liquidation. All insured whose contracts served as a budget or were taken into account in concluding the contract or contracts of reinsurance are entitled to this privilege. The purpose of the privilege is limited to the credit balance between the insurer and the reinsurer.

# Part X. Taxation of Insurance

*425.* For descriptive purposes we can distinguish two major groups of taxpayers: the insurance companies are passive subjects of premium tax; and the insured, injured third parties or beneficiaries of insurance contracts, who are passive subjects of income tax and donations and inheritance taxes.

Law 13/1996 of 30 December on economic policy, tax, administrative and social measures introduced the insurance premium tax in Spain. This is an indirect, real and objective tax, the taxable events of which are insurance and capitalization transactions underwritten by insurance companies in Spain (Article 12). The income levied by this tax consists of the amounts of premium received by the insurance undertaking. The law declares that the operations derived from agreements between insurance undertakings and social security agencies or governmental undertakings that manage some of the social security special frameworks are not taxable. The exemptions established by law concern the obligatory social insurance and collective insurance that implement alternative systems for plans and pension funds, operations related to life insurance, capitalization operations, combined agricultural (crop) insurance, and the exemptions related to international transport of merchandise or passengers.

*426.* The amounts received by the insured, beneficiaries or injured parties with respect to an insurance contract are subject to a complex financial framework in which income tax, donations and inheritance taxes meet. Income tax levies income perceived by an individual during a determined period of taxable time. Components of this income can come from work, capital, economic activity, patrimonial earnings and losses and estate tax from real estate, tax transparency, international tax transparency and image rights.

With respect to insurance, the *Impuesto sobre la Renta de las Personas Físicas* (IRPF)[431] law contains regulations that qualify the amounts received from this type of contract by which the amounts will be classified according to the type of income they represent such as work income, capital income and so on.

*427.* The IRPF law considers as personal work revenue the amounts received by beneficiaries for retirement, incapacity and from determined collective insurance contracts such as insurance contracted with social mutual societies or dependency insurances contracted according to the law for the promotion of personal autonomy and care of the persons in dependency situations (Article 17 LIRPF).

431. Law 35/2006 of 28 November about income tax, corporation tax, non-resident and patrimonial tax.

All income received from capitalization transactions and life or disability insurance contracts are considered as capital income only if they are not classified as work income. Within the IRPF, patrimonial income constitutes an income class that does not properly come from a production factor. It is a residual category in which all incomes that are not part of other categories are placed. It includes income derived from capital obtained accidentally and not periodically and also income that does not derive from capital (e.g., prizes, treasures and interests of indemnity nature).

*428.* In relation to insurance, indemnities or insured capital for loss or damages in patrimonial elements are considered as income and loss. Patrimonial income and patrimonial loss are calculated as the difference between the received amount and the proportional acquisition value that corresponds to the damage.

When the indemnity is not monetary, the difference is calculated between the market value of goods, rights or services received and the proportional value of the acquisition that corresponds to the damage. Patrimonial income will only be calculated when it is derived from an increase in the patrimonial value of the taxpayer and not when it comes from the compensation benefit received as a result of damage.

*429.* Finally, it is convenient to mention the taxes on donation and inheritance, which taxable transaction is the acquisition of a lucrative increase by a physical person though a *mortis causa* transaction or through an *inter vivos* act. The law that regulates the tax (Law 29/1987 of 18 December on inheritance and donations tax) systematizes acquisitions in the following groups: (a) acquisition of goods and rights by inheritance, legacy or any other inheritance title; (b) acquisition of goods and rights by donation or any other juridical transaction by gratuitous title and *inter vivos* (in this second group, life insurance contracts for cases when the insured survives is considered as a juridical transaction different from donation); (c) amounts received by beneficiaries of life insurance contracts when the insured is not the beneficiary, except in cases expressly regulated in Article 16.2(a) of the IRPF law.

*430.* In this third group, the legislative reference to 'life insurance' has applied a deficient legislative technique because under that denomination it is possible to find different types of transactions that classify within the first two groups. For example, insurance contracts covering the life of the insured would be clearly classified under inheritance *mortis causa,* whereas insurance contracts covering the life of third parties and life insurance contracts for survival cases would be classified under donations. According to this law, accident insurance contracts will only be considered as life insurance contracts for the amounts received by the beneficiary if the insured person dies.

# Selected Bibliography


## General Books about Insurance

AA.VV. (Dir Garrido y Comas, J.J.). *Tratado general de seguros: Teoría y práctica de los seguros privados*. Barcelona: Consejo General de los Colegios de Agentes y Corredores de Seguros de España, 1986–1991.
AA.VV. (Dirs. Campuzano, A.B., F. Conlledo & R.J. Palomo). Los mercados financieros, Tirant lo Blanch: Valencia, 2013.
Caño Escudero, F. del. *Derecho español de seguros*. 3rd edn. Madrid, 1983.
Tapia Hermida, A.J. *Manual de Derecho de seguros y fondos de pensiones*. Madrid: Thomson-Civitas, 2006.

## Insurer Undertakings and Market

AA.VV, (Dirs. Cuñat, V. & J. Bataller). Supervisión en Seguros Privados: Hacia Solvencia II, Valencia: Tirant lo Blanch, 2013.
AA.VV. (Dir Verdera, E.). *Comentarios a la Ley de Ordenación del Seguro Privado*. Madrid: CUNEF, 1988.
AA.VV. *Estudios y comentarios sobre la Ley de Ordenación y Supervisión de los Seguros Privados*. Madrid: Mapfre, 1997.
AA.VV. (Dir Ruiz Echauri, J.). *Comentarios a la Reforma de la Normativa de Ordenación y Supervisión de los Seguros Privados. Análisis de la Ley 32/2003 y de la normativa reglamentaria aprobada por los reales decretos 297 a 301/2004*. Pamplona: Aranzadi, 2004.
Bataller Grau, J. 'La desregulación de los seguros privados', *RES* (1999): num. 97.
Camacho de los Ríos, J. *Armonización del derecho de seguro de daños en la Unión Europea*. Madrid: Civitas, 1996.
Carbonell Puig, J. *Los contratos de seguro de vida: Normativa interna y comunitaria*. Barcelona: Bosch, 1994.
Núñez Lozano, M.C. *Ordenación y supervisión de los seguros privados*. Madrid: Marcial Pons, 1998.

## Insurance Compensation Consortium

Barrero Rodríguez, E. *El Consorcio de compensación de seguros*. Valencia: Tirant lo Blanch, 2000.

## Selected Bibliography

Rodríguez Martínez, I. & J. Bataller Grau. 'Il nuevo regime spagnolo dei rischi straordinari da parte del consorcio di compensazione delle assicurazioni', Dir. Ec.Ass., nu'm. 3 (2004).

### Mediation in Private Insurance

AA.VV. (Dirs Cuñat Edo, V. & J. Bataller Grau). *Comentarios a la Ley de mediación de seguros y reaseguraos privados*. Madrid: Thomson-Civitas, 2007.

### General Books about Insurance Contract

AA.VV. (Ed. E. Verdera, E.). *Comentarios a la Ley de Contrato de Seguro*. Madrid: CUNEF, 1982.

AA.VV. (Coords Bataller, J., J. Boquera & J. Olavarría). *El contrato de seguro en la jurisprudencia del Tribunal Supremo*. Valencia: Tirant lo Blanch, 1999.

AA.VV. (Coords Bataller, J. Boquera & J. Olavarría). El contrato de seguro en la jurisprudencia del Tribunal Supremo (1980-2012). Valencia, Tirant lo Blanch, 2013.

AA.VV. (Coords Boquera, J., J. Bataller & J. Olavarría). *Comentarios a la Ley de contrato de seguro*. Valencia: Tirant lo Blanch, 2001.

AA.VV. *25 años de la Ley de contrato de seguro*, *RES* (2005), 2 volúmenes.

AA.VV. *Congreso hispano-luso de seguros*. Madrid: SEAIDA, 2004.

AA.VV. (Dir Sánchez Calero, F.). *Ley de Contrato de Seguro*. 3rd edn. Pamplona: Aranzadi, 2005.

Garrigues, J. *Contrato de Seguro Terrestre*. 2nd edn. Madrid, 1983.

Veiga Copo, A. Tratado del contrato de seguro. 2nd edn. Thomson Reuters Civitas: Madrid, 2012.

# Index

*The numbers here refer to paragraph numbers.*

## Index

www.ingramcontent.com/pod-product-compliance
Ingram Content Group UK Ltd.
Pitfield, Milton Keynes, MK11 3LW, UK
UKHW020140290926
15471UKWH00003B/599

9 789403 539409